BIG

a memoir

QUEER

NUN

Shane
Phelan

A section of chapter 12 was previously published as "A Habit and a Hard Hat" in Herstry, July 15 2021; https://herstryblg.com/true/2021/7/15/a-habit-and-a-hardhat?rq=Phelan.

Paperback ISBN: 979-8-218-34171-8
Ebook ISBN: 979-8-218-34172-5

Cover and book design by Mayfly Design

Published by Companionary Press

Library of Congress Catalog Number: 2023923730
First Printing: 2024
Printed in the United States of America

There are times in life when the question of knowing if one can think differently than one thinks, and perceive differently than one sees, is absolutely necessary if one is to go on looking and reflecting at all.

—Michel Foucault

Only she who attempts the absurd can achieve the impossible.

—Robin Morgan

Glory to God whose power working in us can do infinitely more than we can ask or imagine! Glory to God from generation to generation in the Church, and in Christ Jesus for ever and ever.

—Ephesians 3:20-21

"THIS IS CRAZY."

It's January 2001. I'm 44 years old. I've been in the convent for three weeks. I'm standing in the doorway of my novice director's office. The small room is filled with books in glass-fronted shelves and a big, dark wooden desk. The brick-red Italian tile floor and the old iron-wrought windows lend it a medieval air. And my novice director, all 4'11" of her, fits with the room. Her habit and veil might have come, if not from the 15th century, at least the 19th. She is supposed to guide me in the ways of monastic life, and to help me discern whether I belong here.

For the first time in years, I'm wearing a skirt. Black skirt, white shirt, black sweater; the uniform of a postulant here. If I stay, I'll end up in that same habit that she is wearing, though mine will be a foot longer; at 5'11", 200 pounds, I tower over her.

She leans back in her chair and looks at me. "What's crazy?" she asks.

I show her the first copy of the latest book I've written, entitled *Sexual Strangers: Gays, Lesbians, and the Dilemmas of Citizenship.* Just before entering the convent, I had finished working on this manuscript; now it's arrived, ready to launch into the world. It has a vivid cover, white and purple and red, with lots of nice endorsements on the back. In another universe, it would be the book to launch me into being a full professor. But here?

This is my fifth book on lesbian/gay/queer politics. Recently, a friend called me "the lesbian politics maven" as she invited me to give the keynote address to the National Women's Association annual convention. Until the fall of 2000, I edited a book series on queer politics and theory. I chaired the American Political Science Association's Committee on the Status of Lesbians and Gays in the Profession, and the Gay and Lesbian Caucus. I'm not just queer: I've made a career out of queer.

I say: "I'm this big queer, and now I'm going to be a nun?"

Without blinking an eye, she responds: "So you'll be a big queer nun."

And I think to myself: That sounds like a book title.

But it's hardly fair to start you off here. This isn't just a story about being a queer, or a nun, or big. It's about all of those, but overall, it's a story about salvation, about finding my way through the rubble of a psycho-spiritual apocalypse to a place of healing and—dare I say it?—resurrection. It's a story about swimming toward the light, through twists and turns that belong to me and yet, I suspect, are all too common. I'm a big queer nun, but I'm more than that. You'll have to wait for the story to find out what else, as we all have to wait for our stories to unfold, and sometimes for others to tell us our stories.

Buckle up: We're going for a ride on the redemption highway.

CHAPTER ONE

What's a (Formerly) Nice Girl . . .

As MY PARENTS LEFT and the door to the hospital clanged shut, I felt safe for the first time in years. I had finally managed to get away, even if only for a time.

I didn't know why I needed to flee, why I needed that door between us. I just felt relief.

I arrived there on the day after my 14th birthday, November 16, 1970, after my latest suicide attempt had finally convinced me I needed help. I had tried a few times over the summer, with pills, but never actually got there. This time, though, I had threatened my boyfriend with a knife when he tried to stop me from running in front of a truck. Killing myself still sounded plausible, but endangering Greg was over the line.

My father thought the psychiatrist just wanted our money. I begged, and my mother convinced him that I needed to go.

Because my father's job carried insurance that helped them pay for a private hospital, I didn't go to the county hospital (where 100 people died when the whole psychiatric wing collapsed in the 1971 earthquake, just weeks after I got out). My hospital hosted about 40 patients. Most of the patients were docile, drugged out of their twisted minds.

I shared a room with six other teenage girls. Each morning we had some sort of class. My mother brought me my school homework each week, hoping I wouldn't have to repeat the ninth grade. In the afternoon, we had occupational therapy. I made Christmas presents for my

1

family—ashtrays, candles, macrame plant holders. I loved the candle wax; if you dipped your hand in it, it looked like you were being eaten by The Blob.

As the only girl not diagnosed with schizophrenia, the only one not on Thorazine, I felt left out. My doctor had prescribed Valium, a truly boring drug. I managed to trade meds with another girl one day, to experience Thorazine. As the mist enveloped my brain, I learned I wasn't missing anything. I smuggled in downers whenever I could, using orifices not designed for that purpose.

Once I arrived in the hospital, I could let myself know that I didn't want to die; I just wanted to be out of that house. My official diagnosis was "depressive reaction"; my doctor explained it more simply. "You're furious," he said. "We can't do anything until you release some of that anger."

So, I did. I kicked holes in walls. I threw glass sugar canisters. I broke light bulbs and cut myself with them. I set fire to plastic shower doors. After each incident, I'd sit in a cold rage on my bed and wait for the staff to come and put me into isolation.

I poured out anger, but my sickness seemed to grow rather than diminish. I attacked one of the aides, convinced my father had disguised himself and come to kill me.

On Christmas night, I attacked another resident at the water fountain after a visit with my family. Sharon was making noise and being obnoxious in the hall, and something in me snapped. I shoved her, poking her chest, pushing her down the hall. The staff grabbed me and put me in isolation. This time, they strapped me onto the bed.

Before this, I'd been calm in isolation. Not this time. As I lay there, I became convinced that the staff planned to kill me by pumping in poison gas, or sending black widow spiders through the vents (I'd read this scenario in Nancy Drew novels—it could happen!). I screamed, and they came. When, finally, they released me, I knew I would never go back in there.

That same night I met Mike, a 21-year-old musical genius with a blue Mustang and untreated schizophrenia. Thorazine made him gentle and vague. I fell in love. A week later, Mike's parents had him released so he could go back to junior college with no disruption. This gave me the incentive I needed to get out. I announced to my doctor that I would be released by my brother Dal's birthday, January 24. My doctor said, "Don't worry about dates. Just heal at your own pace." I said yes, of course, but inside I knew: out by January 24.

I told my psychiatrist I felt better. I called my mother and told her the same. I didn't hit anyone or throw anything. I became a model patient.

On January 22, 1971, I left the hospital. I'd been there ten weeks.

That was my second sojourn behind locked doors. My first exposure came a few months prior to that, in the summer between eighth and ninth grade.

Cinder block construction, boring white walls, orange doors: Welcome to the Los Angeles County Juvenile Detention Center. The windows were framed in orange. The plastic chairs had been white at one time, as had the dingy floors. The place seemed designed to discourage. As we entered through the buzzing locked doors, I could feel a miasma of angry despair seeping through the halls.

The uniform reinforced the humiliation of the surroundings: a pair of shorts, a sleeveless smock, evoking a sort of baby doll look. I don't know who designed this, or what they were trying to do; we looked like some sort of porn producer's attempt to mix overgrown innocence with women behind bars. If I were 5'2", I might be rather fetching in this outfit; but at 5'11" and pissed off, I felt stupid. My hair, teased up like all the girls, accentuated the weirdness of the clothes.

I arrived at Juvie the fourth time I ran away, after repeated encounters with the police for suspicion of narcotics and shoplifting. In the end, running away got me locked up. Well, and cussing at the cops.

It was so easy to run away in Los Angeles. I could just walk out the door—and I did.

That first time, I took off with Carolyn Witt. Carolyn's yellow-dyed hair and thick eyeliner suggested sophistication, but she was really just another eighth-grader.

One day, after an incident at school and afraid of her mother's anger, she opted to run away. Fearing for her safety, I went with her. Leaving school, we hit the street with no money and nowhere to go. We started hitchhiking. A trucker picked us up, took us to a hotel room, and left to get us some food. I liked him, but Carolyn was certain he planned to rape us. I blew that off, calling her paranoid. But she could not, would not, stay. She decided to go home. So, I went with her. Standing in a phone booth, with rain pouring down, Carolyn called her mother. Her mother called the police, and the police came and got us.

Of course, the parents each blamed the other child.

Carolyn's mother: "That girl will get you into trouble! I don't want you seeing her anymore."

My mother: "That girl is a bad influence on you!"

Carolyn hadn't talked me into anything. I just wanted to be gone, and she opened the door. Once the exit sign was illuminated, leaving was easy. If I got suspended and didn't want the confrontation at home, I didn't go home. If something pissed me off, I left. If someone offered me drugs, I followed. I hitchhiked all over the San Fernando Valley (I learned to always light a cigarette when I got in, so I had a weapon). I got picked up by hippies living next door to the Manson compound. I slept in a field, under a giant (for L.A.) oak tree, with friends who wanted to ensure my safety.

I'd get caught, or occasionally turn myself in when a sympathetic adult convinced me. It became routine: The police would search me for drugs and call my father. He'd pick me up, we'd argue in the car.

"You can't keep doing this to your mother!"

"I'm not doing anything to her!" I'd shoot back.

"All you want to do is hurt her," he'd pronounce.

By summer, my parents decided they could not cope with me. They told me they were going to have me pronounced incorrigible and placed in juvenile detention. I did what any endangered animal would do: I escaped. Early the next morning, I crawled out my bedroom window and ran. The network of alleys crisscrossing the Valley enabled me to navigate through the city without being seen.

In the months between my first attempt and this one, I'd met a group that seemed to offer the promise of refuge. Doodlehead, Terry, and Greg were a trio of ex-Marines. Greg was actually a reasonably sane and nice guy, and he had become my boyfriend. Doodlehead and Terry spent their days killing their brains with booze and drugs. I'd spent a lot of time in Greg's garage, dancing to Sly and the Family Stone, the Temptations, Smoky Robinson, and the Miracles.

I found Terry and Doodlehead at their friend Jeff's. We piled into Jeff's car and headed to Redondo Beach without plans or money. I hadn't solved my problem of where to go; I had just found more vagabonds to go nowhere with. We ended up at the beach park, trying to fish for food and sleeping outside. After a cold and hungry night, we headed back to Jeff's.

Soon after we arrived, a police car pulled up. *What the hell*, I thought, *I'm going anyway*. Prior arrests, with insults at the station, had taught me to hate "the pigs." Now, as they cuffed me and pushed me into the backseat of the patrol car, I spit all my venom at them. At the station, one of the cops said, "We were going to let you go home. But after that mouthful you gave me, you're going to Juvie."

Okay, I thought; *bring it on*.

Now, as I entered and saw the other girls, I felt less confident. As one of three White girls, I stood out. My size made me a target, someone to be conquered. The other big girls looked like they knew how to fight. I knew how to bluff my way out of fights, at least in suburbia, but this was different.

I didn't let myself know I was afraid. I didn't let them know, either. I used my hate-laser eyes to convince the two Black girls who were my size that they didn't want to fight me.

Aside from the tension of waiting for fights, Juvie was the most boring place I'd been. We spent most of our time hanging around in the TV room. On the outside, the boredom was at least relieved by the drugs and drink. Here, there was no escape from the pointlessness of our daily lives, the ugliness of the place, the ridiculousness of my outfit, the hostility that rippled through the air.

Juvie did offer some novelty, though; here, I had my first encounter with "lesbians."

One day, Peaches, a petite White girl with long, dark hair, approached and asked me to be her protector. She named it as a sexual contract: "I want to be your girlfriend."

This had not occurred to me before. What would it mean, to have a girlfriend? What would we do? Where would we do it, in this place? By now, I was having sex with boys, but I hadn't considered sex with girls.

I knew that if I said yes, I'd be pissing off the big girls who could really fight. If Peaches needed a protector, there was trouble. I didn't need to get between her and it. I had changed my persona when we moved to Los Angeles, but that didn't include fighting experienced street girls. I wasn't cut out to be anyone's protector, or their lesbian lover.

I turned her down. I wanted out of there.

After three days, I had a hearing. My parents were in the courtroom. I said the right words and received a year of probation. I decided I would stop running away. But I didn't want to be home either.

A year earlier, I had been an honors student. Years before that, I got straight As and played with the neighborhood kids.

I remembered these things, but they were not my reality anymore. That girl had vanished.

Once upon a time, outside of Cleveland, a little girl grew up with her brothers and sister in a world of open backyards and apple trees, of running and playing up and down the block. She loved her little brother, and idolized her older sister, and felt awe and a touch of fear for her older brother, a giant who grew to 6'5" before he graduated from high school and left for good. When her brother fought with the other giant, her father, she and her puppy Peanut hid behind the living room couch while they yelled and stomped.

The little girl's name was Barbie.

A happy child, Barbie loved being outside, playing in the trees. Boys liked playing in the trees, running and climbing, shooting squirt guns, exploring—the same kinds of things the little girl liked. Other girls played inside with dolls. Barbie tried dolls, undressing them, then she left them on the shelf. She hated sitting around and acting well-behaved. She wanted to play baseball, and dance, and catch butterflies.

Barbie and her friend Susie started a "We Hate Girls Club." The boys said they didn't belong with them anymore, they weren't boys. Barbie didn't really want to be a boy, but she knew she didn't want to be a girl.

With her family, Barbie attended the Episcopal Church down the street every Sunday morning. Then they came home. Her father and his friend Bob drank and talked through the afternoon. They said grace at Christmas and Easter dinner.

Barbie liked church alright, she loved the hymns, but she didn't feel much there. Her little soul opened outside, among the trees.

Barbie couldn't wait to begin school. Because her birthday fell in November, the school made her wait until the following year. By the time she started, she had learned to read a bit. She was older and taller than most of her classmates.

The day before school began, she sat at the kitchen table, making a name tag, a big flower with seven petals coming out from the center. She colored each petal a different color. In the center she printed her name: "Barbie Baker." She liked art, and music, and recess. As she walked to and from school, she practiced cartwheels and roundoffs.

Barbie got straight As without a lot of effort. By the end of second grade, she read at an eighth-grade level. She received praise from adults, but she felt different from the other kids. Then she got glasses. With her grades, the glasses solidified a new identity. The other kids at school began to call her "professor." Teasing made her withdraw. Her mother told her to ignore it, but she couldn't.

At the end of second grade, Barbie's teachers agreed that she should skip a grade. The principal brought her in with her parents, and made the proposal. She would have to take third-grade math in summer school, but they thought she was ready for the rest of fourth grade. Barbie's parents let her decide.

Barbie said yes. She didn't know that the friends she'd had in second grade would be mad. She didn't know that the new fourth-graders might not welcome her. When one of the neighboring kids said, "They only skipped you because you looked stupid with the third-graders," she tried not to believe her, but it hurt anyway. She was too big and too smart. She told her mother about her loneliness, but her mother quickly responded: "It was your choice, your decision." Barbie learned not to go to her mother for support.

Other things changed too in that year, 1965. Barbie's cousin Pam had moved in with the family when both her parents and her older sister died. Now the house was too small for them all, so they moved into one of the new houses two blocks over. That summer, Barbie helped her father paint the new house. Just the two of them. Barbie began to enter the tomb of her mind.

Third-grade math involved multiplying and dividing. By the end of the summer, Barbie had a blackboard in her head. She could see numbers on it, and multiply them. She developed a special love for the number 9, because it is always 9 no matter what you multiply it by: $9 \times 128 = 1152$, $1+1+5+2=9$. Oh, and 11; now, 11 was cool. 11 makes pyramids when it's squared and cubed: $11 \times 11 = 121$, $121 \times 11 = 1331$, $1331 \times 11 = 14641$. Barbie rolled the numbers around in her head. The numbers would start up, like a song that won't go away, and she'd multiply. For years.

The class allowed for counting too. Barbie counted the tiles on the ceiling, over and over.

In fourth grade, she began learning about social studies. She loved it from the beginning. Other countries, other ideas and ways of life. The world became much bigger than her town, even bigger than the United States. By now, Barbie had been following presidential elections, arguing with her friends about Johnson versus Goldwater.

The social studies books were paperback, theirs to keep and write in. Barbie began drawing mandalas, patterns that radiated from a center. She became so totally absorbed in drawing mandalas that the world around her vanished. One day, she looked up from her drawing to find that everyone had left the classroom. Recess had begun and she didn't know it.

In September 1966, Barbie's family moved again, this time all the way to Chicago. Their new house sat on a circle, enclosed and safe from traffic. The backyard ran along a major road, so they had to be careful not to throw or hit balls out of the yard, but it was big and long enough for decent football games. In the circle they played baseball, and a basketball hoop hung over the garage. Barbie, still the only girl, played all the games.

A few years before, Barbie had routinely walked up to other children and just started to play. Now, feeling alone and awkward, she began to hang out with some of the neighboring girls. Sharon and Debby were the first two Jewish girls she'd ever known. Cindy wore a hearing aid and glasses. They were definitely not the cool girls, but they were friends.

Barbie learned to deal with pain on her own. Playing dodgeball at school, she caught a ball badly and hurt her left little finger. It dangled off to the side. She assumed it was dislocated, so she pulled it, straightened it out, and went home. It didn't occur to her to tell anyone. Years later, she realized her knuckle didn't bend.

In the meantime, life went on. There were still games to play, books to read. There were butterflies to chase with a big, green net, fireflies to catch and put in a jar. Barbie took piano lessons and swimming lessons. She belonged to Brownies, then to Girl Scouts. Life looked normal.

Like a stone thrown into a pond, the change in Barbie was noticeable, but it seemed contained, perhaps a normal part of childhood. Over the next several years, however, the impact of that stone grew. Rather than a stone in a pond, the events of 1965 resembled an earthquake below the ocean: an event unnoticed by all but those with equipment and training, those who look for such things, but an event that shows up later as a tsunami, destroying everything in its path, pulling people out to sea, leaving families bereft and broken. By that time, everyone will have forgotten or denied the original point of impact. It will become a mystery, a thing to wonder while looking at early pictures: what happened to that happy little girl?

Holy One, thank you for holding Barbie safe in your arms. Bless all the children locked in the tombs of their minds and hearts. Hold them until they can hear you calling them out to freedom. Amen.

Chapter Two

Spiralling Down

"I hate you."

This is my first conscious thought, the thought that ushers me into adolescence. The thought, really, that creates me, the one writing this. Well, maybe me; it's hard to delineate exactly when enough change constitutes a new identity.

My name is Barb. I am ten years old. Walking home from Debby's house, I realize: I hate my parents. I'm not sure why I hate them, but I do. Barbie has left. I know that girl existed, I have some of her memories, but she's like someone else. I begin here.

Over the next few years, fissures opened in my life. I looked like a good girl, I did what good girls do, but another person was emerging, looking for a chance to live her life. She was not so good. It would take a while, but she would have her chance.

I continued to excel in school. Music expanded, though not exactly as I'd hoped. I'd been playing piano for three years. In fifth grade, I joined the school band and learned the flute. I wanted to play the clarinet, to sound like the Benny Goodman records my mother danced to around the house. My mother said that I couldn't play the clarinet with a chipped front tooth, but we had a flute, from when Jan had played, so I played the flute, grudgingly. The flute belonged to sweet little girls, polite and demure. I had a shout, a wail really, inside of me that couldn't come out. I was a clarinet confined to a flute life.

More than any instrument, though, singing had become my true "instrument." Singing called the energy through my body, releasing something more direct than an instrument could. I asked my parents for singing lessons. My teacher said I had a real voice in me. I got the occasional solo in church choir.

And, of course, I continued to play sports. For a while.

I got my period for the first time at age 11. I had had the sex education movie at school, but I hadn't paid attention. I'd done my best to forget I had "those parts." Now, blood was flowing from a place I didn't recognize.

I felt confused and afraid. Finally, on our way home from my voice lesson, I told my mother.

"Mom, I'm bleeding." A little croak, a stammer.

"Where are you bleeding?" she asked as she drove.

"Down at my bottom," I stumbled.

My mother gave a short laugh of relief. "It will be alright," she said.

"Am I sick?"

"No," she replied. "You just got your period."

I tried to remember the movie, but nothing. Where was I bleeding from? There's nothing down there.

When we got home, my mother led me to her bathroom, handed me a tampon, and closed the door. I had no clue what to do with this thing.

"Where do I put it?"

"In your vagina, dear."

My what? You mean there's a hole there? I struggled to find it. Eventually, I got the tampon in.

Shame oozed out of every pore. Bleeding was bad enough; now I had this thing stuffed up inside me. What if it leaks? What if people know?

The next day, I marched in the Fourth of July parade with my baton class. I felt certain I had a sign on my back saying, "I am having my period." I cringed as I twirled, my white fringe shimmying across my blue leotard.

The following day, my mother called me in. She said, "Now you are a woman. It's not alright for you to play sports with the boys anymore."

My little brother yelled, "But we need her! She's our best passer!"

But she insisted. Contact sports, even baseball, were inappropriate for young women.

No more football, staining my white jeans as I slid on the grass. No more basketball, reaching over the others to receive and guide the ball in. No more baseball (which had become harder anyway, between my left knuckle and my steadily worsening vision). My shame mingled now with anger. "Becoming a woman" meant not doing things that I loved. It meant leaving the guys, leaving the easy interchange while running around. It was a stigma.

I tried "women's sports"—tennis, swimming, track. No good. I tried cheerleading, but it galled me to be on the sidelines while the peewee footballers got to play. I loved acrobatics, but at 5'4" at age 10, I could see I didn't have a future in gymnastics. Secretly, I felt relieved; I got dizzy trying to do walkovers, and the balance beam terrified me.

I poured my energy into baton twirling. I liked baton, but not like I liked football. I simmered.

Now that I had stopped sports, I read. I read Signature Biographies, a wonderful series. I read mysteries: Nancy Drew of course, and Vicki Barr, an airline stewardess who solves mysteries. I read about baseball. I read Gone With the Wind because I found it in the house (one of the few books my parents had on the shelf). I'm sure I missed a lot, but I loved the challenge of reading it and the complexity of the world it presented.

I read the newspapers.

The papers, like the news we watched every night, taught me about civil rights and Vietnam. I didn't talk with my parents about what I read; my father had his opinions, and everyone else was an idiot. As his drinking progressed, his occasional bursts of bad temper had become a general demeanor. My mother tried to steer clear of political topics, or she seemed to agree with him.

I cheered for Martin Luther King and the struggle for civil rights, and I followed the presidential election. I watched the student protests, and wished I could participate. As 1968 progressed, my anger grew.

Then: April 4, 1968. Martin Luther King Jr. was shot and killed in Memphis. This man had held all my hope for transformation in the world, all my hope for justice and peace. Now, just like that, a sick White man killed my hope. On the day of his funeral, I cut my hair just below my ears, the way my mother liked it. I vowed that I would not cut it again. I was through being cute.

Throughout the spring and summer of 1968, the violence deepened. On June 6, Bobby Kennedy was shot and killed during a campaign appearance. Then, the massive police violence at the Democratic Convention in Chicago, where I had longed to be, nailed shut the coffin of my dreams.

The news of the late 1960s brought me to the breaking point with church. I sang in the choir, of course. I sat in Sunday school and confirmation class, where I heard about a God who is omniscient (knowing everything), omnipotent (all-powerful), and benevolent (all good and loving). So, God knows everything, and has ultimate power, and wills our good.

I looked at the world around me. There was chaos and anger in my family, injustice and violence in my country, war and oppression in the world. Was God not, in fact, aware of this, or was God unable to help, or did God really not care? My teachers at church did not have answers to the contradiction I saw. I concluded that the God they were talking about did not exist.

People at church tried to talk their way around this difficulty, and we children were encouraged to just not worry about it too much, but I couldn't let it go. What we did in church seemed to have nothing to do with the world, with the rest of my life, or my family's life. I sang, I went to a class, I saw friends. I went to confirmation class because everyone expected me to. I didn't expect anything from it; since God didn't exist for me, obviously the whole Christian story was nonsense.

My real goal for the class was to win the necklace, a silver cross with leaves entwined. This prize would go to the first person to memorize the books of the Bible in order. I set to work, and soon I had it. I put it in my pink jewelry box. I got it out from time to time and admired it. But I never wore it. I didn't really like jewelry.

When it was time for confirmation, I asked to meet with the priest who taught the class. He wasn't the senior priest; he was a curate, a young man early in his priesthood. Nervous and excited to be having a conference about my life without my parents, to speak for myself, I arrived at his office. It was filled with books and papers, and felt comforting to me.

He sat down behind his desk, and I plopped into a comfortable leather chair. I said, "I don't want to be confirmed. I don't believe any of this. I don't believe in God."

Confirmation, to my mind, was not, actually, about "being confirmed," like someone else confirming me; it was about *confirming* the faith that was spoken in my name at baptism. This was my chance to speak the commitment on my own. And I couldn't, I wouldn't do it. I would not go through the motions. Dal and Jan, my older siblings, each made confirmation, and Dal seemed to take it seriously, but Jan basically graduated from church and didn't look back. And maybe, if I had just felt lukewarm, I would have done it. But I simply couldn't imagine lying about such a thing.

The priest surprised me. He leaned back in his chair and steepled his fingertips. He looked me in the eye. "That's fine," he said. "You'll do it when you're ready."

I had expected a fight, manipulation, guilt trips. But no. He saw my sincerity, and he respected it. He was not trying to get the numbers up, not trying to make the parents happy. So, as I prepared to leave the Episcopal Church, I carried a memory of pastoral integrity that I would appreciate years later.

My parents didn't seem to mind. If church had ever been more to them than a social obligation, they didn't let me know. When Dave was confirmed (again, that curious grammar) the following year, the whole family stopped going to church. My parents had done their duty, getting us to that point, and now everyone was free to forget about it.

Except me. I never told the priest I didn't *want* to believe; I said I *didn't*. I didn't believe in the God they told me about. But I knew there was a lot more to the universe than what I could see, and I knew I needed something to help me navigate it. Because by now, I was in deep trouble.

As Barbie slept and Barb emerged, she—I—opened the door to forces much bigger than I knew how to handle.

Occult fever was in the air in the late 1960s, and my friends and I were entranced. We watched "Dark Shadows," a soap opera about a vampire and his love life. I read about astrology. I hungered for mystery, and drama, and some sort of power.

For Christmas of 1967, just after I turned 11, my parents gave me a Ouija board. These boards were everywhere. The Ouija board promised direct contact with a world we cannot see, a world full of hidden knowledge.

The Ouija board is sold as a "party game" for two or more people, but I played with it alone as well as with my friends. As I kept working with the board, something started to come on the scene—a voice that wasn't mine or my friends'.

It began slowly, working through the letters. The writer was named Duane. Duane was an American sailor on the USS *Pueblo*, a ship that was captured and held by North Korea in January 1968. I followed the whole story in the papers; the Pueblo and her crew were still being held. Duane Hodges was among those killed. Now, his spirit was talking to me. I had a new, special friend. I looked forward to using the board, to talking to Duane. I didn't tell anyone; they might think I was crazy.

One day in geography class, I heard Duane inside my head. No Ouija board; I didn't seem to need one. There was Duane, friendly and curious. He asked, "What are you doing?" and "What are you thinking about?" It was creepy, but cool too. I felt special, gifted with some sort of psychic connection. I could commune with the spirits of the dead! It was like something out of "Dark Shadows"—only real!

For the next several months, Duane showed up at various times: at school, walking home, in my room. I didn't hear Duane with my friends, or when engaged in sports or music; I had to be quiet and alone (or at least not engaged) to hear him.

After another month or so, I began to see Duane a bit. He was shadowy and vague, like you'd expect a spirit to be. He seemed to float, not because he was levitating but more like he was just a wisp, a mist with consciousness. I only saw him sometimes, usually at night.

Gradually, over the following weeks, Duane's voice started to change. He got more serious, asking about the hurt parts of my life. Duane seemed to know my pain. Then, Duane started talking about dying; specifically, he encouraged me to consider dying. Duane wanted me to join him.

"Where are you?" I asked. His answer was vague. I imagined a blackness, a gloom that would match a disembodied spirit. I thought of Duane as stuck between worlds, in a place without joy or pain, just gloom. A shadowy place.

Then, one Saturday night in July 1968, I was babysitting at the Epsteins' house around the corner from my house. Their two children were safe in bed. I watched TV and ate the snack Mrs. Epstein always left for me.

Suddenly, I heard Duane. "Don't you want to die?" he asked. "Why not kill yourself and join me?"

What the hell? I felt miserable, true, but suicide had not occurred to me. And why would Duane want me to die?

"Join you where?" I asked.

This time I could see the answer, and it wasn't the shadowy place I imagined. The shadows must have been smoke.

Like the door of a furnace opening, Duane let go of his sailor mask and showed himself to be a citizen of hell. Duane's face was distorted and glowing in a sea of fire.

I'd been speaking with a demon who wanted me to die, wanted me in hell. The furnace was waiting to consume me.

"Go away!" I shouted in my head. "Go to Connecticut!!!"

Connecticut? Where did that come from?

My friend Bev had recently moved to Connecticut. Connecticut was far away. That was what came to mind. Later, I felt guilty, as if I had sent a demon toward Bev.

But here's the weird thing:

It worked.

I never heard Duane again. I have no idea what door I closed or how I closed it, but I never heard that voice again.

When the Epsteins returned, I managed to look like nothing had happened. There were no fires, no floods, no scorched cushions or slimy counters to show what had occurred here. There was just me, saying goodnight and running out the door, racing home to my room, desperately hoping to be free of that voice, afraid that I might hear it again.

I stopped using the Ouija board. I stopped hearing Duane. Nevertheless, gradually at first, then with aim and force, I headed toward the fires of hell. Over the next few years, I lived out much of Duane's invitation anyway. I dwelt in the land of darkness, in the furnace, and I burned.

I lived in a small town where it was hard to change places and identities. Inside I had a bad girl, an angry rebel, but I didn't know how to let her out. I started experimenting.

I had my first cigarette at age ten. In sixth grade, I got thrown out of Girl Scouts for smoking in the bathroom during a meeting. In seventh grade, I joined again, only to be expelled for talking back to the troop leader.

Around age 11 or 12, I began to drink a little. I stole a wee bit of my father's Scotch. I didn't like the taste, but I liked the feeling of relaxation and silliness that came with it. I didn't want to risk getting caught, so for then, that feeling was just a promise for the future.

In seventh grade, I began acting out in gym class. I didn't hate school; in fact, I loved learning. I began taking French in seventh grade, algebra in eighth. I participated in the University of Chicago's Great Books program, meant to introduce students to the history of Western literature. Perry Kaplan and I raced one another through our speed-reading course.

But all my rage about sports surfaced in the school gymnasium. I hated our stupid royal blue one-piece uniforms—baggy and down to our knees, like old-fashioned bathing costumes, ensuring that our delicate frames would never tempt the boys. I hated the teacher, for no real reason except that she presided over this miserable substitute for the sports I wanted to be playing. I started talking back, refusing to play my part.

I began shoplifting. I started small. Certs breath mints were a big deal in my school. I gradually progressed to stealing several rolls at a time and selling them to friends. It's true—I was a preteen breath mint dealer.

But Certs were not that meaningful to me. Music was my real desire. I spent all my allowance on albums, and I asked for more at birthdays and Christmas. I had all the Beatles albums, the Monkees, Herman's Hermits, Paul Revere & the Raiders, some Rolling Stones.

Those were the days of 45 rpm singles. Groups with one hit might sell a single and never be heard from again. Do you remember Bubble Puppy? Strawberry Alarm Clock? I had them all. I didn't pay for any of them.

The record store in town had listening booths. I would enter the store and pick up several singles, some I wanted and some I didn't. I'd ask to hear one or two, and carry the others into the booth as though considering my purchase. While listening, I would put some of them in my schoolbooks. Afterwards, I'd leave the booth and make a show of returning some. Occasionally, I'd buy something. Then I'd leave, my heart pounding.

I never got stopped.

Sounds crazy, doesn't it? Not crazy that I did it; crazy that the store manager never stopped me. Yes, there were many customers in those days, and we kids went there after school, so they might have been distracted, but really. Were they running some sort of charity for us? I must have had 40 records by the time we moved away.

Each day after school, after my daily fix of HoHos or Hostess cupcakes or Suzy Q's or berry pies, I'd go up to my room. I had fallen in love with the Monkees, and my walls were plastered with pictures of them from all the teen magazines. I had poster-sized pictures of each of them on my ceiling; tiny clips from newspapers lined the walls.

Each day, I entered my sanctum and twirled my baton to the rhythms of my stolen music. (You can, in fact, twirl a baton in close quarters; you just have to be careful with the tosses.) I twirled to them all, but my favorite was Bob Seger's "Ramblin' Gamblin' Man." I loved the ramped-up energy of the song, but I loved the words too: words of freedom and defiance. I'd twirl, and sing along:

> 'Cause I was born lonely down by the riverside
> Learned to spin fortune wheels, and throw dice
> I was just thirteen when I had to leave home
> Knew I couldn't stick around, I had to roam
>
> Gotta keep moving, never gonna slow down
> You can have your funky world, see you around

Take that, suburbia! Take that, Mom and Dad! I'm on the move. Oh yeah, leave me the fuck alone. That song was more than a song to me; it was an anthem.

The baton thumped on the ceiling.

My mother sensed that all was not well with her daughter. In seventh grade, while I stole and twirled, she wrote the first of several letters to me. She wanted to help, she wanted to be there for me, but she just—didn't talk to me. She wrote letters instead, typing them with her italic script. In the first one, she wrote that she was concerned about where I got the money for my records. She had noticed I had them, she had suspicions, but she left it up to me to discuss it if I chose.

I didn't choose. I threw out her letter.

She never mentioned it again.

In the winter of seventh grade, I began my plans to run away. I couldn't say why, but I knew I needed to get away from my family.

I dreamed of San Francisco. Hippies, Haight-Ashbury, Janis Joplin! And no snow. San Francisco had already been decked out in the imaginations of others, and I wanted that glamour and love. Most especially, I wanted to get away.

All I needed to do was get there.

I planned to buy a plane ticket. I practiced signing my mother's signature. Her handwriting was idiosyncratic, round but not in a childish way—just a unique curly hand (which my writing approaches more and more as I age). It was hard to match. It didn't occur to me that the airline agent wouldn't know her signature.

Over the next several weeks, I actually got pretty good at it. But somehow, I never actually took the step. It was just too ambitious, too complicated a plan.

I twirled my baton. I listened to the Beatles singing "She's Leaving Home."

It wasn't just my parents I wanted to flee from; I wanted out of my whole life, my life as a suburban White girl, a good girl with good grades and activities. I didn't know how to be anything else in my small town. I pushed at the edges, but I couldn't really jump. Inside of me, though, someone else was growing, someone not so good or careful. She just needed some help to come out.

November 16, 1969, the day after my 13th birthday, my brother and I went to the Rolling Stones concert in Chicago. Not my older brother Dal; I went with Dave, aged 11, and one of his friends, and my friend Chris. This was my birthday present from my parents. I wore my coolest outfit: a lime green long-sleeved shirt under my brown, faux leather hot pants jumper, with a zipper running all the way down. I wore matching brown boots. My hair was growing long. I could feel sexual energy surge through me, and by now, I knew what it was.

This was the *Beggars Banquet* tour. I played that album obsessively, as I played so much music, grinding every note and every verse into my memory. The songs depicted a world unlike mine, but a world I identified with somehow: druggies, prostitutes, fighters, losers. The album stood like an ensign at the inauguration of my new life.

As we entered the arena, the smell of marijuana hit my nostrils for the first time. I didn't know what it was, but that very fact intrigued me.

Our seats were on the upper level, directly to the left of the stage. We looked down at the sea of bouncing heads and the haze of smoke rising from below. I basked in the energy flowing through the amphitheater.

The Stones opened with "Gimme Shelter." I danced through the whole concert, singing along to "Street Fighting Man" and "Sympathy for the Devil."

Somehow, I crossed a border at that concert. The people they sang of were my people now. Release from my good-girl identity was no longer an idea; it was a promise. And it was waiting for me, for real, without my needing to forge a check. The next week, my parents paid for my escape.

Chapter Three

California Nightmare

SOME PEOPLE EXPERIENCE THEIR ADDICTION as a slow, downhill slide. They start with a little drinking or drugging in high school or college, and gradually progress. That wasn't how it was for me. I saw the edge of the cliff, took aim, and jumped. I wanted to be numb. I would do whatever it took to get there.

A week after the Stones concert, we moved from Chicago to Los Angeles. This is what is known as a geographic cure. My parents thought my father's drinking would be better there. It wasn't.

It was a geographic cure for me too. My fresh start had come, all expenses paid! California, here I come!

I thought, "I can be anyone I want to be." I wanted to be Janis Joplin, all hair and song and anguish, drugs and alcohol and sex, living the electric blues.

As the Stones headed west, to California and disaster, I followed. Like them, I didn't know what awaited me.

A year later, I landed in the hospital.

Along the way, I learned a lot that first year in Los Angeles. School was a snore, way behind where I had been in Illinois; my real lessons were elsewhere.

I learned how to smoke for real. By my first summer in California, I smoked a pack a day. The cigarette machine in the gas station charged 35 cents. In an era filled with anti-smoking posters and warnings, with a mother who had to quit because she was in danger of losing circulation to her extremities, I inhaled heartily. In the face of the warnings, my friend Pam, another tall girl, posed with me for a photo. The caption was, "Smoking stunts your growth." We laughed at our own joke. My mother took the photo. I confronted my parents to let me smoke in the house; they caved. I smoked in the car, and outside school.

I learned to do drugs. When you're a teenager, drugs are easier to get than alcohol. I had my choice: do I want to go up, or down, or psychedelic? I definitely wanted to go down, to sleep, to numb out. Once I got high, nothing mattered and anything was okay. Mixed with alcohol, I could totally check out for hours. I could escape the wailing in my head.

I learned to have sex. Once drugs and alcohol entered the scene, any inhibitions I had vanished. I had kissed David Bloom, and during the summer before we left, I had engaged in heavy groping with a 17-year-old boy at the Wisconsin resort we went to. Now, my education advanced.

My first real boyfriend, Rick, was calm, matter-of-fact, I think because he was snorting heroin. We followed the typical teenage sexual path: Rick pushed, I resisted. But one fine sunny afternoon, at my friend Karen's house, we managed to get into her bedroom alone. Under the influence of the downers, the desire that rose in me was stronger than any reservations. The next thing I knew, we were naked and Rick was entering me. Blood gushed out.

Over the next few months, Rick and I had sex a few more times. One time, in a backyard under the moonlight and some reflected street lights, I came close to an orgasm. As it approached, it scared the hell out of me. What was happening to me? It had to stop! We had to stop!

Rick tried to coax me into continuing, but I couldn't. For all that I wanted to lose consciousness, I didn't want whatever that was—some sort of craziness, dizziness, awareness. We stopped.

That's the closest I ever came to an orgasm with a man. But I didn't know it was an orgasm; I didn't put it together with what I heard about, or my partners experienced. I strained, I pushed, I did my best to go there, but that's not a place you can push to. I could not let go into that well of sensation. Even drunk, even aroused to the point of pain, I couldn't go there. I couldn't be absolutely certain, but I suspected something was missing.

I learned to fight—or, really, how to be prepared to fight without having to fight. I'd never seen girls fight before, but my new schoolmates demonstrated the possibility. I learned to head off fights by threatening dire punishment for touching me. My anger, and my size, served me. I learned to carry a hunting knife.

I learned to cut myself. I made an improv tattoo of Rick's initials by repeatedly scratching them into the back of my hand. Then I turned over my hand and began taking whacks at my wrist.

With all I learned in that period, some things got lost.

I stopped wearing my glasses. Since I no longer read the blackboard, I didn't need them. I memorized landmarks all over the Valley so I wouldn't need to read the street signs.

I left piano and flute. I hated the orchestra leader at school, so one day in January, I accidentally left my flute in an alley near school where I'd been hanging out with friends. The piano was okay: I had graduated from Grieg and Mozart to Simon & Garfunkel and the Beatles. But really, piano takes practice. I didn't have time for that.

I learned to run away, to cuss at cops, to attempt suicide. I learned how to get out of the house, for a while. I did my best to get out of my mind.

Where were you, God, in those years? I believe you were there. I aimed at destruction, but somehow never reached a final end. Were you in me, keeping me from taking the truly disastrous steps? Were you beside me, picking up the pieces? I don't believe you stop us from choosing our paths, but perhaps you open us just enough for us to find a handhold if we reach for it.

Maybe I don't need to know. All I know is, thank you for not letting me die yet.

When I left the hospital the director told me, "You may have fooled your doctor, but you don't fool me. You'll be back." I suppose he was right, but I was bored and in love. The locked door opened, and I returned to my parents' house. "Don't tell anyone where you've been," my mother ordered me.

I went out with Mike until March, when he tried to run me over with his blue Mustang. He had threatened to strangle me, but it seemed an idle threat.

After we broke up, I tried to return to the hospital. My doctor wouldn't let me go back, even when I hinted that I might feel suicidal. "You're not crazy," he said.

I felt crazy, though. I had faked my way out of the hospital, but I hadn't really dealt with anything. The only difference was that now I had Dr. Jacoby, whom I saw every week. I came to his office, and we went down the elevator and outside to the coffee shop next door. There, in the glistening red leather booths, we talked. He told me about making jewelry. I have no idea what I told him. Once or twice, I came to see him on LSD; I don't know whether he knew or not.

In April, two months out of the hospital, I cut my wrist. I didn't mean to kill myself; it was just a very hard day. I wanted to feel some external, concrete pain to ease the volcano inside me. I had been cutting with pieces of glass for a year or so, with nothing more than gentle scars to show for it. But this time, I used a razor blade. I sliced, and my wrist had a gaping wound. It looked to me like my hand was dangling off. There was a lot of blood. No one else was home. I called a friend at UCLA, on the other side of L.A., and said, "Doug, I'm going to die." He told me to get a towel, to go to a neighbor's, and go to the emergency room—all of which I did, with great speed. Our neighbor drove me the two miles to the hospital. I hadn't, in fact, cut anything crucial, so they stitched me up and sent me home. All the while I cried, afraid of my father's anger.

Meanwhile, Doug had called the fire department. My parents drove up just in time to see the firemen trying to force open our front door. This did not sit well with my parents. My mother took to her room, to my Valium tablets. My father pursued me into the bathroom. I sprawled on the floor, sobbing. He stood over me and demanded to know why I did it.

"I hurt!!" I yelled.

"You've never hurt in your life," he said. "You have no feelings to hurt. You just do these things to hurt your mother."

Running away, trying to kill myself, cutting: for him, these were all attacks on my mother.

After Dr. Jacoby heard about this, he asked to see my parents with me. During the meeting, my father repeated what he had said, that my only aim was to make life hard for them. And then—Dr. Jacoby told him to stop talking. He told him that was an unacceptable way to talk to, and talk about, his daughter.

My father stopped! I'd never seen anyone stand up to him except my brother Dal, who'd left, and myself. We hadn't made a dent in him. But Dr. Jacoby was a man, he was older, he was as big as my father, and he told him to stop the poison. I don't know if my jaw dropped as visibly as it felt inside.

I knew that wouldn't end the litany of abuse at home, but it didn't matter. In that moment, Dr. Jacoby became someone I could trust. I knew it vaguely in the hospital, but now it was clear. There was a place, an hour each week, where an adult was on my side.

Just after leaving the hospital, I went to Santa Barbara to visit my sister and her husband. I met a drug dealer on the beach in Santa Barbara. Ken offered me drugs, and we went to his house. I didn't think to tell my sister where I was going. I just followed the pills. For three days, we had sex in his bedroom, the walls lined with tie-dye fabrics and the pillows piled everywhere. I had no awareness that my sister might be concerned; I had no awareness. That was the point of sleeping pills.

Later, Ken came to visit me. We drove up the canyons to the abandoned missile sites around the San Fernando Valley and got high. The lights in the Valley twinkled like a basin of stars, encircled by more mountains. I gradually got more dependent on downers.

While running away and drinking and drugging, I also visited churches. L.A. had churches I'd never seen in Illinois, like the Church of the Nazarene and the Jehovah's Witnesses. On my way to the mall on Sunday mornings, I would pass these churches and stop in. They always welcomed me, but they didn't fit my new lifestyle.

After I left the hospital, my search continued. The downers had become a problem, and I wanted help. My friend Pam and I met someone from a "Jesus freak" church, so we went and told of my need. They prayed over us. I still wanted drugs. They told me to pray harder. I prayed harder, but I still wanted them. The church people said I lacked faith. I said goodbye (well, words to that effect).

That was the last time I went to church for almost twenty years.

But God is sneaky. I wouldn't come to God, so God came to me.

I began high school the next fall. In November, Ken drove down and gave me a baggie full of downers. Hundreds, enough to keep me high for months, or at least weeks. I took the bag with me to school; I had learned that my mother went through my pockets and threw out whatever drugs she found.

Sitting outside before class, I feel the bag in my pocket. Suddenly, I hear a voice: "You'll be dead before this bag is done."

The voice is just behind my left ear, like someone whispering, quiet but distinct. It's not outside of me, but it isn't me either, not like me thinking a thought. It's in that space between inside and outside, me and not-me. The message is definite and clear. And I know, I know in my gut, it speaks the truth.

If I start on this bag, I'll end up dead.

I get up, walk into the school, into the lavatory. The pills swirl as they drain from the toilet.

From now on, I thought, only alcohol! I knew I had been addicted, but that was over. Drinking is a normal American pastime. Okay, so I got drunk a lot, but so did all my friends. Even my family was relieved when they heard I was "only drinking."

I didn't know what that voice was, where it came from, or if I'd ever hear it again. But I knew it spoke truth, and it aimed at life.

I had just had my first conversion experience, complete with the arrogance of the convert. I began to look down on those dope fiends, those druggies. Keep your filthy drugs away from me! Only losers do drugs.

When I met Steve, then, I had to explain. I don't do drugs. I drink.

Chapter Four

Life, Death, Life

WAS STEVE PART OF MY DOWNWARD SLIDE, as my parents thought? Or was he actually an oasis in a life that might have been worse? Or, more likely, both? It may be a cliché to say that people are not all good or bad, but clichés arise for a reason. Good and bad are always woven together in moments and in lives.

In all, Steve was a blessing to me. No one else would have stood for the chaos and anger I brought with me. For the next five years, I knew Steve would have my back when I got lost.

When I met him, Steve was 17 to my 15. His hair was as long as mine (we would occasionally measure), halfway down his back. He dressed in dirty jeans, flannel shirts, and biker boots—a match for my jeans, flannels, and cowboy boots. He had a scraggly teenage beard, wire-framed glasses, and a bad attitude. He was the leader of our tiny pack, the one the others deferred to and accepted insults from. He smoked and drank at a pace matching my own. He was my idea of the perfect boyfriend.

His only drawback was the lack of a car, even a license, after he drove a car into his garage door. The door was never fixed. The hole went with the unmowed lawn and the fading paint on the house.

When we first started having sex, we used the crawlspace over the garage. Steve had made it up with a mattress and a sleeping bag. We could be in there with no one knowing. Later, we stopped hiding and just moved into the house.

Our days fell into a pattern. After school, we'd go to Steve's house. We'd have a snack and play cards while listening to music. Our shared taste ran to Alice Cooper, Deep Purple, the Steve Miller Band, Black Sabbath. Then we would head to his room.

Oh my God, his room. I cringe now to think of it. Of all the things I did, all the ways I sold myself short, going into Steve's room stands out for me. Like many teenage boys, he didn't see the point in cleaning up. Unlike many mothers, his mother didn't see the need to make him do it. He wasn't a hoarder, I think; he just didn't bother to take anything out. His room was a jungle of boxes, papers, old clothes, unwashed clothes, maybe washed clothes. The only clear area was a little path to his bed, which may never—really, I don't know—have been washed. We spent day after day in that room, on that bed. We lay in there until his parents came home. Then we would come out, have dinner with them, watch some TV.

My parents couldn't stand Steve. They couldn't stand his dirty clothes, his flat expression, his house. But especially, my mother had a bigger problem with Steve. Steve had gotten his previous girlfriend, Debby, pregnant. She was having the baby, without Steve, and had dropped out of school. My mother thought he'd get me pregnant and leave me too. I thought Debby was a bitch for chasing him around and hassling him. I wouldn't get pregnant, and Steve wouldn't leave me.

I was half right.

In February 1972, partway through tenth grade, I missed my period. After a few more weeks, I went to the doctor. Sure enough, I was pregnant.

I knew that I could not raise a child—and I didn't want to. If I wanted the baby, I would have had to leave home; my father would have thrown me out that very day. In fact, he might have tossed me just for being pregnant. At 15 years old, I knew I couldn't raise a child. So, unlike Debby, I didn't ask Steve to become a father. I just wanted him to stay with me. When I told him I was pregnant, he shrugged and said, "Bummer." I told him I planned to get an abortion, and he answered, "Cool."

Then I told my mother. She was livid.

"How could such a smart girl be so stupid?" she spit out.

This was not the first time I'd heard that line.

"We used a condom," I offered.

"It didn't work," she snapped back.

We lived in California, where abortion was legal. But that didn't mean it would be easy. My mother was determined that I would get an abortion without my father knowing. That meant we couldn't use our family insurance or money. So off we went to the MediCal office, the place for people with no resources. My father worked for DuPont, he had resources, but I didn't.

My mother had to go with me and give her approval. The office was not like anywhere my mother had ever gone. Rows of chairs on a concrete floor. Public health posters on the walls. Clerks behind a desk, telling us to take a number. This was an education for her, and for me.

We sat in the waiting room—me, my mother, and Steve. I sat between them, like a referee between angry boxers. On my right, Steve held my hand, smoked, and stretched out his long legs. On my left, my mother sat upright, stiff as a board, her shoulders pulled up to her neck. I could see the steam rising from my mother's ears. I knew she was mad that Steve got me pregnant, but I also had the feeling that she was furious that he hadn't left. Not only because it made her wrong, but more because she just wanted him gone.

I, on the other hand, felt loved. Not by my mother, who was doing the huge hard work of caring for me alone, but by Steve, who sat by my side and let himself be named as the father. I felt vindicated.

See? He loves me.

Now, the agonizing waiting began. The abortion was scheduled for spring break, another two weeks away. I would go to the hospital, have a simple procedure, and be home. Easy.

As the day approached, I felt uneasy. I could feel something in me I hadn't expected; a spark of life, of possibility. I knew I needed to do this in order to have a life going forward, but I hadn't known my heart might break. I pushed down the feeling, as I had pushed so many before.

Then, on the day before the abortion was scheduled, I began to bleed. In the ordinary course of things, my mother would have taken me to the hospital—but then my father would find out. So instead, she drove me to my friend Neil's house. The plan was for me to lie on the couch and bleed until it was over. Neil's mother worked during the day, and she accepted our cover story that I had been temporarily ejected from my parents' house. My mother told my father that I was visiting a friend.

Steve stayed with me. My mother checked on me each day. We hung around, watched TV, and listened to music, like any other spring break (or any day after school).

At the end of the break, I was still bleeding, but I needed to go home. That night, I finally lost the fetus. It was tiny, almost formless, but it was clearly not just a blood clot. I stared into the toilet, and then I flushed. I told my mother.

I went to my room, closed the door, and sobbed—quietly, in case my father heard. The reality hit me. Beyond judgments, beyond right or wrong, something had begun in me. Without even knowing it, I had somehow let myself care about it. And it was gone, expelled into the sewer. I had no idea what to do with this feeling, and no one to share it with.

The next day, we went to our family doctor. This kind, patient man had seen me through cut wrists, a motorcycle mishap, and the pregnancy test. Now he examined me and said everything looked fine. He assured me that there was no reason I couldn't have children in the future.

As we got in the car, my mother stared ahead and said, "I guess it's time we got you on the pill."

I looked out the window and replied, "I guess so."

And that was that. We never discussed it again.

Mom, I'm so sorry. I couldn't see how hard you worked to save me from my teenage self. As I write, I realize, and regret. Thank you for all you did to shelter me. Please God, be with all the girls and women who lack the resources to make choices or receive support. Bless all those who try to help them, and the children they bring into the world. Please, please, please.

Steve's parents sort of adopted me. I don't think we told them about the pregnancy, but soon afterward, I began talking with Steve's mom, Sylvia, over cups of Emperor's Choice tea. She listened to me without judgment, without advice. I'd stay for dinner, and then Steve and his father would drive me home in Vern's little yellow Datsun pickup. Squeezed between two men who were on my side against my parents, I felt safe.

Vern and Sylvia were "alternative" sorts, into meditation and psychic phenomena and the occasional marijuana binge. They were part of a monthly group that met for meditation and spiritual sharing, and they began inviting me along with Steve. I learned about past lives, reincarnation, Seth, A Course in Miracles. They treated me as someone in my own right, on my own path.

Among the group was a middle-aged, overweight lesbian couple, possessed of 20 cats. They were a couple, but sex didn't really show up for me in their relationship. We called them "friends," and they acted like that when they joined us in meditation gatherings. They were dwelling in that netherland of semi-closeting so common at the time, abiding with their neighbors, seen but not acknowledged. I didn't want their lives, but I liked that they were accepted by the group. In a world where lesbians were generally invisible, I now had two pictures: women in jail and sexless cat lovers. That's as far as that went for years.

Curiosity about psychic phenomena and ideas, this desire for the strange, was a big part of my bond with Steve. This bond would persist long after we officially broke up the next year. Like me, Steve was hungry for something—some experience, some aliveness. I gave it to him.

It began a month or so after we became an item. One afternoon, as we lay together on a twin bed in Neil's house, clothed but breathing hard,

Suddenly, something like a shroud comes over me. It seems to me that I'm in the back of my head, watching, listening.

Filth begins to pour out of my mouth. I turn my back to Steve, and I say terrible things, hateful things. My mind is filled with hatred, and it spills all over him. But not only Steve: I am speaking of myself in the same way. But not as "I." Instead, I'm referring to myself as "she," as alien to the person speaking. And that's how it feels. The "I" who is watching is not the "I" who is speaking, though it isn't anyone else either.

From "my" place in the back of my head, I laugh. I think, this is some weird game I'm playing on Steve, venting. I think, I could stop at any time. Isn't this bizarre?

But I can't stop. I can't just stop and roll over. I can think of doing that, but I am powerless to do it.

After a while, the other voice subsides. I return to the front of my head, drained, exhausted. I'm freezing. Finally, I can turn toward Steve. I need a blanket and a hug, from this man/boy I'd just attacked so viciously.

I don't know how to talk about what just happened, so I pretend I don't know. Steve tells me a little. Because my exhaustion and cold are real and evident, he can believe that I had undergone something.

After this, the—what can I call them? Attacks? Invasions? Insanities?—recurred for several years. At first, they were frequent, maybe every month or two. Later, the intervals got longer, and I began to know when they were coming. If they began while I was home alone, I'd get in the car and go to Steve's. We'd drive into the hills surrounding the western San Fernando Valley, and sit and let it pour out. I knew I needed a safe companion at those times, and he was the only one I could trust with it. Steve didn't ask questions. Each time the cycle—the voice, me watching but frozen, coming out into cold. He said he knew when it was coming, because the air around me got cold.

I never told him I could see what was happening. I felt too confused, ashamed. Was I perpetrating some kind of fraud? Maybe I could have stopped it, fought it . . . I pushed it all away.

Of course, you might be diagnosing me, her, as you read this. The language we use determines the attitude and solution we bring to the situation. Medical: this girl is dissociated. She needs a skilled psychiatrist! Spiritual/supernatural:

this girl is possessed. Get her to an exorcist! Or, my father's: this girl is seeking attention and abusing others. Don't reward her! Call her bluff. Ignore her.

You choose. I'm just telling you how it was for me.

These episodes weren't the only frontier for psychic drama, however. My antennae were out, all the cracks in my own psyche somehow providing access to a reality I knew but couldn't pin down. Sometimes I stood in the fields beyond our house and felt the energy of the universe streaming around me—neutrinos on their long journey, electrons swirling. I walked through the ruins of a burned-down house in that same area, and sensed pools of anguish or long-ago celebrations. During these times I'd be present, but extended somehow. Steve was my witness, my anchor, when this awareness would come pouring in. I relied on him to be steady and non-judgmental.

We got hooked up with someone who claimed a local house was haunted, and asked for help in cleansing it. I had no clue how to do this, but I wanted to see what was up. Off we went in Neil's car. The house was set apart a bit from its neighbors. It had a neglected air, as it had been unoccupied for several years. We had been given a key, and so we walked in.

As we walk in, the house seems to breathe. The main rooms are unremarkable, just empty, but with a forlorn air. But as I walk down the hall toward the bedrooms, I sense something different. The hair on the top of my head goes on alert. My arms are tingling, a subtle sensing.

I turn into the second left bedroom. At first glance, it is as empty as the rooms I've passed. But in the far corner, as through a mist, I see a child in a low rocking chair. This boy, maybe nine years old, is hunched over and crying. He doesn't acknowledge me.

I know he's the "ghost" who is coloring the atmosphere of the house. Had he died here? Or had he been left behind in some other way? Whatever his plight, he is clearly stuck.

I want to hug him, but I can't. I reach out somehow, and tell him I'm sorry he hurts. His life isn't here anymore. It's time to leave.

Steve calls to me. Our friends are ready to go. I don't tell them what I've seen. As we begin to drive, though, we all sense that we are not alone in the car. Neil says, "I feel like I'm being shown where to drive." He follows this prompt for several miles, until we end up on another quiet street, this one with houses lit for the evening. Neil stops across from one of them, a nondescript white house with green shutters. The car feels different then, like our passenger has gotten out and gone toward the house. Then I tell them what I had seen in the house.

Of course, we wanted to know more! We wanted to go to the door and ask if they had a son, if they'd lived in the first place, what had happened there. But we didn't. We never knew, I never knew, if we shared a real event, or followed a lot of suggestible ideas. That seemed true for a lot of my life during those years. Was I crazy? Psychic? Both? How would I know?

I had given up on "God," but I hungered for contact with the energy of the universe. I knew there was something, another reality alongside this one, that I couldn't name or access.

It was confusing, but at least it wasn't boring.

Boredom, in fact, has been part of my journey toward healing. When I landed in Juvenile Hall, I saw how boring that life would be. Hospital, same. And then, what I had with Steve grew stale. There was only so long I could hang out, even with all my interior drama.

The opening wedges happened in the spring of tenth grade. In school I took all the basic classes, with no plan to go to college or even learn anything in high school. My grades were okay, but they involved no study. I took Comparative Religion as an elective, and wrote a paper on Satanism.

I spent my days with Steve and his friends. Without a car, without money, and without any dreams or plans, we didn't have much to do. Boredom stretched out before me.

At home, I read. I read anything I could get. Steve introduced me to Robert Heinlein, and I read every one of his books. But I also consumed any novel I could get: Arthur Hailey, Leon Uris, James Michener. Then I plowed through my sister's high school books, the ones she read for her classes. John Steinbeck, Sinclair Lewis, Hermann Hesse. Reading

Exodus, then *Mila 18*, I learned of the horror of the Shoah. In an effort to understand how this happened, I read books about Hitler, about Germany. Soon, I had taught myself modern European history.

So, in school, I was officially not interested. I had bursts of curiosity and cooperation, but without social support for them, they died out. My identity as a rebel demanded that I not care about school. But that identity carried with it a commitment to truly numbing levels of ennui, interspersed with sex and hormonal rages. There was only so long I could live like that, but I needed more than a prod.

It's not enough to know what not to do. I needed something in front of me, a possibility for my life, before I could shift course.

In the spring of tenth grade, that possibility came through three teachers.

Singing was the only activity that transferred with me from Chicago to Los Angeles. Somehow, when I wasn't running away or locked up, I continued singing lessons. My mother found a teacher in Westwood, a good 45-minute drive from our home. Adele was Lebanese by heritage, Italian by training, operatic in her expression. She emphasized technique and beauty over power.

She expected great music from me—me! She pushed me. She terrified me. I ran into her bathroom in tears when she told me to do something I was sure I couldn't do—not the only time that would happen to me. She stood outside the bathroom door and coaxed me back out.

Adele assigned me music that was "appropriate for my age." Voices take a long time to mature, and they need nurturing. I sang songs that gradually extended my range while I developed vocal technique. They were nice, and I enjoyed singing, but they didn't rock my soul.

In high school choir, we sang age-appropriate music as well. I liked to sing, but the music was pretty tame. I bided my time, waiting for something—I didn't know what.

Then one day, an earthquake hit my little world. Mr. Greb, our teacher, handed out some sheet music. Before we started looking at the music, he played a recording.

The top of my head came off.

The music soared, and dipped, and ran around the room. It wove a shimmering fabric of sound, a fabric that kept changing like light on a moving glass.

What is this? What is this beauty? What is this power? Oh my God. THIS is not just music. This is a foreign land I never dreamed of, a continent of immense area and height. This is how eagles fly. This is rolling waves of sound, up and down. This is dance. This is energy, more energy than the hard rock I love, channeled and made into a mountain.

It was the "Sanctus" from Bach's *B Minor Mass*.

Then we sang it. One practice and I fell in love. To feel the notes moving up and down my head cavity, to hold the posture I needed to reach the high notes, to maintain the technique and awareness needed for the runs—that was what it was to be alive. I stood in the midst of dozens of voices and sang my heart out. I quivered like a tuning fork to the music that ran through me and around me. I wanted to be surrounded by this sound. For the first time in years, maybe the first time I remember, I felt fully alive.

Adele was furious. "This man, he will kill your voice!" She planned to call my director, to get him to stop. I prayed that she would fail.

From that day, my world changed. I still listened to my old music. But now my money went into buying the *B Minor Mass*, and later to *Bach's Greatest Hits*. The following year we sang Vivaldi's *Gloria*, and I bought that.

From then on, there was a counterpoint to the anger and chaos that had consumed my life. Bach introduced me to ecstasy, an ecstasy that was nonetheless ordered and sane. I did not suddenly convert and become healthy and happy, but I had a lifeline.

The second opening for possibility showed up quite differently. One day in choir, Kathy sat down next to me. She was as close as I came to a friend who didn't drink. She was neat and tidy and dressed like a normal high school girl. She worked as a student assistant in the English department.

That day, she leaned over and whispered, "They had a meeting to talk about you."

To say I challenged my teachers would be an understatement. I came in late, I made noise in the back row, I slumped and shrugged, and failed to turn in homework. For some reason, it peaked in English class. My school had designed tenth-grade English in modules, six weeks on poetry, ten weeks on European literature, you get the idea. Each module was taught by a different teacher. I might read voraciously at home, but I wanted nothing to do with my English class, or the teachers. I got by on the tests, but I wasn't really learning anything. The teachers were sick of it.

Kathy said, "Some of the faculty wanted to just give you credit and get you out of the rest of the year. But Mr. Rifkind told them that you were learning something, and that you'd come around someday when you felt like it."

That hit me like a bomb. Mr. Rifkind stood up for me. For an adult, a teacher, to profess faith in me! To see something in me buried underneath my flannel shirts, dirty jeans, and boots! To hear something beside the taps on my shoes as I walked down the school corridors to the vice principal's office!!

Mr. Rifkind became an object of devotion. I had a new father figure: short, slight, dark, gentle, Jewish. Pretty much my father's opposite.

I wanted to please Mr. Rifkind. I started behaving a little better, and I decided to take Mr. Rifkind for American Literature in eleventh grade. I decided to work in his class.

That same spring, Mr. Wilhite, my math teacher, went off book. Having no interest in college, I sat in "High School Math," the class for dummies, covering material I did in seventh grade back in Chicago. There was lots of room to be bored.

Mr. Wilhite wasn't much to look at—he was a slouchy, sloppy dresser, kind of hunched, high balding forehead, glasses. He had a quiet, sort of shy demeanor. He was nice without being afraid of us.

One day he came in and announced: "You all are too smart for this stuff. I'm going to show you something else." Graceful shapes appeared on the blackboard, with letters and numbers.

I vaguely remembered seeing these shapes and letters a few years back, when I had been in eighth-grade algebra, before the move. But they hadn't mattered then; they were just part of the next assignment. Now, there was no "supposed to"; there were just these beautiful equations. Quadratic equations: even the name was delicious. Quadratic; Ecstatic. I rolled the name around in my mouth, and felt vaguely intelligent. Somehow, I knew, the beauty on the blackboard and the beauty of Bach were connected.

I decided that I would go back to the beginning and take first-year algebra with Mr. Wilhite the following year.

The pilot light was on—and so was the fight for my identity. Could I be a pissed-off rebel, Steve's girlfriend, and also a student?

No. Not exactly. Steve and I broke up the following fall. I began to talk about things he didn't know about and didn't care about.

The final nail in the coffin of our relationship was *The Fountainhead*, by Ayn Rand. I read it in the summer of 1972, after tenth grade, in the wake of these epiphanies, and I got one message loud and clear: I am worth something. It didn't matter that I didn't fit in. My anger was a sign of something deeper, something creative. I related to Howard Roark's tortured soul, to Dominique's passion, to the promise of creativity and energy. Ayn Rand let me still be a pissed-off rebel, *and* a student. I inhaled her writing: *Atlas Shrugged*, *Anthem*, all her non-fiction books. They led me to philosophy and politics and economics.

Her message fit well with my alienation: I don't need you! I don't need anyone! Just get out of my way! So there.

Steve wasn't interested in politics, or history, or ideas. As I began to wake up, we drifted apart. I wanted conversations: conversations! About ideas! He wanted things as they had been. I became "too much hassle" for him, and he became not enough stimulation for me.

We broke up, and he found another girlfriend. That didn't interrupt our spiritual adventures, or our drinking, or even our sex. I eventually became "the other woman," a fuck buddy before we had that name. I didn't have another steady boyfriend for years. But slowly, I began to have a bigger vision for my life.

Without Steve holding my identity in place, I began to shift.

I painted my room, finally erasing the mustard color that had been there before (and who on earth thought that was a good color for a bedroom?) and taking down the black paper poster. Now my walls were a pale blue, coordinating with my blue-and-white desk and bookshelf set that had come with me from childhood. I got a quilted blue-and-white bedspread, complete with little flowers on it. My mother breathed a sigh of relief. "This is beautiful!" she cooed.

My clothes changed too. I didn't abandon my jeans and flannels, but I expanded. Some days I wore—wait for it—a skirt. I got a blue-and-white pleated miniskirt and navy-blue laced shoes with chunky heels. I felt quite sexy in this, in a sort of schoolgirl way. I loved the bounce of the pleats as I walked.

I had begun wearing glasses again when I started going with Steve. He wore them too, so it seemed to me it would be hypocritical of him to reject me for wearing mine. The rectangular wire frames enabled me to look sort of cool while seeing the world.

I worked in my classes, and my grades rose. I decided to go to college after all. I hadn't had any of the college prep classes, so I planned to go to the local state school. I found that if I took summer school and an extra course each semester I could graduate a semester early, and that suited me fine.

As a sort of punishment, students who completed early were barred from the graduation ceremony. I would get my diploma in the mail. But I wanted to be part of the party, even if I wasn't invited. The choir was going to sing the "Hallelujah Chorus," which I knew by heart, so the teacher let me join them. I threw on a choir robe over my jeans and cowboy boots, and let my soprano soar.

Once Steve and I broke up, my parents let me learn to drive. By spring 1973, I was cruising in my father's gold 1970 Impala—not exactly cool, but it was wheels. I could go places, lots of places, without my parents knowing exactly where or with whom. I could get to parties. When I started hanging out with Steve again, I lied to my parents about my plans. I made some girlfriends, introduced them, then used them as my named destinations. My parents would ask for a phone number, and I just never quite managed to give it to them.

I spent the summer of 1973 in summer school, writing essays and grinding valves at school in the morning, and reading in the afternoon. The evenings—the evenings were mine. I may not have had friends, not like people you hang out with or share meaningful conversation with, but I had people I could drink with.

We met on turnoffs, plateaus in the Santa Susana Mountains just outside the Los Angeles city limits. It was a thing: "I'm going to the plateau." Thirty or forty of us, ranging from high school into directionless 20s, every Friday and Saturday night. I'd drive up and down the canyon in a drunken blackout, and arrive home safely. Not a ticket, not an accident in all those years. (Yes, God, thank you.)

One night, that same little voice that got me off drugs spoke up. "Leave now," it said. Just behind my ear, like before, "Leave now." I got in my car and left. Later, I learned that one of our friends drove off the side of the road and slid down the canyon.

That voice didn't keep me from returning the next week, however, or the weeks after that.

Late that summer, a guy showed up. He was just a face, a big guy who was high and wanted everyone else to get high. He pressed some uppers into my hand and said, "Take them." I said, "I'll do it in a minute," so he'd leave me alone. I hated uppers! I hadn't taken pills in years. I put them in my pocket.

About an hour later, the county sheriffs showed up to break up the party—the first time that had happened to us. They went through the crowd, and they searched us. They found the pills in my pocket, and that was it. Off to the Malibu sheriff's station.

I sat in the cell and waited for my parents. I had tried so hard to clean up my act, and *now* I got arrested! Back when I had actually been using drugs, I never got caught. *Now* I got caught because I didn't take them! Something was wrong here.

I sat alone in the cell, humiliated. My parents came and took me home. I went to my room. I planned to never come out again.

The next morning, I remained in my room under a blanket, waiting for the ax to fall. Instead, my brother Dave came in and said, "Come out. We believe you."

My mother went with me to the probation office for the preliminary hearing. She brought my eleventh-grade report cards, my vastly improved report cards, and said to the probation officer, "Are these the grades of a girl who does drugs?"

The probation officer looked at them and said, "Well, they could be."

Undaunted, my mother plowed on, telling him how I had changed, how responsible I had become. Yes, I had a record, I had been on probation before, but that was three years ago. Now, she said, I'm a model citizen, except for this one incident.

The officer was not overwhelmed by this testimony. But as he walked me through the arrest, he found that the sheriffs had no probable cause to search me. I hadn't been close enough to the drug dealer to warrant such blanket suspicion. Or maybe he just didn't want to fight my mother. At any rate, the case was dismissed. I still had the arrest on my record, but no conviction.

On my 18th birthday, my mother filed a request to have my records sealed. When it was granted, she took me to Benihana of Tokyo, my favorite restaurant, for sukiyaki. Her relief was greater than mine: I didn't really know the consequences of that record, the questions and rejections that I would have faced. I learned later, as I applied for jobs and schools. And over time, like so much in my family, it just receded from consciousness, if not from memory. Let's just forget about it.

I had another glimmer of light in high school. It didn't seem like much at the time, but eventually, it would change my life.

I loved all sports. I loved playing, and I loved watching (except for golf, which I disliked in any form). When the Olympics came on, I sat glued to the set.

At the 1972 Summer Games, an Australian swimmer named Shane Gould took several medals. I liked her, but what really lit me up was her name. I had never heard it before, but as soon as I heard it, I knew: that's my name! I had never been comfortable with Barbara, with its diminutives and variants. I lived with Barb now, but it had never felt right. I knew that the root of the name was Greek for "stranger," and I didn't like that. Even without that, though, it was the sound of it, the push-pop of the Bs at either end.

Barbed wire. Sharp. Serious, studious. For me, Barbara was a spoiled name, the name of someone I didn't want to know.

I heard the name "Shane," and I knew that was me. Of course, I didn't tell anyone: only crazy people changed their names when they didn't have to. I hugged that name to myself.

Soon, Shane became a figure in the stories I told myself each night. Since the age of eleven, I had trouble falling asleep. I saw monster faces when I closed my eyes, but I had learned that visualizing a story could keep the faces away until I fell asleep.

In these stories I was strong and powerful. When I began them, I was also angry and destructive. But as Shane, the stories shifted.

Now, I remained strong and powerful. Conflict surrounded me, but I didn't initiate the fights. Often wounded, I would still manage to drive to my lover's house and get bandaged up. I could communicate telepathically with him, so he knew when to expect me.

Shane was gifted, a target, and resilient. And, though she had this boyfriend, she—I—was fundamentally self-reliant. Shane didn't need others, nor did she wish them harm. She just wanted to play pool, drink a few beers, have sex, and see into the mystery.

I told versions of this story every night I went to bed sober until I moved in with an actual boyfriend. It felt weird to tell myself stories while lying next to him. I found I could sleep now without the monster faces appearing.

I didn't tell anyone about the monster faces, or about the stories, or Shane. Who would I have told?

Chapter Five

College

IN THE ROOMS OF 12-STEP PROGRAMS they tell people to "act as if." If you don't believe in God, act as if you do and see what happens. If you still feel like a beaten-down addict, act as if you are a responsible citizen and, over time, you might find yourself becoming one. In church language, people might call this "formation." If it works, you can actually become healthier. Or, you might just fake your way through life.

Sometimes, both may be happening at the same time.

I entered California State University in the fall of 1974, after a summer bingeing on booze and sex. I left as a married woman. I entered as a Young Republican, and left as a Marxist feminist. College, we are told, can change lives.

Cal State actually was perfect for me. The classes were smaller, the teachers were available. Best, they had a great music department, especially their voice department. Because my high school had a strong reputation for voice, the director of the University Chorus wrote to invite me to join the Chorus in singing Verdi's *Requiem* that fall. I didn't know the piece yet, but I knew I wanted to do it. Throughout my undergraduate years, I sang in the Chorus: Mozart, Mendelsohn, Beethoven. I loved, loved, loved the feeling of singing at the top of my range with 120 other people, surrounded by waves of sound. We practiced three times a week, and I never missed.

I didn't know it then, but that was my first healthy spiritual practice. When I sang, I didn't think. I didn't want to drink, or escape. I didn't worry about classwork, or feel lonely or pissed off. I was present. Singing connected me to myself, and to the universe. The energy was powerful, but contained and directed.

As much as I loved to sing, I decided that it would be a leisure activity for me. I had wanted to be a voice major, but I couldn't work up the courage to audition. I'd given up my voice lessons two years before. I didn't think I could support myself from music. And, really, I wasn't sure I wanted to spend my life around the people I knew from choruses.

I turned to my other love, politics. I majored in political science, thinking I might eventually go to law school (once my records were sealed, of course). That first year, though, my poli-sci courses were boring! Lots of memorizing and multiple-choice exams. I wanted to pursue the ideas that I had begun to learn by reading Ayn Rand: individual freedom, free markets, objective truth.

As part of the poli-sci major, I had to take macroeconomics. Here, I found the clarity I sought. Graphs and formulas—patterns, not just items. And truth, not just a bunch of opinions. You could prove this stuff. I switched my major to economics.

Economists have a saying: "If you can't quantify it, it doesn't exist." It's sort of a joke, but not entirely. As I continued to wrestle with my psychic/psychological drama, economics, math, and logic provided a clear and sturdy place to stand. I told myself that all the events and perceptions of earlier years were fiction. I tried to just put them aside.

And yet, I continued to be drawn to people who were seeking a bigger meaning. I usually met them while drinking (well, that's how I met everyone, really). I read all of Carlos Castaneda's books to that time. I read about Native American spirituality and history. This gave me words for a bigger reality than what I could see, and a respect for the earth. It also fueled my anger at oppression and injustice. I continued to go to the fields and the canyons, stretching toward any shreds of aliveness I could find there. I went into the hot desert hills and read Dostoevsky.

Now, though, I also read philosophy. Locke, Hume, Berkeley. I read Plato's *Dialogues* during my shift at a local gas station. I read Milton Friedman and Carl Hayek, leading proponents of free-market capitalism. While one side of me was standing in solidarity with indigenous people, another part was pushing for some individualist Eden in which values such as solidarity and community didn't really enter. I lived a double life, still or again.

During registration week, I saw the table for the College Republicans. I went over to sign up.

A pair of conservatively dressed young men looked at me with suspicion. They thought I was teasing them. There I stood, in my jeans and boots and T-shirt. I didn't fit their picture of a Republican.

"What?" I demanded. "Is there a problem here?"

Finally, Gary shrugged and handed me the sign-up sheet. He gave me a flyer saying when their meetings were. I'm sure they never expected me to come.

Within a few months, I became the vice-president of our local chapter. I got involved with the Young Republicans in our area, and was put in charge of liaising with other college campuses. I served as a delegate to the state conventions of both bodies. At the end of my freshman year, I received a scholarship from the Republican Women's Club, and got my picture taken with Fred, the cockatoo from the TV show "Baretta." I won a scholarship to summer school at Georgetown University, in a program sponsored by Young Americans for Freedom, an ultra-conservative group. My parents beamed.

I spent the summer in Washington, D.C., taking classes in the morning and working at the Capitol in the afternoon. I spent my afternoons with mountains of data, trying to make a case for abolishing the Federal Reserve System.

After that, I needed a drink! I gathered with the other students at the pub on the Georgetown campus. The drinking age in D.C. was 18, so I drank legally for the first time.

As always, I found the real drinkers. Not everyone who came to the pub was a drinker. You had to stay till closing and see who stayed with you. I found Rick. He didn't really drink like I did, but he seemed happy to be with me while I did. We took six-packs to the lawn outside my dorm and lay under the stars and talked. (At least I think we did; sometimes I blacked out, and found myself back at my dorm room.) By the end of summer school, we declared ourselves to be in love.

Rick came from a conservative Christian home, and went to the local Catholic college. But somehow, his path resonated with me. He shared my interest in Native American spirituality. Fascinated by traditional arts and crafts, and the promise of self-sufficiency, he introduced me to the *Foxfire* series of books about traditional arts and crafts. I learned to make jam.

For a year, Rick and I wrote each other four times a week. I professed love, and meant it, while I continued to have sex with Steve and the clerk at the liquor store. In the summer of 1976, I took the bus from California to Pennsylvania to see him. I met his parents, and went to their church. I got some exposure to a world very different from my West Coast beaches-cars-sex world, a world of German and Irish immigrants, of coal miners. People generally stayed put, generation after generation.

I was glad to see Rick, and happy to leave there.

Rick graduated college the next semester, and in December, he came to visit. Well, actually, he moved to L.A. He stayed with me and my parents, then he found a job as an apartment manager. When he moved there, I moved with him. It didn't occur to me to tell my parents or discuss this; I thought it was obvious.

After a few days, my mother called. "When are you coming home?" she asked.

"What do you mean?"

Her question shifted. "Are you staying there?"

"Oh, yeah. I thought you knew that."

She didn't explode. Whatever my father said escaped me.

That spring, Rick proposed and I accepted. It seemed to make sense. He was 25, four years older than me, and he wanted to settle down.

Over the next year, even as plans for the wedding progressed, I began to see that life with Rick would be a settling down indeed. He loved the things I loved, shared my views, but . . . honestly? His horizons were smaller than mine, or different. I wanted to set fire to the world with ideas, and he wanted a steady job and a happy marriage. I tried to ignore the uneasiness in my bones.

The spring of 1978 had brought two men into my life, each of them shifting my path in big ways. It was my last semester in college. In January, I began applying to graduate schools in economics, hoping to leave Southern California for someplace with seasons. Rick and I were scheduled to get married in June.

By the time I graduated in May, my life was a mess. My neat plans were falling apart. My mistake was to let myself think new thoughts, and feel new feelings.

As I progressed through the economics major, I began to get impatient with what I heard. My school's economics department was filled with acolytes of Milton Friedman and the University of Chicago, where he held sway. As long as I stayed in that camp, all was well. But I began to notice the wall around the camp, and feel the scrape on my face when I hit that wall.

I had left the Republicans two years earlier, after I got kicked out for refusing to go along with a stolen election. I tried the Libertarian Party, then just forming. I went to a convention in the spring of 1976. Everywhere, I saw people who didn't fit in, and who just seemed to want to be left alone. I began to question the motivations behind the libertarian philosophy, and to return to my earlier concerns for a more robust social justice.

Then, in the fall of my senior year, I ran smack into the boundaries of my teachers' ideas. I had looked forward to taking History of Economic Theory, in which we read the writers who had shaped modern economics. We read Adam Smith, Thomas Malthus, and David Ricardo, early figures, examining their ideas closely.

Then we got to Marx. Our teacher assigned the Communist Manifesto, in which the young Marx made some predictions that had not—so far—played out. Our whole exposure to Marx amounted to reading the list of things he had been wrong about, and dismissing him.

Outrage spurted up from within me. I knew we had been cheated, left ignorant of a hugely important thinker and system of thought. The other students complained too, but the professor did not address our objections.

In the wake of that incident, I began to notice the times when I'd ask a question and the professor would answer, "Well, if you knew more economics, you'd know why that isn't a problem." They never, however, seemed to want to teach me that "more." I thought that maybe I'd learn it in graduate school.

The next semester, my final one as an undergraduate, I decided to take two philosophy courses that fit my interest: Philosophy of Social Science and Political Philosophy. Both were taught by a professor I had never met.

I entered the classroom with my new stack of books. I hadn't heard of any of them, but they looked intriguing. They had titles like "The Dialectic of Sex." This was new terrain, intriguing and challenging.

Right on the dot at 2 o'clock, Alan entered. He too was different from my usual crew of professors. For one thing, he was cute. Black hair, worn just a little long over the ears with bangs—sort of a Beatles cut. Matching black glasses framed his narrow, intense face. Slender, vibrating health, he contrasted sharply with my usual slouchy teachers. He looked like a man with a passion. His leather jacket, too, was not usual attire for professors at Cal State. Clearly, he wasn't from around here. It turned out he was a refugee from the East Coast, trained at Harvard, somehow landing at this California second-tier school. Someone asked why he came there. He replied with a line from *Casablanca*: When asked why he came to Casablanca, Humphrey Bogart answered: "I came for the waters." His interlocutor exclaimed: "But Casablanca is in the desert!" Bogie shrugged. "I was misinformed," he drawled.

He had me right there. This guy was smart, and funny, and edgy. He felt ready for a contest, for debate. He wanted us to challenge him and one another. After all my math and logic classes, with one right answer, Alan offered an open space to explore.

He said he was a Marxist, and that we would be reading several books from that perspective. Of course, I had been disgusted with the dismissive treatment of Marx in my history of economic theory course, but I was still wedded to monetarist free-market theory. I saw the contours of the contest: In arguing for "my side," I would get to confront directly the challenge presented from another perspective.

I didn't know then that this meeting would change my whole trajectory. I couldn't know that in another year, I'd be walking out of my graduate fellowship and calling Alan for help.

As I knew from personal experience, earthquakes open new cracks in the ground that seem solid and fixed. If finding Marxism and feminism was the first earthquake of 1978, the second was falling for Blake. Like the first, this one began below ground, with subtle vibrations and tensions, until one day, the earth split open.

Blake was brilliant. Period. He was a philosophy and math major, like most of the circle of friends I had found. Each day we would all gather at the cafeteria on the roof of Sierra Hall and play games— bridge, hearts, pinochle, backgammon, Risk, depending on who was there and how long we had. Blake was clearly the smartest of a bright bunch, and he radiated energy. His long black hair and scraggly beard made him seem safe to me. His intense engagement with everything he encountered was a magnet for me.

Blake was a falconer, training and rehabilitating eagles and hawks, and he knew everything about that. He had a prodigious memory, which he turned to learning every Monty Python routine and every Tom Lehrer song. He loved any sort of challenge.

Sometime before college, Blake traveled down to Central America just out of curiosity. In a Guatemalan bar, he saw a scarlet macaw sitting over the row of bottles. He bought the young bird, and put him in a cardboard box, and brought him home via local buses. Scarlet macaws can live up to age 75, so Blake had a bird for life. He named him Big Bird.

In short, Blake was interesting. I fell for his curiosity about the world, for his energy, for his active intellect.

As the semester progressed, I found myself thinking about Blake. I sat in the hallway of the philosophy department, hoping to run into him. I didn't let myself think about what I was doing. Of course, I wouldn't get involved with him! We were just hanging out, right? I told myself that—right up until the night we had sex in the back of my van.

When I got home that night, I saw the wedding dress hanging on the closet door and the invitations, printed and waiting for addressing. I knew I had crossed a line. The next day, I called off the wedding. I don't think I told Rick about Blake. I told him I couldn't get married yet, and that I needed to leave.

"I'll wait," he said. "If you need more time, I can wait."

"That's not it," I confessed. "I don't think I'll be back."

"Don't you love me?" he pressed.

"I don't know."

I left the next day. Our nice apartment, filled with my parents' donated furniture; our two cats, Quincy and Thorstein, who loved to go camping; the future we might have had—I left it all, with Rick sitting at our kitchen table. I took my clothes. I moved into a friend's studio apartment for the summer.

We never spoke again. Rick was furious, and I had no words. I felt ashamed to be hurting this faithful man, but I knew I couldn't go forward with him.

The following fall, I entered UCLA's graduate program in economics. I had wanted to go away, but UCLA offered me the best support. Now that I had left Rick and wanted to be with Blake, I felt content to stay in Los Angeles—for a while.

I entered with an Alan-sized chip on my shoulder. As a recent convert to Marxism, my aim was to go and learn their theory so I could contest it from a place of thorough knowledge. No more "if you knew more"; I would learn the more, in order to demolish it.

I learned that that was not a good reason to go to graduate school. I felt alienated from my classes and my classmates, the distance we kept between the equations we derived and the people whose lives were embedded (and submerged) in the equations.

I also learned that I didn't have the preparation in math that I would need to really make it. I had taken calculus and linear algebra, but here I was surrounded by math majors.

Perhaps most important, I learned that I'd need to work my ass off to keep up. This was not undergraduate work anymore. Blake didn't need to study to get A's in his classes, so he had lots of free time. He wanted to spend it with me. I tried to get by with a few hours of study each day, but it didn't work.

At the beginning of March, after two quarters at UCLA, I dropped out. I handed in my econometrics paper, and I went to a phone booth.

I called Alan in tears. "Now what?" I wailed into the phone.

Alan thought for a while.

"Should I go to law school?" I wondered.

Alan's reply has never left me. "You'd love law school," he replied. "But you'd hate being an attorney."

A powerful distinction. I knew he was right.

"Then what?"

"I think what you want is political theory."

I had never heard of it. Political philosophy, yes. But political theory is taught in political science departments, and I had left political science years before. Political theory involves philosophy, but it also draws on history, literature, and culture—really anything—to analyze how humans organize themselves. Questions of justice, of course, but more fundamentally of identity—what is it to be human? How should humans live together? How is it that we fail so spectacularly, so often? Political theory is a very wide net.

I applied to Cal State again, this time as a political science major. I binged on political theory for the next year. I had found my field at last.

As it turned out, I did have an interesting time with Blake—but it wasn't always a good time.

In January of 1979, he drove us deep into the Anza-Borrego wilderness east of San Diego, driving a VW bus down a trail marked "four-wheel drive only"—and going the wrong way on a one-way trail. Convinced he could do it, he ignored my pleas and my fears as we careened down 60-degree inclines. At one point, I got out of the van before he went down, afraid the van would turn over. That didn't stop him. Then, we got stuck between two hills and had to hike out—10 miles? 15? I lost track. Eventually, because I had a student VISA card, I paid to have a tow truck get in there and winch out the van.

Two months later, I married him.

Neither set of parents was too enthusiastic. Blake's mother told me, "You should have a man who's taller than you, and older. Blake's too young." My parents didn't say anything. But we—I—were determined.

We met with the minister who would do the ceremony, Blake's mother's pastor. He asked us questions and listened to our answers. After an hour he said, "I've rarely met two young people so well prepared to face the challenge of marriage."

Yup, we knew the words. We had the idea, alright.

We got married on a hilltop in Topanga Canyon on a sunny March day warm enough to do without coats. After a really simple reception, with no alcohol (my father was trying not to drink), we got in my bright blue 1962 Ford van and went up to the mountains—to the same town I had reveled in five years earlier.

I woke up the next morning and thought, "Shit! What have I done?" I knew that many newlyweds have that feeling, but it didn't help. I had been on the rebound—from Rick, from UCLA—and looking for a sense of forward movement. Marriage was not supposed to be the answer to a problem. I felt I loved Blake, but this level of intimacy was terrifying.

On the way home from our honeymoon, a drunk driver rear-ended us on the freeway when he fell asleep at the wheel. The van didn't have headrests. Whiplash left me barely able to move my arms. I spent the next two months flat on my back except for basic chores and driving to physical therapy three times a week.

Blake was going to school and working nights in a hospital. Newly arrived in our tiny mother-in-law apartment behind the house of one of Blake's friends, a fellow falconer, I was miles from any friends or family. In the yard, we kept Mike's three hawks and one of Blake's. Later that year, we housed a golden eagle that had fallen from its nest in the desert and walked to a train crossing. The L.A. Zoo asked Blake to foster it and teach it to hunt, so it could return to the wild. Buddy joined the hawks. Once he healed, we began driving him out to the desert north of L.A. to train him to hunt. He was awe-inspiring to watch, and terrifying as he approached Blake's glove; it is not unheard of for raptors to grab the faces of those who are in their path.

And then there was Big Bird. While Blake and I were dating and engaged, the macaw had lived with Blake at his parents' house. Upon our marriage, I learned that Big Bird was coming with us, and he needed a cage. A big one. A chain-link, outdoor cage. Somehow, we found the money. During the day, Big Bird was outside, screeching and calling to the world. Blake assigned me the job of Big Bird's care while he was gone.

I slowly got better, and took an internship with the Interstate Commerce Commission. In the fall, they made it a regular staff position, helping customers deal with moving companies. It wasn't exciting, but it gave me time to read between calls and on buses. As fall approached, I needed the time. I returned to Cal State, in political science, while working full-time downtown.

I lived on the bus. From North Hollywood to work downtown, then from there to school in the Valley until 9:30, when Blake and I would drive home.

That year, I found the Women's Center on campus. One of the professors invited me to the Socialist-Feminist Study Group that met monthly at UCLA. I learned about women's history, about feminist anthropology, about dreams for collective living and action. I fumed over women's oppression, and stretched my ears toward possibilities for change. For the first time, I met women who didn't act like "women," deferring to men, but like people—women who said what they thought, who stood for things, who organized. I liked these women a lot. They showed me I could be a woman and be powerful, I could give voice to my anger, and have companions who understood and shared my concerns. I met lesbians who were not in jail or surrounded by cats.

All this activity could almost distract me from my distress about my marriage. I began therapy, thinking that if I changed, everything would be alright. After a month or two, I edged up to the truth that I didn't want to be married. I couldn't face that truth, so I ended therapy.

In the spring of 1980, one of my lesbian friends from the Women's Center told me I should come out, that I was clearly one of them. I thought, "I've got enough trouble in my marriage without that." I put aside her remarks.

Then, when Blake and I both applied for graduate programs, I saw my chance to gracefully separate.

I applied to only two programs, ones my professors knew about and that seemed interesting. One was still in Southern California. I applied partly because Blake was applying there. But I didn't really want to go there.

I never got used to the climate in Southern California. I remembered Massachusetts from vacations when I was little. Plus, the university there had one of the few radical economics departments, and one of the first feminist political theorists.

As soon as I got accepted into the political science program at the University of Massachusetts with a fellowship, I said, "I'm going to Massachusetts. You can come if you want." Blake too had been accepted and offered support at UMass, but he also had four-year offers to Stanford and UCLA. I told him, "You should go to one of those. We'll both be working hard during the school year, so it won't matter that we're apart." What I couldn't say was that I knew our marriage wasn't going to last, and he belonged in Los Angeles.

He didn't buy it. He decided to go to UMass with me. Much later, he told me that one of his professors warned him not to let me go to Amherst alone—he said I'd turn into a lesbian!

Imagine that.

Chapter Six

Coming Out, Dropping Out

I THINK THERE IS SOMETHING REAL about geographic resonance, that feeling of fit that we feel in some places. Later, I'll tell you about locational astrology; for now, let's just say that some places feel like somewhere we can blossom, and others are barren. Some are "home," and some are just a place to park. We each have those places, whether we're aware of them or not.

For me, it seems that the Northeastern U.S. is home. I can blossom, in all sorts of ways. But blossoming can be messy, and slow.

Blake and I (and Big Bird) arrived in Massachusetts in the fall of 1980. We both had received University Fellowships, which allowed us to study without teaching or doing research for professors. But none of our brainpower could navigate our emotional reefs, or my drinking.

On the night before classes began, I had two grand mal seizures from alcohol withdrawal. I didn't know it was withdrawal for years to come, nor did my doctors. I went home from the hospital with a prescription for Dilantin, which I took for 25 years, and likely didn't need.

The label on the bottle said, "Don't drink while using this." I took that to mean, "Don't drink too much." Then I went back to my regular drinking.

During that first year, I poured all my energy into reading and writing. I loved my classes and my professors. We read at a dizzying pace—Hegel, Nietzsche, Foucault, Freud, along with Plato and Aristotle, Augustine, Hobbes . . . two millennia of thinking about politics.

Every day, I read. I read on the bus, and whenever I ate alone. I read in the office I shared with another student. I probably read in the bathroom. Even on the nights after my class went out for beer, nights when I drank hard, I got up and read.

I learned to write. As an economics major, most of my work had involved numbers and tests rather than extended papers. My classes with Alan were my first forays into philosophical argument. Now I had to not only read, but respond, and perhaps even think an original thought.

That first fall, my professor assigned an essay on an article we had read. Baffled, I went to talk to him.

"There's a flaw in this argument," I said, "but I'm not sure what it is."

"Trust that," he said. "Let it roll around in your mind, and it will come clear."

I did, and eventually, it did. I started to trust my intuition, to let ideas emerge rather than force them. I began to believe that I could do this work.

If my grades were perfect, my life was in shambles. I became seriously depressed. I spent the first summer there doing research for one of the professors and reading for my comprehensive exam in the history of political theory—"Plato to NATO," as we used to call it. I read, I wrote, I drank. I cared for Big Bird.

As our first year at UMass came to an end, I kept trying to leave Blake, but I didn't know how. I left for one day that summer, but I had nowhere to go. One night sleeping in my office at school sent me back.

Finally, in November, right after passing my major exam with distinction, I found myself lying on the green shag carpet of our apartment, too depressed to move. I looked at the carpet. I thought that if I could get to the phone and call someone, I'd feel better, but I couldn't get there. I couldn't quite lift my head. I don't know how long I lay there, but when I managed to get up, I knew I had to leave to go on with my life.

When I came to get my things, Blake cried with me. This young man somehow loved me. We stood in the walk-in closet and hugged, and kissed, and cried. I still loved him, as I hadn't loved Rick, but I just couldn't live with him. I thought maybe I couldn't live with anyone.

Blake, thank you for opening my eyes to the wonders of nature. Thank you for silly songs and phrases I still use: "You cheat like a rug!" Thank you for trying to love the very damaged woman I was. I don't know what else I might have done at the time, but I do know I hurt you, and for that, I'm sorry.

Earlier that fall, I had begun therapy with a counselor at the student health center. Soon after I left Blake, I went for an appointment. The therapist sat me down. I had been to the health center for something else, and she had connected with that doctor. They learned that I had told them two different stories—about what, I don't remember.

"Do you know that you told us each a different story?" she asked.

No, I didn't know that. I hadn't meant to lie or embellish; but I had, somewhere along the line.

Years later, I went back and asked to see my records. I learned that she had diagnosed me with multiple personality disorder, based on incidents like that and my dramatic changes in clothing and affect from visit to visit. MPD was just beginning to be a thing in the therapeutic community. It's a blessing she hadn't told me that diagnosis; I would have gone to town with it, filled with images from popular movies. All I knew at the time was that I needed help.

That therapist referred me to Carolyn. On my first visit, I saw this would be a very different experience from the health center. Her office was a large, open studio with a hardwood floor and a fireplace in one corner. The "therapy corner" held two comfortable chairs and a Persian rug. At the other end of the room lay a giant log.

"What's with the log?" I asked.

Carolyn replied, "I'm carving a totem."

That got my attention. I became willing to try to open up to her.

Over the next year and a half, Carolyn and I began to drill down into my psyche. As we dug into my history, I hit boulders of resistance. I didn't have memories, but my body did. I'd find myself bereft of thoughts, curled up in a corner sobbing. Sometimes, I'd be furious before I even got there, and I'd spend the hour in hostile silence. Carolyn gave me books to read—Alice Miller's *Prisoners of Childhood* and *For Your Own Good*. They resonated, as she knew they would, but the resonance didn't bring assurance; it brought anguish. It stimulated feelings in me that didn't have memories attached. I'd read and cry, read and freeze up. I didn't know why; I just knew it was so.

Slowly, images began to surface. They were like dreams, vague and ghostly. The characters were not always clear. The tone was of a vague danger, a threat that was not immediately apparent. They featured a man whose features were unclear, like the monster I used to see when I tried to sleep. Over time, they took a more definite shape.

Carolyn was not my only new relationship. When I left Blake, I commenced sleeping with not one, but two other graduate students, one married and one not. Oddly, it was the single one that I kept in the dark about the other one. The married man had a bisexual wife with whom he shared no secrets; they were both doing their best to believe in open marriage. I hung out with both of them.

Through them, I met more lesbians. Many of them assumed I was a lesbian, even as I kept insisting, "I'm straight!!!!"

I hadn't given my sexuality a lot of thought, actually. My insistence was partly based on not wanting to be bothered, and partly because my married lover's wife wanted to sleep with me, and I didn't want to have sex with her. Being straight was my excuse.

Then, some cracks opened in my world.

I marched in the 1982 pride parade in Northampton, as an ally. Men from some conservative church were at the march with signs that read, "God created Adam and Eve, not Adam and Steve." They tried to push us and disrupt the march. I realized that this was what my friends put up with on a daily basis.

I didn't wear a sign saying "I'm not one of them," and so I got abuse hurled at me just as my lesbian friends did. "Dyke!" young men on my block called. I had been identified as other. It stirred something in me.

I got what my lesbian friends faced, and I got angry about it. I identified with my friends. But still—is that a basis for sexual orientation?

Some part of me was in motion, though. Later that summer, I went out to California to visit my parents and some professors. The visits were disappointing, disillusioning to say the least; I went out to dinner with a professor I liked, and ended up drunk and in bed, feeling used. I felt a chapter of my life closing behind me.

I don't know what happened, really. I don't want to say "I faced the truth," as though my life before was all false. I can say I had had some really horrible encounters with men, and I had had enough. But it wasn't about men, exactly. It was something deeper—not so much a fleeing from anything as letting myself stop aiming in a direction that didn't work for me.

I'm standing on a corner in Westwood, in old jeans and a yellow T-shirt. As I watch pedestrians swirl around me, I realize suddenly that the world I'm watching doesn't match me. Now, I have a name for the gap: I am a lesbian. I want to be with women. I do not want, or need, to fit into this heterosexual world.

I don't have a simple story of always feeling one way and finally facing it. I had been heterosexual simply because that was what I knew. That was the single item presented on the menu I had been given. Any feelings for women had been safely submerged. Now, someone had put another item on the menu, one that was fresh and sweeter than what I had been consuming. So, I chose.

I could have chosen differently. I could have continued to insist that I was heterosexual. God only knows what my life would have been like. I don't want to think about it. I wanted a fulfilling life, and this door opened. Had I continued to be with men, I don't believe I would ever have really been alive. I would have been convincing myself, lying about how I felt. I was pretty good at that, but in this one moment, I chose more life.

In the wake of this shift, my world centered around being a lesbian. I became radicalized more every day, as I encountered hatred more directly now. I "looked like a lesbian"; my hair was short, I was tall and dark and (at that point) skinny, dressed in jeans and T-shirts. Now, I let out the part of me that had "hated girls," the tomboy. I began to wear vests and jackets I found in used clothing stores. I felt free, and strong. I looked in the mirror, and I saw with shocking clarity how much I looked like a dark-haired version of my father.

As I walked down the street, boys threw full beer bottles at me and yelled. That word again: "Dyke!" I wore it, we all wore it, as a badge of pride. Yeah, I'm a dyke. So what? Fuck you.

My inner crusader had a new venue. The anger that I had simmered in me my whole life now had a legitimate target: I'm mad about heterosexism and homophobia! I'm mad about the way men treat women, and the way some women let them get away with it! I had a righteous focus for my anger. I felt vividly alive.

My thirst for drama, for the simulacrum of aliveness, found outlets all around me. Our local feminist bookstore received bomb threats, so we organized into teams that watched the store overnight from the church across the street. I signed up to be a peacekeeper at our annual pride march. I got the thrill of danger without participating in violence.

And, importantly, I got to be part of something bigger than myself. After years of isolation, I had found a community.

Of course, I found the lesbian bar, and the occasional lesbian dances at local bars we rented for the evening. Convinced that my relationship problems stemmed from trying to be with men, I began to explore relationships with women. With women, I would bond in glorious ease. Uh huh.

At my first dance, I spotted a woman I found attractive. Compelling, really, more than attractive. Something in her intensity matched mine. I asked her to dance, and that night we found our way to bed in the house where I was house-sitting. Well, I know we got as far as the kitchen, standing at the sink. I think we eventually got to the bed.

The next morning, she did not want to leave. In fact, she was desperate not to leave. She was alone and in pain; surely, I would not abandon her?

I let her stay another night.

When I insisted that she leave the next day, the haunting began. She took a taxi with money she couldn't afford to spend. She stood in the driveway and yelled:

"I'm going to kill myself right here because of you!"

I let her in.

For the next several months I had a shadow, knocking on my window at home, calling to me to drink and have sex with her. I would refuse, then relent and go to the bar under the railroad tracks. We had sex in the alley outside. Then the game would begin again. My roommates were losing patience.

It turned out that Delores had recently been released from Northampton State Mental Hospital, diagnosed with borderline personality disorder, and she lived in a boardinghouse. She had a counselor. I met her once, with Delores, and learned of the diagnosis. I didn't know what it meant, other than that she was not getting better. She had two children, conceived when she was drunk and had sex with men. Both had been removed from her care.

By mid-fall, I was considering dropping out of school to get away from her. I told one of my professors. She took me to breakfast and leaned across the table.

"You can't leave," she said.

"Why not?" I asked. "I'm miserable. I can't take this."

"We need you," she answered. "The world needs your work. Your misery will pass, but we need your intellect and your passion."

As an African-American female academic, she knew about facing challenges and contributing. She had fought for every achievement in her life. She saw something in me, and dared me not to give up.

I decided to stay, but I couldn't seem to get free. Delores haunted my window and the streets.

Soon, though, the fever broke. After months of feeling guilty for Delores' pain, I met someone who saw what was going on and said, "Oh, she's on to you now." She meant that Delores made the rounds, looking for someone to save her. I wasn't special. It was just my turn.

I learned to walk down the main street of our town, ignoring her calling after me. It took a year or so, and another girlfriend by my side, to stop her.

So much for the ease and beauty of women's relationships.

In coming out, I found a whole world waiting for me. Not only the sex and the community and the drama of the struggle for justice, but the ideas!! I read about lesbian history and philosophy and erotica. I listened to raging debates about sadomasochism, a topic that was increasingly splitting lesbian communities. Was lesbian s/m "feminist"? Was it in line with "lesbian values"? Was it a dangerous virus of the patriarchy?

As I listened, I wondered: How did this connect—did it connect—with my study? Pretty much anything is a potential source and topic for political theory, dealing as it does with questions of justice and belonging. And sure enough, philosophically inclined lesbians were theorizing about what it meant to be lesbian, what lesbian community meant, about sexual ethics, lesbian culture—everything that human beings occupy themselves with. But they were largely doing it outside the halls of academe, in lesbian publications, in community centers, and living rooms.

As interesting as all this was, I didn't plan to write about lesbian anything. I planned, maybe, to write my dissertation on Plato. I had taken years of Ancient Greek to prepare. Or I planned, maybe, to write something about feminist community, but I didn't know what.

As the next two years moved along, I got more confused and lost. My therapy with Carolyn had progressed, and I had become clear that something awful had happened to me. Whenever I got close, I'd slam down the door. I'd go to therapy at 9 a.m., then return home and drink to numb the pain.

Drinking had become essential to my daily life, and it was wearing me down. By the spring of 1984, I had vague ideas about a dissertation, but I couldn't think my way through it. Joanna, my current girlfriend, and I broke up. That fueled my drinking, and my confusion.

In the past, I had been able to work well while my personal life was a mess, but I couldn't do it anymore. My brain just wasn't going to keep going while the rest of me was in chaos. So, in the spring of 1984, I quit.

Well, I asked for a year's leave from school. I didn't think I'd be back. I wanted to "find myself," to move beyond academia. I told myself that political theory was part of the patriarchy, that academia was corrupt. I wanted to do something besides read and write. Something that didn't need so much brainpower, power I seemed to be losing.

My exploration was short-lived. I had no idea what else I could, or might, do. I didn't know how to look for anything else, or risk anything. I took some house cleaning jobs to tide me over. Then, after my money ran out, I began working full-time at Kmart.

When I applied, the manager said, "You're overqualified."

I replied, "I need a job. I'm not going anywhere."

I started in housewares, organizing the warehouse and stocking the shelves. I loved it. I loved making order where there was none, I loved being in motion, and I loved being able to leave when my shift was over, whether my assignment was done or not. The manager started moving me to various departments to get them cleaned up. At first, this upset me: I just got this in place, and you're making me leave? What will happen to my pots and pans, my cutlery and can openers? After another move, I got used to it. Finally, I encountered the mess in the garden shop. There, I could wear a Kmart T-shirt and jeans instead of the stupid smock all the female employees wore. I got to throw around bags of soil and build my muscles.

I thought I was doing well. Along with running and riding my bike everywhere, I walked around 12 miles a day on the floor. I wasn't eating sugar. I felt strong and competent, fueled by a pot of coffee every morning and tequila and beer at night. Now I had more money for booze, and a job I could do while hung over.

During the year I spent at Kmart, a few customers came in and said, "Why are you here? You don't belong here." I wanted to say something smart about their snobbishness—"What's wrong with honest work?"—but gradually, I knew the answer.

I was there out of fear, and inertia. I was an excellent student, but inside, I was still someone who worked at motels and gas stations. I never even considered trying anything more challenging. I felt stuck, unable to move forward or backward. My horizon stretched out, flat and hopeless.

I met Karen the summer I dropped out. She was a senior at a local college majoring in computer science, combining her love of math and writing. She was smart, shy, waiting to bloom. She was quiet, not giving away much. She had glasses that worked to correct a wandering eye, so it could be hard to make eye contact. She wore jeans and baggy shirts like most of our group, so I didn't realize for a while that she had a classically womanly body: 5'3" and curvy, she would have been a pinup girl in the 1940s. In the 1980s, with glasses and short, straight hair, she was hidden. To me, she was just a nice person on the edge of our little group.

But Karen pursued me. She came to my softball games, and we showed up at the same parties. Over the course of a few months, I became aware of this quietly funny woman. Finally, we began dating—if that's the word for drinking and dancing together. I love to dance, and she kept up with me at the lesbian dances in town. As we talked, I realized that this was a deeply observant, gentle, but strong woman.

I liked her. But one summer day, in a flash, that turned into love.

We sat on the football field at the high school, our unofficial town park. Other pairs and groups gathered too, but at a distance. The trees and the grass were at their mid-summer gleaming, and a gentle breeze toyed with the leaves. Karen got up and walked away a bit, toward the goalpost. She started doing cartwheels. She didn't care if anyone was watching, or what they were thinking. She wasn't an Olympic athlete, or even a high-school gymnast; she was just a young woman turning cartwheels.

Watching her, my heart turned cartwheels too. I saw the beauty of her spirit, the little girl in her who would move because her body demanded it. This quiet woman was also a wide-open, joyous soul. My heart landed between those goalposts as surely as if she had aimed it there. I fell in love.

Gradually, we opened up to one another. She shared an apartment with two other women, so the only privacy we had was in her room. That tiny room contained a mattress on the floor, a chair, a desk—and a lot of stray papers and books and clothes strewn here and there. We added to the pile of clothes as we lay on her bed and—talked. Karen slowed me down, and showed me how to relate beyond sex. We explored each other in different ways as well, but these talks were the deepest, most intimate conversations I had ever had with another person. I began to tell her about my anger and pain. I opened up to her as never before.

Lying there naked, seeing her and hearing her, my love deepened.

"You're beautiful," I said.

"I wasn't beautiful until I met you," she answered.

Karen wanted to know me, and to be known. With her I felt safe to show my brokenness (as though I could hide it), and I could hold hers. Something began to open up in me.

Chapter Seven

Sober

"Thank God, you made it!"

That was the greeting I got at the door of the meeting on July 22, 1985. The greeter happened to be someone I knew, a bit. Moira and I had drunk together one night, a few years before, at a party given by friends. There wasn't anything remarkable about that party, except maybe for the black knit, skin-tight, full-body jumpsuit I wore.

Somehow, though, Moira remembered me.

Her greeting pissed me off. She made it sound like I really needed to be here! Maybe she said that to everyone who looked new, but it felt personal. What did I do that night, anyway?

I can tell you my story now because I got to the door of that meeting. People like Moira welcomed me. Because I stayed, and stopped drinking, and gradually grew up, I might just have something to share with you.

That night was pivotal in my life, but the turn actually began months before. First, I had to claim myself.

On November 15, 1984, my 28th birthday, I became Shane. I had finished trying to be straight. I had finished, I thought, with academia. I could let myself have what I wanted, be who I wanted. After all the years of internal stories featuring this wonder woman, I let myself be Shane.

I needed a last name to go with it. Shane Baker was still pretty dry. Phelan was a town out in the California desert that I used to drive through. For me it evoked the spaciousness of the desert, and it sounded good with Shane.

I became Shane Phelan. I didn't know I was making myself Irish, or male. The Shane I had seen was female. Once I knew these things, I didn't care; I liked the androgyny of it. The last name introduced a new layer of mistaken identity: Irish people assumed I had Irish heritage, and over time, I stopped telling them different.

I changed my name legally that year. My family worked to honor that change, and Karen was great. The people at Kmart already thought I was strange—a lesbian grad student lugging potting soil—so they went along with it.

I checked in with Carolyn, my former therapist. "Does this sound crazy?"

"Not at all," she said. "In many societies, changing your name is a sign of initiation into adulthood. Trust this impulse. I think this will open something that needs expression."

Barb didn't vanish like Barbie did. Shane was continuous, with Barb's memories and opinions and activities. Somehow, though, Shane developed in ways that Barb likely would never have considered. Don't ask me to explain; I don't have a clue.

That winter, I began to remember more. Images at first. A large man lying by a pool. A large man in a basement. The face of the large man, shadowy at first, slowly taking shape.

A voice began to run in my head: "Nothing happened. Nothing happened. Nothing happened." But my body said something happened. I curled up and cried as I had before in Carolyn's office, alone and bereft.

For years I had had a memory of my father taking me down to the basement during a tornado and leaving me there, to keep me safe. He hid me under the washbasins. No one else remembered that tornado. No one else went to the basement. Just me and my father.

Barbie was still in the basement. Her father put her there.

I fought against this new memory. This had to be a cover, an excuse

I made up to explain my feelings and my craziness. Of course, I was making it up! These memories were under discussion everywhere; I was jumping on some bandwagon, seeking attention.

Alternatively: something happened, but it was my older brother who did this!

My body kept cringing, trying to expel something.

Finally, I opened the door a crack. I saw the monster. I saw the man I thought wanted to kill me, the man I loved and hated. I told Karen, in a little-girl whisper: "I think my daddy hurt me."

> Oh God, just putting those words here! I want to turn to my siblings and apologize for writing this. I want to say, "I'm sorry. I shouldn't be saying this. I don't have enough proof." But I know that's the voice of the incest. Eventually, years later, I learned in therapy that that voice was characteristic of trauma denial. "Look away. Don't look here." Since then, when I've heard the voice speak in that way about anything, I know I'm treading on ground that is so painful some part of me doesn't dare to look. At those moments, I actually feel verification—if there were nothing there, there would be no energy clustered around it. I may not have the details right, but I know I'm in a dangerous, delicate neighborhood.

> For a long time, I couldn't say the words: "My father molested me. I am an incest survivor." I couldn't even think them without freezing up or crying. When I could say them, the feelings around them froze up. In order to say them, I had to make them distant—I had to make myself distant. Now I say it regularly, routinely, and other people thank me for my courage and tell me their stories in turn.

> My father molested me.

As the memories started to solidify and I let myself believe them, I started to wonder. What made him do that? My father wasn't a monster, though he had felt that way to me. Now, as I watched him age and decline, I saw the sad, even pathetic man behind the bluster. How could this person have done those things?

The only thing I knew for sure about my father was that he was an alcoholic. I knew from my own experience that people do things when they're drunk that they might not do otherwise. I began to think that the incest was related to his alcoholism.

I needed to learn more, terrifying as it was. I went to the town library. I looked in the card catalog, and I found a few titles about children of alcoholics. That was as far as I could get that day: I went home and cried, overwhelmed by the prospect of facing what had happened to me.

The next week I tried again. I looked up the call numbers, and I went into the stacks. The books weren't there. I went home and sobbed into my pillow.

The following week, I looked up the numbers and went to the stacks. The books weren't there. I went to the desk with my heart in my throat.

"Oh, there's a waiting list for those," the librarian told me. "Do you want to get on the list?" I hesitated, and then mumbled, "Yes." Then I went home and collapsed, shaking as the energy of shame poured through me.

By May, I had the books, and I began to read.

The next month, Karen came to me. "I'm going to stop drinking," she said. "You don't have to stop, but I won't be drinking with you."

I felt some nameless terror rise up in me, but I wasn't about to show it or listen to it. "Okay," I said. "Who knows? Maybe I'll stop too."

I said, it, but I couldn't really imagine it. I had never considered stopping. No matter how sick I got, no matter where I woke up or who I woke up next to, I never once said, "I will stop this," or even, "I need to stop." I knew I'd do it again. That's just the way it was.

Because it hadn't occurred to me to quit, I had never felt the fear of stopping. Now, my palms sweated. But I loved Karen, and I wanted to be with her. I felt the terror, and I shelved it.

At the end of one of the books, the author had included the Johns Hopkins test. This was a list of twenty questions about your drinking, to help you see whether you had a problem with alcohol. I took the test, and answered yes to three questions. That seemed safe. Then, at the end, I read: "If you said 'yes' to any one of these questions, you likely have a problem with alcohol. If you said yes to three, you are an alcoholic."

No. My father is the alcoholic. For years I had said, "My father's an alcoholic. I have an addictive personality." I had been a pillhead, but I stopped at age 15. Now I just drank. Okay, I drank more than some people, but not more than the people I hung out with.

I took my outrage to Karen. "This test says I'm an alcoholic!" I ranted.

She looked at me.

"Well, duh; you know that." Immortal words.

"No, I don't!" I spluttered.

"You say it when you're drunk," she replied.

Oh.

Here's the thing. I can dance around something forever, but once it's there in front of me I want—I need—to move on it. If it was possible that I was an alcoholic, if I might be my father's daughter in this way, I needed to do something.

I looked at my father's life. This gregarious and happy man, who majored in medieval history, had spent his life in a job he often hated. He had drunk in the car during his lunch hours. The man I knew was isolated, bitter, and defeated. Now he was almost 70, and life was draining from him.

I heard my mother's voice in my memory. "You're just like your father," she'd say with exasperation. I knew, now, that it was true.

The lightning bolt hit hard and suddenly. I would not live fast and die young. I faced the more awful, far less romantic prospect of 50 more years of slow and growing misery. That scared the hell out of me. I went to a meeting.

On a Monday night in June 1985, I snuck into the giant parish hall of Grace Church. About 150 people filled chairs across the length of the hall. Up front, a podium held a microphone. I liked the size of the space, and the group: I could hide.

As I watched people come in, I noticed two things. First, people were talking and laughing and hugging. This was a happy place, not the dour scene I'd anticipated. I liked that part. I saw the coffeepot and the cookie plate, where many of them gathered, but I didn't want them enough to risk being talked to.

Then, I saw a group of men come in. They looked like I expected alcoholics to look; shuffling, in baggy clothes, unshaven, bleary. The meeting itself was uneventful. I don't know what was said. I know they used the word "God," a problem for me. I thought, "I'm a 28-year-old lesbian feminist atheist. I'm young and strong and athletic. I don't belong here." I snuck out before the end.

Still, I knew I needed something. Maybe it was the program for families of alcoholics. I knew I qualified for that!

On a Wednesday evening I went to a very different venue. Down a side road, in a little church parlor, I found six middle-aged women. They were prim and proper, sitting in wing-back chairs with their feet and knees held modestly together. I strolled in in my tight Levi's, Hawaiian shirt, and running shoes. When I saw the scene, I wanted to just turn around, but I couldn't let anyone see I was scared. I sat down on a little beige love seat by myself, crossed my leg over my knee, and waited to escape.

All these shifts were colliding in me: my father's drinking, Karen stopping, noticing my own use, facing my fear of not drinking. My tidy, tiny world was exploding. I became desperate for something, some sort of movement. I decided to try again.

I found out that there was a beginner's meeting before that giant meeting. I came in, and Moira greeted me. I headed for the coffeepot and the cookies. Balancing my styrofoam cup and plate, I took a seat at the end of one of the tables, at the angle, as separate as I could get. It didn't work; people sat on either side of me. Now I was glad Moira was there—not because I knew her, but because she was another lesbian. At least I wasn't alone in this strange place.

The meeting opened. The leader told a bit of his story. He had drunk like I had, messy and loud. He drove drunk and slept around.

His life was full of chaos. Other people shared in turn, and I heard more stories like mine. I didn't say a word.

This time, I stayed for the big meeting. The guys from the hospital didn't come. I felt a little more comfortable. I listened to the speakers tell their stories of destruction and recovery. I wanted what these people had. I wasn't sure I belonged here, but I wanted to. I thought, "I hope I'm an alcoholic."

After the meeting, three women grabbed me before I could escape. "We're starting a lesbian Step group tomorrow night," one of them said. I had heard the Steps read at the meeting; now I learned that some groups read the step book and reflected on it together. They helped me buy a book, so I was ready. They told me where the meeting was, and gave me their phone numbers if I needed help.

That night I began to read. Of course, I would have to edit the damn book; it was full of "men," and "he," assuming the alcoholic was male. I didn't know what to do with the God part. But I was curious, so I kept reading. I got to Step Six: "Were entirely ready to have God remove all these defects of character." I thought, no way! No way am I ever going to be ready to let "God" mess around in me!

The next night, Tuesday, I went to the meeting. I told them about Step Six. They laughed. Susan, who eventually became both my sponsor and my softball coach, said, "You're not on Step Six yet. You're on Step One. Just settle down."

Settle down? It was all I could do just not to drink. The craving in my chest, the tightness that I had always soothed with tequila or beer, or anything really, that craving was up all the time. I had never noticed it before, really, because I drank as soon as it happened. Now my body was screaming, "Where's the booze?"

Still, I couldn't be sure I was an alcoholic. True, I had abused alcohol. And true, it was turning out to be hard not to drink. But really: isn't it sort of extreme to call myself an alcoholic? Powerless over alcohol?

Three weeks later, Karen and I had a fight. In my anger, I started looking for a drink. In the apartment she shared with two other drinkers, I found the liquor bottles: a tiny bit of Kahlua, a drib of peppermint schnapps, the end of a bottle of crème de menthe. I put them in a glass and took a swig.

I didn't spit it out, but I didn't take another sip.

There was no way I could tell myself that I drank that for the taste. I had used that line for years, as I slowly drank a bottle of Guinness or sipped a balloon of brandy. I conveniently ignored the cases of Meister Brau and the tequila in my backpack. But now, after a few weeks of meetings, my defenses broke down.

I was—I just might be, maybe—an alcoholic.

That was August 8, 1985. So far, I haven't had a drink since.

No words, God, can express my gratitude. Tears come closer. Thank you for saving my life. Keep me sober today. Amen.

I began to notice the ways my disease showed up, including the voice in my head that said, "You don't need to stop yet. You're young. You can come later." I realized that non-alcoholics probably didn't have this argument with themselves.

Then I heard a friend, another lesbian close to my age, speak at a meeting. She talked about all the energy she had put into trying to control her drinking. I could relate to that. Then she said, "If you have to control it, it's out of control."

I went to Joanna, my former girlfriend. She and I had drunk together, but she didn't drink like I did. I asked her, "How do you know when to stop?" She answered, "When I don't want any more."

What?

That stunned me. I never, ever, didn't want any more. I might run out, I might blackout or fall asleep, but I never didn't want any more. Throwing up might slow me down, but it didn't make me stop wanting to drink.

Slowly, I let myself remember and feel. I remembered the times I squatted down to pee in parking lots, and the times I threw up in parking lots or in my bedroom trash can.

My face tightened as I thought about sneaking into my friend's house at midnight and stealing pizza from his refrigerator. I faced the public fights and screaming matches, the falling down in restaurants, times I drank alone. I let myself be horrified by all the times I drove in a blackout, or seriously drunk.

I squirmed as I made a list of all the men I remembered having sex with, and compared it to the list of those I actually knew and cared for. I sobbed and shook as I recalled lying on a hotel bed, crying and saying, "No," too drunk to fight back, while a man I thought was my friend penetrated me. I let myself know how close I had come to being raped at other times, drinking with strange men.

I took the Johns Hopkins test again. This time, I said yes to 17 out of 20 questions.

From then on, I went to a meeting every night. I felt guilty about joining Karen in "her" program, like she had this one place to be separate from me, so we worked out a schedule of meetings that were together and those that were separate. Since we lived in separate towns, that wasn't too hard. But I worried what it would do to our relationship.

For sure, it messed with our sex life, and our dancing life. We had always gone dancing, at least once a week, drinking and engaging in what some would call suggestive, even lewd, dancing. Now, without alcohol, I didn't know how to do that. I had to stop going to bars, and that meant no dancing.

I didn't know how to enjoy sex without alcohol. I didn't have to go to a bar for that, thank God, but it was still awkward at first.

In fact, I felt awkward everywhere. I had lived with a bottle nearby for fifteen years.

A month after I stopped drinking, I had another place to feel awkward. Call this serendipity, or synchronicity, or coincidence. Some might call it God.

Just as I entered recovery, my department chair reached out to me. In a blatant attempt to get me to finish my Ph.D. he asked, "How would you like to come back and teach a class, on anything you want?"

I had realized that Kmart was not good for me, so I said yes. No great desire to teach and write brought me back; I wanted to get out of Kmart.

Now I had a month to design a class, order books, and write a syllabus. I had to begin to draft a dissertation proposal.

What did I want to teach? All I wanted to talk about was recovery. I didn't think that would fly in a political science department, even one as wide open as mine. I had had classes on Freud, and I had read Jung, so I decided to do a course on "Psyche and Politics." I think I managed not to talk about the Steps, but I'm not sure.

Suddenly I found myself back in an environment in which I was supposed to be able to think. I had left when my brain was drowned in alcohol, and during the subsequent year, I hadn't read anything harder than novels. Gradually, though, I found I could read and think again.

This time, sober, I found I had a dissertation topic in front of me.

I considered the Plato project. I knew it would be really hard to say something new about Plato, and to make anyone care.

I thought about the prospect of looking for a job. As a lesbian, I had to think ahead. When should I come out to prospective employers? I knew I was not the type who could live in a closet.

I decided that if I wrote about lesbians, any department that gave me an interview would already be signaling their willingness to include me. True, I would miss a lot of job opportunities, but the ones that might come would let me be me.

Also, it was much easier to say something new about lesbian feminism than about Plato. The debates were swirling around me; I just had to connect them to topics in political theory and show why they mattered.

I won't give you the details of the dissertation. What matters is that I learned how to do these new things—teach a class, write a dissertation—in the meetings I went to each day. There were professors there, along with the carpenters and truck drivers, and they coached me. They taught me how to set reasonable goals, so I felt good at the end of each day. They reminded me to get to meetings and work the program.

Twenty months later, I received my Ph.D. and my first real teaching job—a year's position at a prestigious school in Pennsylvania. Another year, and I had a book contract and a tenure-track job in New Mexico. Clearly, something was working.

My academic success was wonderful, but the real action in my life was spiritual. Not drinking certainly made my mind work better, and my life circumstances improved. But, although I didn't know it at the time, finding God was the gift that would keep on giving.

I walked into "the rooms" an atheist. I had been disappointed by the Church when I was young. I had flirted with Judaism, but the 1973 war and occupation of Palestine turned me away from that. I believed that reliance on God was for weaklings.

Over the early months of sobriety, I saw that I was one of those weaklings! My life was a mess, not only because of drinking, but because of all the things I used alcohol to avoid and all the ways I hadn't grown up. I needed help.

But not, I thought, "God" help. Father God? Old man gray beard God? I needed another way.

As I sat in meetings and thought about my life, I slowly realized that although I didn't believe in a "higher power," I definitely believed in a lower power. I had experienced it. That was the power of confusion and loneliness and pain, the power that told me to kill myself. I believed in that.

Then, as I reviewed my drinking history again, I began to see where something else had been helping and protecting me. My little voice that told me to stop taking drugs. The simple fact that I had never even had a ticket, much less a crash, while I drove in blackouts and brown hazes. So many people around me had killed themselves, or were still lying in ditches of misery where I had left them years before, but I was alive and getting another chance. I thought, that is not because I'm so smart. Something smarter than me, something that loved me more than I love me, must have been at work. I didn't think it loved me more than the ones who didn't make it; I just gave thanks that, as Moira had said, I made it this far.

I didn't know what it was. I thought it might just be my unconscious mind. Whatever. What mattered was that I had access to a source of strength and wisdom that I hadn't known about. I had a higher power, and I "came to believe" that it "could restore me to sanity," as Step Two says.

I proceeded on to Step Three. Here, things were trickier. The word "God" was in there, but the people and the literature seemed to say that I didn't have to use that word. All I had to do was try to "turn my will and my life over" to that power.

I realized that I wanted to do that. My will had led me to disaster more than once. More than ten times. Aside from the results, however, the sheer exhaustion of trying to run everything, trying to make things turn out how I wanted, was a burden. I could (try to) offer myself to this higher power and see what happened.

I began to work on the next Steps. I wrote an inventory of my history, my wrongs, my resentments. Reading it over helped me to get just what a mess I had been, how much I needed help. Now for the next Step, sharing this inventory with my sponsor.

My sponsor, at the time, scared the piss out of me. Serious and smart, she looked at me with eyes that seemed to see into me. She wanted to help, but she was not going to be gentle and sweet.

The day of our meeting to go over my list, I could barely get out of bed from the terror. I locked my bedroom door and got down on my knees in front of my brown, refinished armchair. People had told me to get on my knees before, but I don't think I ever did. Now I knelt and said, "Whatever you are, please help me."

No, I didn't "say" that; I pleaded. Please, I'm terrified. Please, I don't know what to do or how to do it.

All at once, I felt a rush of energy enter my feet. It coursed up my legs and my spine and filled my chest with warmth. It shot up through my throat and poured out through the top of my head. In its wake, I felt peace and ease.

"What the hell was *that?*" I wondered. Somehow, it didn't matter. Whatever it was, it had answered my prayer. It heard me and answered me. I was still nervous, but the tsunami of fear was now a pond with some waves.

I knew I wasn't alone.

I decided that this something needed a name. I needed to be able to talk to it, to address it. I decided to call it God.

I can't say that this experience made my Fifth Step with my sponsor perfect and fulfilling. I was still nervous, and there were things I didn't tell her. That didn't matter. My big lesson that day was that something—"God"—knew me and loved me. And now I knew it, a bit. I wanted to know more.

One of the members of my home group, Dan, was an Episcopal priest. I went to him to see about books that might help me. He took me to the little bookstore at the church and picked out volumes by Kenneth Leech and Morton Kelsey. I also found a little book on meditation that wasn't Christian.

Then Dan bought me a copy of the *Book of Common Prayer*, the prayer book for the Episcopal Church. "There are a lot of good prayers in here," he said. "And there are forms for praying each day, and the psalms. Just see if there's something you like."

I felt vaguely stupid with these books in my arms, but I stuffed them in my backpack and got them into my room without being seen.

I looked through the prayer book and found many beautiful prayers. Some of them said things that really spoke to me. The only problem was that they all ended with the phrase, "through Jesus Christ our Lord." That was too much. I started saying some of the prayers, leaving out the ending. I could pray to the God "in whom we live and move and have our being" without having to get on board with Jesus as God.

As I began to explore this world of prayer and meditation, I found myself back with the questions that had not been answered in Sunday School. Now, however, they were combined with questions of how to respond. How was I supposed to live? What did this higher power—God—want me to do? I've turned over my will and my life, so now what? I wanted to please this new God. I wanted to be perfect—without too much disruption to my life, especially my relationship with Karen.

I told my new sponsor, Skip, about my concerns. His answer was simple and direct. "You don't get to do theology for at least a year," he pronounced. "The questions will make you drink. Just do the next right thing."

Soon, I had a joyful relationship with this unknown God. People told me to "utilize, not analyze," so I let myself feel grateful without pinning down to whom or what I was grateful.

That's the key for me. Gratitude is prayer. Gratitude opens us to beauty and love and power. Gratitude enables us to endure hard times and celebrate good ones. Paradox here: thank you, God, for giving me gratitude.

In the spring of 1987, I got a job teaching a class at a liberal arts college. Twice a week, I drove the 60 miles in our new blue Nissan truck.

On a bright, sunny day in February 1987, I pulled out of our parking lot and popped a cassette into the tape deck. *Aretha's Greatest Hits*, my favorite. The road was plowed after the previous day's blizzard, but the little Nissan slid like a bobsled, bumping against the walls of snow on either side of the road.

Aretha sang as I drove, and I sang with her. I still sang with community choirs, but singing with Aretha was like sticking my finger in a socket. The wall of energy hit me, and I wailed with her.

As I careened up the road, I thought how close I came to missing all that I was experiencing. The satisfaction of using my brain, belonging to a recovery community with whom I didn't need to posture or hide, gradually maturing in my relationships, prayer—in a short year and a half, my life had changed beyond my wildest dreams.

Aretha had belted out "Respect" and "Think." She'd caressed the notes of "Say A Little Prayer." Now, gently, she headed into my love song.

Looking out on the morning rain
I used to feel so uninspired

And when I knew I had to face another day
Lord, it made me feel so tired
Before the day I met you, life was so unkind
But you're the key to my peace of mind
'Cause you make me feel
You make me feel
You make me feel like a natural woman

I belted it out with her, every cresting wail and sigh.

This was my love song—not to my lover, who had put up with me during my drinking and my early recovery—but to God. The God I didn't believe in, the force that strengthened and sustained me and seemed to protect me when I wouldn't take care of myself—to that one, I sang the deepest song of my heart.

Bach, Beethoven, plainchant, and hymns had all helped me express the love in my heart. Janis Joplin hollered out my pain. Grace Slick shouted fierce truth. But in this song, Aretha named my deepest joy at being saved. Listening to her, I touched the divine.

I guided my truck into the parking lot and gathered my things. As I prepared for class, my heart continued to sing with gratitude for the gift of an ordinary day. I whispered as I walked: "You make me feel..."

This new relationship with God brought me joy, but it also brought tension into my relationship with Karen. She was still sober, but she was much less willing to "get spiritual." She had been raised Roman Catholic and still felt the scars of the God she'd been told about. I had never heard the punishing messages that she, and so many, had heard. My problem hadn't been a punitive God, but an irrelevant one. Now I had found a God that filled me with desire and delight, and she was nervous. We eventually reached a sort of entente, where we met on the ground of recovery but didn't go into the specifics of spiritual growth. My path would be my own. As in my family, we didn't talk about it.

Home wasn't the only place of compartments, though. Where before I had had lowdown drinking partners on the one hand and academics on the other, now I had the academics, the too-smart-for-God folks, and my recovery community where God was central. I had a new closet.

The gap was accentuated during the year I taught in Pennsylvania. Karen stayed in Massachusetts. I commuted every three weeks or so, slogging my way up the New Jersey Turnpike between trucks, everyone bumper-to-bumper doing 70 miles per hour (that sounds normal now; back then it was unusual), usually in rain or snow. In between trips, we would talk on the phone. I had plenty to do with teaching three new courses and revising my dissertation to make it a book. I also had lots of time to meditate and read about prayer and meditation.

I met Phil, an Episcopal priest, at my new Saturday morning meeting. He invited me to church. "A lot has changed since you left," he told me. I thought that might be true; after all, he was gay and seemed to be out. (I didn't notice that he did not have an actual position in a church.)

The next day, I arrived at the church. Phil and his partner, Charles, were waiting for me. Phil introduced us. We went in and got seats about halfway back in the large, cone-shaped sanctuary. Unlike the churches of my youth, this church was big, modern, gleaming with lights and polished wood. The altar seemed miles away.

The service began. I focused on following the hymn during the procession, so it wasn't until the priest began speaking that I saw:

The priest was about 5'5".

The priest had long hair pulled back.

The priest was a woman.

I had left church before that door opened, just as I had left before this prayer book came out. I didn't know it had happened. Now, in front of me stood a woman in full Eucharistic regalia.

I began to cry. I hadn't known I wanted this. I hadn't thought of what a difference it might make for my relationship with God, or with the Church. I let the tears flow.

Something stirred in me that day. I began to attend the weekly morning prayer service when I could. I didn't engage in the larger congregation in any way, but I liked the small group that gathered for prayer.

I told Karen what I'd been doing. She didn't want to know. So, while I was in Pennsylvania, I attended church. When I was in Massachusetts, I didn't. I didn't think about what I would do when we moved back in together.

That spring, I was offered a tenure-track job in New Mexico. But first, I returned to Massachusetts for the summer. Karen and I would pack up and leave in July.

I didn't go to church during those summer months, but I definitely had a Sunday morning service. One of the old-timers, who had known Bill W., had a cabin nestled up in the Berkshire Hills, and every Sunday morning he hosted a meeting. In the winter, we crammed into his living room around the fireplace. Sometimes there were 50 of us in this room, spilling into the hall, to hear the wisdom and humor that lived in that house. In the warmer months, we met outside amid rolling hills lush with maples and oaks. It was sometimes hard to hear outside, but it was worth it. The beauty of the place spoke of God's glory as much as our sharing did.

In May, on my first Sunday back from Pennsylvania, I went to the meeting. Somehow, the topic that day got around to our relationships with our fathers.

I had not spoken to my father for a year at that point. I hadn't spoken to my mother either. It started this way.

My father had acted like a spoiled child (or an active alcoholic) at my Ph.D. graduation. For him, the big deal about coming to visit was food: He wanted lobster, and he wanted pizza. Neither of those were on his low-protein, low-salt diet. When he ate protein, with his damaged liver, the toxins built up and he acted drunk.

Of course, my mother felt sorry for him, so we had pizza the first night they were there. The next day, on the way to my ceremony, my father insisted that we have pizza again—and maybe lobster. When my mother said no, he went into a sulk that lasted through the day. He refused to meet my department chair, or anyone else. He stood to the side and waited until I finished greeting people, and then he turned to the car.

Steam poured out of my ears. Really. This was the first time I had achieved something that felt like an accomplishment, rather than just doing the next thing. For once in my life, I felt proud of what I had achieved. And here my father was pouting about pizza.

We didn't fight then and there. Instead, I sent him a letter, basically saying I was sick of his behavior. I said I didn't want any contact with him unless he got some help. He called me and told me what an idiot I was, how out of line. I got madder, and found myself yelling at him about his abuse of me. He denied it, calling me a liar, and we hung up on each other.

Soon afterward, my brother called. My parents were hugely upset about my accusation. No, not "my" parents; "his" parents. He reprised my father's line from my teenage years: "We all agree that you are incredibly self-centered and that you don't care about anyone else." Then he laid down the law, "I don't want you coming near them again. You are no longer part of this family."

I froze. When I could breathe, I said, "Fine."

All my life, as far as I could recall, I had felt that I didn't belong. Now, as I hung up, that feeling crystallized. But I needed to be sure.

I called my sister Jan and asked, "Do you think this too? Do you think I don't care about anyone?"

In her sane, blunt way, she answered, "No. I don't think you're more self-centered than the rest of us, but you talk about your feelings. You say things we're not supposed to say."

Then I asked, my heart in my throat, if she believed me about the incest. "I don't know," she replied. "But my therapist thinks it's true, just from what I've told him about the two of you."

So, one door had closed in a big way, but another had cracked open. Someone else believed me.

The next winter, Dave called again. "Dad is going downhill," he explained. "There may not be much time for you to see him."

The last I had heard, I no longer belonged to the family. Now I was supposed to go see the monster? And anyway, this guy had come back from two comas, two times he almost died. I didn't know what to believe. And, given our last encounter, why would I go out there now? What would I say if I did?

"Call me when he's dead," I said.

I pushed it all out of my mind, giving my attention to my work, to Karen, to our upcoming move.

Then, on a beautiful day in May, I sat at the meeting on the mountain listening to people talk about fathers. Most of the people there had at least one alcoholic parent and lots of family conflict. I realized I didn't want to be cut off anymore. I drove back down the mountain thinking, "I'm going to call Dad."

I walked in the door of our apartment, and Karen greeted me.

"Your mom called," she spoke gently. "Your dad is dead."

I collapsed on the couch. I had missed my chance. Just like that, just when I felt ready to reach out, he was gone. Any chance for reconciliation had died with him. I struggled for air. Then I cried and cursed.

I called my mother.

As usual, I didn't know what to say. "I'm sorry?" I grieved the timing, but I couldn't honestly say I was sorry he was dead. I was sorry he died without any closure on my part, I felt sorry for myself, but I didn't have a place in my heart for him to be missed.

I said, "Hi, Mom, I just heard," and let her talk.

As she went over the events of the past week, I realized that my father had been in extremis for several days. Dave and Jan had been there with my mother at his bedside. They knew he was dying, but they didn't call. They didn't give me a chance to say anything! I had forgotten that I had said to call me when he was dead. Really, I didn't remember.

My grief mingled with outrage. I quivered with the wrongness of being excluded. I wanted to yell, to hit something, to do—something—with this adrenaline shooting through me.

I went to my sponsor.

"Why didn't they call me?" I wailed.

"They probably thought you would have made a scene," he said. He let me think. "Would you have?"

I paused. "I would have said, 'I hate what you did, and I love you'. That might have seemed like a scene."

Skip answered, "They didn't want that."

A light bulb went on. If I wanted a relationship with my family, I needed to act in a way that didn't scare or anger them. I needed to consider their feelings.

I called my mother. This time, I knew what to say.

"Mom, I get why you didn't call me to come out. I promise you that, in the future, I will not make a scene, I won't make things harder for you. Please promise me that if you get sick or hurt in any way, that you will let me know."

She agreed.

We had no funeral for my father. My father's ashes were disposed of at sea without any of us attending.

I was the only one of my family who got a memorial service. I returned to the meeting the next Sunday. On a beautiful sunny day, with a gentle breeze blowing off the hills, I told everyone what had happened. After the meeting, we stood in a circle around the flagpole, about 40 recovering alcoholics who knew what it was to miss a big chance. I got a few minutes to say to my father what I would have said: "Dad, I love you. I am so like you, in so many ways. I hate what you did to me, I hate what this disease did to you and to me. I am so mad at you, and I'm so sad that we never got to speak again."

Then, around the circle, other members spoke to fathers, dead or alive; some spoke of their fathers. Some spoke of their own fatherhood and how they were trying to do their best now that they were sober. I cried, and some others joined me. We all laughed. We said the Serenity Prayer, and we hugged. I got what a funeral should bring—comfort, companionship, and hope for a future.

Oh Dad, I'll say again what I said then, what I would have said to you had I been there with you. I love you. I hate what you did to me, not only the incest but the scorn and dismissal. I hate what alcoholism did to you and to your father before you. I'm so sorry that you grew up with your horrid mother. I am so like you, not only in my addictions and my height and athleticism, but in my spiritual hunger. I saw that in you, when you lay in the sun. I wish you could have found peace. I pray that you have found it now. Love, Shane.

A few weeks later, I went out to see my mother in California. My mother asked me about the abuse. I described where it had happened, but didn't give her details. I still had trouble talking about it. This time, she received it, and apologized for not being there for me. A miracle.

Just before my father died, my mother got the news that, after several years of remission, her breast cancer had returned, and metastasized. My mother allowed that she had actually been looking forward to my father's death so she could travel and do things she liked. Now, she learned that she had months, maybe a year, to live that vision. I again had her promise that she would include me in her final time.

In the meantime, we talked. I learned things about my mother I had never known. I learned that she, like me, had majored in political science and economics.

I never knew she had any interest in politics! She had so thoroughly retreated in the face of my father's pronouncements and dismissals of disagreeing views, that I truly didn't know she had any of her own. I couldn't blame her, actually. I hated being told I was an idiot when I disagreed with him, especially when I majored in economics and politics. Now, it floored me to think that I had inherited these concerns from her. What else did I not know?

I returned home to Massachusetts and prepared to move to New Mexico. The next months were a whirlwind of activity and of emotion. I never wanted to leave the "happy valley," as many people called it. This is the anguish of most Ph.D.s as they head off to another position after years with a cohort of smart people interested in what they're interested in. It's part of the path.

That didn't make me like it.

Karen and I went to the 4th of July picnic our friends held each year. We hugged and cried and promised to write (a promise I mostly failed at). Then, the next day, we set off in our little Nissan truck with the bumper sticker that read, "Bush is pro-life until birth." We had a futon in the truck bed and food for simple breakfasts. We headed west to a new life.

Chapter Eight

Lost in the Land of Enchantment

"SOME WANDERED IN DESERT WASTES; they found no way to a city where they might dwell. They were hungry and thirsty; their spirits languished within them." (Psalm 107: 4-5)

In 1975, I passed through New Mexico on a cross-country bus trip. I thought it was the most beautiful place I'd ever been. The huge western high desert, with its mesas of red rock under cerulean skies, sang to me of spaciousness. In the face of that immensity, I felt somehow in tune with my real size, and I took comfort in being just another tiny creature on the planet, rather than a big suffering self-absorbed mess.

My interview had confirmed the attraction. I loved everything I saw there. I loved the sunshine. I loved the adobe houses and the way the buildings on campus were designed in Pueblo style, whether they were made from adobe or cement block. Some were more modern than others, but all were painted in some shade of desert sand. There was a harmony here, a spaciousness and simplicity, that spoke to me. I felt myself breathe and expand.

The culture was equally compelling. The history of occupation and domination, with its continuing contests among the indigenous peoples, mestizos/as, descendants of the Spanish, and the later Anglo colonizers, was utterly unlike what I knew from my bi-coastal experience. It was complicated and fascinating. I wanted to explore this land, meet these people, learn this history.

The town hosted a feminist bookstore and other great small bookstores, a food co-op, funky coffee shops, and theaters. The best of western Massachusetts, with a job. Surely, I would thrive here.

Now, Karen and I were driving to our new future. We camped our way across the Midwest, dropping down to follow the old Route 66 out of Chicago. With no air conditioning, the drive was stifling and exhausting. Everything was dry, high desert, dusty tan dirt meeting the few desert plants, pale green under a blue sky.

As we came over the pass through the Sandia Mountains and looked out over the Rio Grande Valley, my heart sank. Instead of the vista I had noticed on the day of my interview, I gazed at one-story houses as far as the eye could see, clustered in the lower parts of the valley and thinning out up the sides of the foothills. I saw the cottonwood trees, a narrow band of green in the midst of brown, but they seemed different that day. Wide boulevards cut a grid through the valley. I looked and saw a miniature Los Angeles. "Oh shit," I thought. "What have I done?"

As a teenager in Los Angeles, I had missed the change of seasons I had grown up with in Ohio and Illinois, and years in western Massachusetts had deepened my love of the cycle of nature through beautiful spring blossoms to summer fullness and autumn glory. Even the long, hard winters brought a perverse pleasure, as February made us all desperate for spring. The cycle of loss and replenishment was a yearly miracle, and I loved each part of it.

As fall came without the red of maples, as the sun beat down relentlessly, I longed for New England.

In New Mexico, I met lesbians and gays in recovery who had been raised in religious traditions that actively excluded and demeaned them. This was new to me, coming out of my little progressive corner of Massachusetts. No one had really talked about that struggle. But here there were a lot of refugees from evangelical and fundamentalist churches. Many of them couldn't get sober because they had heard that God hated them. For the first time, I felt grateful for my lukewarm religious upbringing. I hadn't been exposed to the promise of spirituality and religion, but I also hadn't been harmed. My vague God worked for me.

When we got to New Mexico, I went to the closest Episcopal Church. The people there were doing stuff that felt like the Jesus Freak church I had gone to as a teenager—raising their hands, praising God in ways I associated with conservative religion and politics. I might have gone to another church further from home, but I frankly didn't want it enough to face Karen, to dive into a world that I felt would separate us. God was already a touchy subject; I didn't want to know what this would do.

I went back to my solitary generic prayers. I didn't talk to anyone about my hunger. I especially didn't tell my academic colleagues that I prayed or thought about God. I didn't even write about these thoughts in an abstract way. I didn't open the door that might connect my two worlds. I had my recovery community, where I could talk about relying on God—I could be "spiritual," if not "religious"—and share my personal struggles. And I had my colleagues at school, for whom such talk was anathema.

Soon, though, I would need God and that spiritual community.

My mother's cancer was progressing. She used her remaining time to do what she most wanted. In October, she took the train out from California to Albuquerque, traveling with a female companion. We went to the Balloon Fiesta, and she watched Karen and me float through the sky. I cried out my homesickness, and she hugged me and told me it would get better.

Then, in November, she went to Egypt. She had always wanted to see the pyramids and ride a camel, and, with my brother's help, she did these. By the time she made it home, we knew there wasn't much time.

She died in December, just before Christmas. This time I got to be there, with my brother and sister, and experience our coming together in a new way.

Suddenly, I went from being an outcast in my family to being an "orphan" with two siblings. I felt that yawning space in front of me where another generation had been.

Then, three weeks later, I learned that I needed an emergency hysterectomy. I had had occasional sharp abdominal pain since my teens, but the X-ray in 1975 didn't catch it, and college doctors agreed with me that it was just stress. In fact, I had developed a systemic infection and cysts. Not until the surgery were they sure it wasn't cancer. Later, my doctor said, "If you had come in five years earlier, this could have been treated medically." But I had grown up learning to tolerate pain. I had mastered the art, to where I was barely aware of it.

If the door to the past had closed with my parents' deaths, the door to the future—to any children I might have had—closed at the same time.

My colleagues at the university did not visit me in the hospital, nor did I expect it. My new friends in recovery, though, came to visit, bringing me stuffed animals and cards and flowers. They amazed me: so, this was what people did for one another! I had another reason to be grateful for having found "the rooms."

But my deepest experience of relationship in the hospital was with God. After one day in the surgical unit, they moved me to the obstetric ward (a cruel, or at least unthinking, transfer). The nurses said, "You're not that sick, and you need to move. If you want juice, get up and get it. If you need to go to the bathroom, get up and go."

Filled with gas from the surgery, my stapled tummy screamed for Percocet. And I was supposed to get up?

The first time I had to get up, I lay in bed and prayed. I prayed for the strength to stand the pain. I begged: "Just help me sit up." Eventually, I managed to struggle to my feet, sit on the toilet, heave myself up again, and stagger back to my bed. I felt that God had indeed been with me, giving me the strength to do these things. Over the next few days, the pattern took shape. Pray. Brace. Push up to an elbow. Sit up and swing legs. Stand. Shuffle. Give thanks.

Thank you, God, for holding me in my pain. Thank you for holding me in all the other pains and fears since then. You don't remove them, you don't cause them, but I know I'm not alone in the hard times—or the easy ones! I know that if I stick close to you, you will sustain me. Help me remember.

Let's recap. In eight months, both of my parents had died, I had up-rooted and moved twice, started a new job and begun revising what would become my first book, and had a total hysterectomy.

I was a mess.

I began therapy in March when my depression was overwhelming. I thought that grief over my parents was the reason, but of course, my pain wasn't only about the past year. I began to open up, which meant I fell apart. I re-entered the pain of incest, the sense of alienation from my family, and the consequences of my alcoholism.

Each week, I went to my therapist's office and entered hell. I dissociated even before I left my campus office, sneaking out the back way so I wouldn't meet anyone and have to try to speak. When I arrived, I sat on her light blue love seat while she sat across from me in an office chair. Usually, I left her office still dissociated, struggling to drive home.

Then, one day, Coyote showed up in the office.

We had begun doing active imagination work. It's like dreaming and like memory, only you're awake and involved. I don't know how this session began, but it quickly developed. Louise asked me to relax, and then to open my "inner eyes" and see the scene: where I am, how old, what my surroundings are like.

I'm eight years old. I'm alone in an attic playroom, with sunlight at the windows, lying on a tan-and-ecru couch. The room is meant to be a playroom, but I'm not playing. I'm paralyzed from the waist down. There's a box of toys near me, but I can't reach it. Even if I could, I wouldn't bother. I have no interest in the toys. Sunk in misery, I lie on the couch and look at the window—not through it to a wider world, but just at the rectangle of light.

Suddenly, a coyote is in the room. He isn't the animal you might see in the desert or on the edge of a field; he's brown and scraggly, six feet tall, able to walk on his hind feet. This is not just any coyote.

Coyote doesn't say hello or ask how I am or ask what's wrong. He doesn't ask me anything. He just starts looking through the box of toys. His eyes light up as he pulls things from the box, but he returns them before I can see them.

As I watch him, I get curious too. I get curious enough to roll off the couch and drag myself over to the box. Inside, there are all kinds of toys: a jack-in-the-box, ready to spring out at me; board games and miniature tennis balls; and jacks and . . . toys I had never seen before. The next thing I know, I'm beginning to move my legs a bit to play with the toys.

Coyote never asks about my movements. We just play.

Then, it seems that it's time to leave the attic. For the first time, Coyote speaks. He asks if I'm ready to leave the attic. I'm afraid—my father is somewhere in that house. I don't want to meet him. But Coyote coaxes me. "I'll go first," he says. "If we meet anyone, I'll take care of it. You will be safe."

Down the steps we go, the staircase winding to the second floor before straightening out for the final stretch. My legs are still wobbly, but I can make it with the banister.

Sure enough, my father is coming up the lower stairs, ready to put me back in the attic. But Coyote is ahead of me. We all stop on the stairs. Then, Coyote kicks the shit out of my father and throws him to one side, over the banister, as I scoot out the front door. Just like that.

This six-foot-tall, hairy beast with giant feet has made me safe. He has rescued me, without ever asking a direct question or giving me a sympathetic look.

After the session, I got curious. Why a coyote? I knew nothing about coyotes. I had no associations with coyotes. But Coyote clearly knew me.

I began to notice coyotes wherever they were; not just the live coyotes who roamed the Air Force base south of us, but coyote fetishes and patterns.

I read Coyote stories. In many indigenous North American traditions, stories are told of Coyote's role in creating the world. Coyote is full of appetite and self-will, and clever and devious. But he is often fooled by his own cleverness, not seeing what is clear to others. Coyote makes big plans to get one over on others and gets run over himself.

Just like the Roadrunner cartoon, Coyote is the sacred clown who keeps getting run over, pulled apart, and still shows up again. Coyote gets banged up and bounces back, but he doesn't necessarily learn anything from the experience. There's no path of development for Coyote; he just keeps chasing, falling, getting up. He bumbles through life, and dies, and rises again.

Coyote is an image of our sacred humanity. We are clever, and sometimes devious. We chase dreams, we plow into trouble, and we get up and try again. Coyote is also another face of God. This God is prone to do things that seem like disaster, and to whisper outrageous possibilities into our ears.

As I absorbed all this, I got a sense of what Coyote was doing in my life. Since I had stopped drinking, I had become serious and driven. I was drowning in reliability. I needed some Coyote medicine.

I got it. I wrote about Coyote, but I didn't know that Coyote was writing my life at the same time. I kept looking like something I no longer was, deceiving other people and myself, until I found myself running on thin air over the cliff.

Coyote, are you a face of God? What kind of God is it who deceives and plots, who makes fools out of others—and becomes one itself? I know many people consider you a divine force, but you sure don't look like the God I was raised on. You don't even look like the strong, reliable God I want to stay close to.

Still, you bring me such gifts. Laughter at myself, willingness to be surprised, and your bizarre capacity to survive even when the sky is falling on you. Your resilience, your naïve desire, seem to me a part of the God I've come to know.

I don't know what the theologians would say. I don't have to know. I only need to give you thanks for showing me another way to new life. Keep me alive to the ridiculous and unlikely. Shelter me from my seriousness. Thank you for releasing Barbie. You crazy Coyote, I love you.

For the first several years in New Mexico, I gave thanks every day for the privilege of earning a living doing something I loved. I had a stable relationship with a wonderful woman. We had three adorable and mostly well-behaved dogs, three shaggy balls of fluff. Each day, I walked from my lovely adobe Pueblo-style house through the university neighborhood and across the playing fields to my office, taking in sunshine and the mountains to the east of town, and I marveled that I had landed here. I got tenure. I was publishing, and I had an intellectual community. I was teaching and writing about things that mattered to me.

Somehow, it wasn't enough.

I wanted to be where the action was, imagining it to be someplace else. I wanted, really, to return to what I had in graduate school, to be surrounded by people who cared about what I cared about, who shared reading histories and conversations. I wanted to be with other political theorists.

It wasn't only the job, though. I liked New Mexico well enough, but I didn't want to live there. The dryness was too much of a good thing. The sunshine that had invited me when I interviewed in the winter had become oppressive. In the summer, I'd complain about the heat, and my friends would say: "At least it's a dry heat."

"It's like living under a broiler," I'd reply.

I started applying for jobs at other colleges. Each year, I applied for what looked attractive, the two or three jobs in the country that fit. Each year, nothing happened. It turned out that not everyone felt my research was what they needed in their department.

My dissertation was published as a book in the fall of 1989. Voila! I'm a lesbian political theorist! I'm using the word "lesbian" at meetings of the American Political Science Association! I was asked to speak at conferences, and challenged to name a vision for lesbian identity and community. I began to see answering those questions as a contribution to the world. I kept writing. In 1994, I published another book on lesbian politics.

I didn't only write on lesbian politics. I wanted to express the mystery of our being, while still trying to sound like a "political theorist." I wrote about other thinkers and topics in feminist theory, and dreamed of a book about ideas of nature. I brushed up on my Greek in case I wanted to write about Aristotle. Still, it was the lesbian work that got attention.

At the same time, I became active in advocacy in my professional associations. I chaired caucuses and committees. I co-edited a massive volume of original sources on the history of LGBT politics. I edited a book on queer legal and political theory. Soon, I was a big fish in a tiny, marginal pond. I was a big queer.

I found myself boxed in. The more I wrote on lesbian, then lesbian and gay, then LGBT/queer politics, the less academically mobile I became. I'd hear from friends at the places I was applying: "They say you're too feminist," one told me. "They think your work is marginal to the field," another said, explaining that her colleagues basically didn't want to know about lesbian stuff or do the work to relate to the larger issues I was writing about.

My career seemed to be growing, but I was coming up against the limits of the box I had created for myself. As nice as it felt to receive affirmation for opening a new field, I felt unsatisfied. I wanted to address deeper questions of identity, of our being. I had been drawn to write about queer life in part because it was directly involved with these questions, and because sexuality and gender seemed to me arenas of deep mystery. Whether I was writing about sexual politics or nature or Coyote or—anything, really—I was drawn to the mystery of Being, and being. I scented a return of sacramentality in the world, a renewed appreciation of wonder and mystery and humility. Without the apparatus of religion, I still sought those places where poetry and narrative and gesture are more appropriate than analysis. I didn't connect this to the God I knew from recovery; I just knew that life, aliveness, fullness, lived in that space beyond us and yet in our midst. I wanted to talk about that, to write about it, to dwell in it, but I didn't know how.

My personal life, too, was drying up. Karen and I had each grown during the first years of recovery, but that brought new tensions. As for many couples, our big issue was intimacy—sexual and emotional.

After a very torrid beginning, we had entered into what people call "lesbian bed death"; we became loving friends with very little sexual contact.

I don't know; maybe it was harder to relax without alcohol. Well, of course it was.

Maybe it was my weight. When I got sober, people told me to eat sugar when I wanted to drink. I got really good at eating sugar—and lots of other things. When I first got sober, I weighed about 140. After a year, I was closer to 160. I was still running, though not much. I no longer rode my bike; we had a car now.

Then, we moved to a hot, dry place where running was no longer fun. I had the hysterectomy, and I got out of the habit of exercise. I walked to and from work each day, and I walked our dogs, but it wasn't enough to compensate for the amounts I was eating.

By 1992, I weighed 208 pounds. I began to run—well, to trot—and to use the faculty weight room. I got down to 192. I had an assessment at the athletic center, and I learned that I was officially obese. Somehow, that didn't make me try harder. I was willing to exercise, but not to look at my eating. My therapist suggested I attend Overeaters Anonymous. I went to one meeting and saw people much bigger than me, talking about a desperation I didn't feel. And, underneath that, some fear stirred. I didn't return. I would hover around 210 pounds for the next twenty years. So, for sure I was no longer the athletic young dyke that Karen had been attracted to.

But I don't think my body was the real issue. Sobriety had also meant facing early situations of abuse for us both. For several years we took turns growing and pulling the other along. But by 1996, we were seriously stuck.

My healing work had progressed. I had ended psychotherapy at Louise's suggestion. "I think you might find some body-centered modalities more useful at this point," she said. I began with acupuncture, which relieved the pain I felt from too much typing. Then, my acupuncturist sent me to a holographic repatterner. (This was New Mexico, after all.) Using crystals and tuning forks and scents, the practitioner aimed to clear out past pain.

Shockingly, things started to move. First, I realized I had been blaming Dave for taking my parents away when he was born. I wrote and apologized. Then, I began to wake up to the energy in my body, to desire. I wanted passion and contact in my life. Being celibate partners was not okay with me.

I sat with Karen and our three dogs in our living room and said, "I need you to go here with me. I need more intimacy."

She stroked Sparky's fur and looked down, "I can't."

Very clear, as she always was. No animosity, just the statement. She was not prepared to go where I felt I needed to go.

I loved Karen deeply. We had been through so much together, so much pain and truth and growth. But this next step I would have to take alone, if I were to take it.

One day, after a repatterning session, I was walking home. That little voice, the voice that saved me from pills and disasters, spoke up. *"I need to leave Karen."*

The voice had shifted over the years. Where initially it addressed me as "you," now it seemed more a part of me speaking to my conscious self. "I need" rather than "You need." But it brought the same finality and clarity as when I was 15. My love, her love, our history, were not enough. Something was waiting for me, and I would have to go alone for a while.

Karen moved out in June. When she left, I began to think about dating, but I didn't know how or where to begin. All my friends were in pairs. I wasn't going to go to bars. I wasn't playing softball because it was too hot. And, really, I was terrified. I began to suspect that Karen wasn't the only one with intimacy issues.

I was alone. I worked, I watched basketball on TV, I worked on the house.

Dear God, I believe you were at work here, but the path has been hard. It's one thing to give up drugs that are killing me; it's another to leave a loving, if stale, relationship. I hurt Karen, though she found new life. Bless her. Thank you for sending her into my life. Guide us all as we navigate the seas of love.

One night, a few months later, I was talking to my brother Dave. He was teaching at a medical school, researching public health questions like the impact of having language translators in emergency rooms. As we talked, I realized he loved his work—he really loved his work. He saw the difference it made. He worked really hard, as he always had, but he was not thinking about getting ahead; he was thinking about the people who needed translation.

I did not feel that way about my work. I believed in what I did, I knew I was making a difference, but my heart wasn't there anymore.

Dave was on a mission; I had a job. I wanted to feel like Dave felt, about whatever I did.

Bit by bit, in ways I didn't see at the time, my life was headed for a Coyote-sized change.

I spent the spring semester of 1997 in Hawaii. Water! "As the deer longs for the water brooks" (Psalm 42), I longed for the water and the company of the wonderful faculty they had there.

In Hawaii, I woke up. The landscape was the opposite of New Mexico: water everywhere, everything lush and green, scents of jasmine filtering through my open apartment door. I learned to snorkel, flying over miniature cities of coral with fish moving like multi-colored sequined fabric. I learned the pleasure of drinking lattes and eating papayas.

I had come to teach courses on LGBT political theory and women and politics. As I learned from the students about the racial and economic dynamics of Hawaii, I was struck by how the patterns resembled New Mexico: both places had indigenous populations that had been colonized, oppressed, exploited. In both cases, they resisted and fought for their land, their language, their culture. Both had complicated histories around women's roles in maintaining traditional cultures against the onslaught of colonization. As I shared Chicana literature with my students, they wrote papers in pidgin. Together we crossed boundaries and blended identities.

I had stimulating colleagues, including three women who were also visiting for the semester. The four of us began exploring the island, but gradually, I began spending more time together with Carole, another lesbian theorist, without the other two. We drank coffee and argued political theory. The combination was electric. Just enough conflict, just enough contest, just enough hard mental work. Soon, we were in bed together. We spent the rest of the semester entwined.

I had been out of the game for years, safe in my sexless relationship, while Carole had been exploring. As she shared her experience with me, I found myself disappointed. I didn't want stimulation, as nice as that was; I wanted ecstasy of a sort I couldn't name. I hungered, but I didn't know what I craved. When we returned to the mainland, our attempt to maintain a long-distance relationship soon dried up.

I became the Director of Women Studies at the university. I had ambitious plans for the program, including getting approval for a Women Studies major, and I knew this work would demand a lot from me. I decided to be celibate during my tenure as director. I thought I would not have the energy to build a new intimate relationship while giving myself to this work. So, having left my ex to find hot sex, I became celibate. Somewhere I could hear Coyote laughing in the wings.

Oh, but Coyote wasn't done. Coyote was just getting started.

Chapter Nine

Coyote Speaks

"THEN THEY CRIED TO THE LORD in their trouble, and God delivered them from their distress. God put their feet on a straight path, to go to a city where they might dwell." (Psalm 107: 6-7)

You've been waiting for the "nun" part, haven't you? It's coming.

Over the next two years, I gradually sank into ennui. In my beautiful adobe house, I was not so much at home as in hiding.

I longed for home without knowing what that meant. None of the jobs I applied for sounded like home; mostly they were just a change of scenery. The promise of home did not exist for me, not as a place I might arrive in. Family wasn't home; I loved my siblings, but our relationships were not that close. Their homes were not home. In fact, my family's houses had never been "home" in the sense I needed. I had little practice with home. Karen had been the most "home" I'd ever had, and I had left her.

Like a stray dog left in the desert, fending for itself somehow and gradually going feral, I retreated into my house. I could get by alone, but dogs need a pack. A dog alone is less than a dog, somehow; and I alone, in my big house, was somehow less than myself.

I sat with friends and drank tea and talked. Through the dogs, I met neighbors who became friends. I had some folks I regularly met at our shared breakfast place. I had friends who included me in their lives. Their kitchens were almost home, but my deeper homelessness led me away from them, out to the desert, where I could watch the clouds over the mesas. Alone, I went to the wildlife refuge to watch the cranes migrate. Alone, I visited the Very Large Array of radio telescopes. Alone, I went to the movies and out to dinner. It didn't even occur to me to share these with others. I had learned early on to be alone, that connection was dangerous and self-sufficiency was best. Early lessons die hard. I didn't really know about friendship, so I only dimly got that I was missing something.

I knew, however, that something was missing in my professional life. I looked successful: I was publishing, getting things done in the Women Studies Program, mentoring Ph.D. students and junior colleagues. I was editing a book series and writing another book. All these were worthy activities in themselves, but I knew that I was no longer following a vocation. I was working.

I knew professors who kept teaching while their hearts moved to something else, who had a job rather than a vocation. I flirted with that, wondering what I might do that would bring fulfillment without calling on me to leave my secure position.

I experimented, a little.

While Karen and I were together, we barely advanced beyond our graduate school furniture. Now, living on my own, I could indulge myself. I built a nest. The living room and dining room became a little Hawaii, with dusky rose walls and lots of plants. I bought a brown leather couch and love seat, with matching wooden end tables and black iron table lamps.

I painted the back bedroom and bought a futon couch. I started collecting antique teapots, and I found a glass-fronted wooden cabinet to hold them. The room became my meditation space, as I looked through the French doors to the backyard.

Decorating gave me a certain sense of solidity and depth. I'm not just a workaholic; I love teapots! And tea. And decorating. And basketball. And my dogs. I'm a three-dimensional person, right?

Searching for lovely things became my way out of boredom and loneliness. I would head to the local antique stores and walk through, like visiting a museum. Now and then, I'd see a teapot I liked, or a painting—big, splashy things to fill space on my barren walls. And for those hours, while I wouldn't dare broach a conversation with anyone, I could share the energy of the place and the people and the things. I could visit life.

I started decorating for others, just simple movements and additions to help my friends. I realized I loved to work with color and shape and space. This was huge growth for me; for years, I couldn't have told you what color the walls were. I had been covered with bruises from not paying attention to corners. To be aware of the world was an awakening of sorts.

I imagined starting a side business, offering redecorating for lesbians who needed some help and had a small budget to work with. I designed a flyer to post at the local feminist bookstore. I never posted it, though; somehow, I didn't feel equipped. I liked helping friends rearrange and paint and brighten, but I was not ready to make a thing of it. My senses were more awake than before, but that wasn't translating into a career path.

In fact, though, following that road of beautification to its dead end moved me along a lot.

One day, walking through my lovely house, I felt a very different feeling. Standing on my sunporch, with its bookshelves full of paperbacks and its sunken area for a wood stove, I was stopped in my tracks.

I lived alone, in this enormous house. I alone had dominion over a kitchen, dining room, living room, bedroom, study, and meditation room; I enjoyed the sunporch and the basement where I kept my exercise equipment (and sometimes used it); I shared a two-car garage with no one, using it for storage. At the university I had two offices, both filled with books and files and computers. All of this space was occupied by me, decorated to my taste, filled with items which, if not top-of-the-line, were luxurious beyond most people's imagining.

That day it hit me: This was sin. What had been a delight was now a burden, an indictment.

By letting my appetite for this sort of beauty run free, I had found its limits. I had awakened to something, but this road wouldn't take me where I wanted to go.

If I could set this time to music, it would begin as a single note. It would be a wooden flute, or maybe an oboe, gradually opening to a fuller cry. Not a wail, just a piercing clear question. As it continued to build, the note would be scaffolded with thirds. The notes would begin to rise and fall, to blend with each other in a not-too-pleasing way. Not discord exactly, but an atonal communion of sound, hovering on the verge of resolution but never tipping over into it. It would be the sound of longing that doesn't yet dare to shout or plead or pray. It would become a slow fugue of elements, never quite dancing with each other but sharing the space. This music would not be heard as music to everyone's ears; like a Schoenberg symphony, it would offend many. No theme, no melody, nothing to hum—what sort of music is this?

This is the sound of flies hovering, of hope rotting on the shelf, of refuse gently settling into a compost not yet fertile.

Depression is a name we give to the deep emptiness that precedes a new life.

My efforts at finding a sideline weren't panning out. Really, I didn't want to live that way, earning a paycheck for work that deserved more from me. I needed a vocation, something like what Dave had. I needed a life with meaning and purpose beyond my own security.

Tenure—"golden handcuffs," as some call it—called me to security. No one I knew had left a tenured position; sometimes people in business or science who started a company based on a discovery might do this, but not people in humanities. All I knew was academia.

I sensed I was at another tipping point. Something had to give.

One day in the summer of 1999, while I was walking home from acupuncture, I heard the little voice. Clear as a bell, it said: *"I have to leave New Mexico."*

When the voice speaks, it ends debate. It's as though something in me finally gives way so I can know and face what I haven't been able to see. The little voice doesn't say, "I want to," or "I wish"; it's not tentative. It's clear. "I need to leave."

I filed it away, near the top of my mental desk.

A few weeks later, my friend Rebecca announced that she was leaving her career as a massage therapist to go to law school in Boston. The news jolted my sleeping imagination. People changed careers! I knew that, but I didn't know anyone in academia who had done it. It just wasn't an option.

Now I saw the whole picture. I was staying in a place, a climate, a situation that didn't satisfy me because it never occurred to me that I could do something besides teach and write. Now I heard the possibility that I could choose my life again. But how?

One day, outside the local metaphysical bookshop, I told my friend KC about my desire, and my fear. KC was born in Michigan, and had moved to Mexico with her partner. After a few years, they decided they wanted to return to the U.S., and they came here.

"I don't know what to do," I told her. "I want to leave. I only know how to teach and write. And decorate a little. What do I want to do? What would I do if I wasn't here, doing this? And if I don't know, how can I do anything? What if it didn't work out?"

KC cracked open my encrusted life and showed me possibility.

"Look. If you don't like point A, where you are, you go to point B. If you don't like point B, you can't go back to A, but you can go to point C. You don't have to be stuck with B."

This was a revelation. I had unconsciously assumed that my choice would have to be perfect and permanent. That belief had paralyzed me. Now I knew, I would never know how the next step felt until I took it.

I asked for an unpaid leave of absence for the 2000-01 academic year, beginning in June 2000. I planned to leave town and go east, toward the water, and find out what else might be waiting for me. I began to pray to know what to do.

The next month, I heard about a lecture on locational astrology at the bookstore. I had been curious about astrology since I was a preteen, but I'd never actually applied it to my life.

The premise of locational astrology is that the planets are not stationary in the sky, but are tracing orbits. By looking at their paths at your time of birth, you can see that the influence of some will be greater in some locations than in others. Do you want to emphasize love? Get on your Venus line. Need more focus? Look for a place with a lot of Saturn.

I went to the lecture. Then I went for a private reading with the astrologer, Arielle, up in the Santa Fe Hills. I had sent her my birth information, and she was prepared for an extensive conversation. She had printouts of maps showing the course of the various planets over the country and the world, and lists of locations by longitude and latitude, emphasizing one influence or another.

Gazing out her windows at the brown hills beyond, I sat on her comfortable red-striped couch and sipped peppermint tea. Arielle began with some general information about my chart and what she would expect from my life given what she saw. I was impressed with how much rang true: the concern for politics and community and my tendency to color along the boundaries of institutions, neither fully inside nor fully outside. We talked about some of the possibilities open to me, and how restless and ambivalent I felt about them.

Then she got to the point. "Of *course* you can't get anywhere here!" she announced. "It's a great place for you to go on retreat or vacation, but it's not a place to find a relationship or put down roots. You need water."

Yes. The openness and spaciousness I had felt on my visits was real, it called to me, but not on the level of daily living and creativity. Since coming to New Mexico, I had gradually dried up. I had used my intellect, almost by force of will, but my heart and soul had struggled. My soul was desiccated.

But where would be better? We had a map of the U.S., on which I could see the lines of influence. Hmmm. Arielle verified my sense that western Massachusetts had been a place of growth and transformation. That whole area, from the Hudson River to the Connecticut, was pretty alive for me. Of course, Alaska was on her list too. And I had loved visiting Alaska. But somehow, that didn't seem like the most obvious place to start to build something new.

Location alone was not the issue. A lot would depend on the second question: What did I want to do? What song was waiting for me to sing it? Arielle could tell me what my chart said my strengths were, but she couldn't tell me where my heart lay.

Over the next few months, the song began to surface. When I found another path and followed it, it was to be the queerest thing I'd ever done.

In recovery, I learned to pray every day to be of service, to be delivered from self-absorption, to help others by my example of recovery. I didn't know exactly what I was praying to, but I knew it was there. I was comfortable calling it God.

Now I began praying differently. I learned to feel the energy moving through my body. I sat in silence, breathing and releasing thoughts, trying to be in the presence of—whatever. "God," whatever/whoever that meant. The Force. And I prayed to know what to do.

My suspicion of Christianity had grown over the years, as awareness of anti-Semitism had expanded to feminist analysis and listening to anti-queer bigots speaking in the name of Christ. I just couldn't see aligning myself with this lineage.

Nor, however, could I jump into anything else. Given my mother's heritage, I knew I "qualified" as Jewish, but I had never seriously explored Judaism as a religion. In graduate school, my best friend was an observant Jew, and we talked, but again mostly about the politics around identities rather than any faith.

Then, in 1997, during our brief fling, I went to services with Carole. When we did, I got it. My mother's roots were Jewish, but Judaism was not my religion.

The following year Pam, a friend who was on her way to becoming a Buddhist nun, had invited me to her local center. The people were lovely and the teaching was interesting, but it was too mental and disembodied for me. I wanted a path that united body, mind, and spirit.

I prayed. I meditated. I drove my little red Festiva up to the airport on the mesa and looked at the clouds. I wrote poems about them, awkward fumbling that failed to say what I felt. I knew that what I was craving was somehow bound up with awareness of the beauty of the world, but I didn't have pictures or words for it. My poems went into the trash.

Then, just as I was making plans to go on leave, two women asked me to sponsor them in working the Twelve Steps. I didn't have a sponsor, but I wanted to sponsor them, so I got a new sponsor.

Anne challenged me to get clearer about who or what I was praying to. "That vagueness was fine when you were early in sobriety and couldn't afford to rock your boat," she said. "But now, 14 years in, it's time to get clearer. Who is the God of your understanding?"

I had no idea. I was, really, a little afraid to have an idea, afraid it would trap me into some sort of dogmatic rigidity. But I trusted Anne. I pondered.

As I thought of my friends' paths, I gradually saw an opening. I read Marcus Borg, who compared religions to languages, and I realized that, despite my best efforts to reject it, my language for God was Christian. I remembered someone saying that opposition is one way to be inside a tradition. My opposition to Christianity was a wrestling with, not a standing outside. I had been immersed in this tradition, and not simply as an enemy. I was an opponent, a wrestler, like Jacob wrestling with the angel.

I saw that I had let the haters define this tradition. I had let the anti-body, heaven and hell types set my agenda. While I was opposed to the oppressive strain in Christianity, I could oppose it from within as well as without. And, just like being queer, I could claim this identity without ceding to others the right to decide what it means.

I am a Christian. That's my language, my doorway into the mystery.

Of course, there are lots of Christian dialects. I spoke Episcopal/

Anglican, and even that was rusty. But I could hear the beauty of the universe and the love of God in it, so I was ready to learn more. I became grateful for my years away from church. Through my time in recovery, I learned that God is bigger than church, beyond doctrine.

Now, wrestling, I could come in freedom. Just like my earlier coming out, I knew that I didn't have to claim my Christianity as inevitable. I could have chosen to stay outside, as I could have chosen a heterosexual life. In each case, though, I would have lived a lesser life, a life half-submerged. I would deny myself joy in order to cling to the life I knew.

I decided to let go.

I began to read again the books that my priest friend had bought me in my first year of sobriety. Their framework wasn't quite familiar yet, but that language was the closest I had come to words about God. It was a vocabulary of love and hope and resilience, everything I sought and saw in the rooms of recovery. The authors promised that more of these qualities waited for me if I would let down my resistance and let God speak.

I hugged my budding awareness close to my heart, sheltering it as a cocoon shelters a butterfly that is forming within it. I sensed, somehow, that my bifurcated world was about to come together in a way that would disrupt my security but lead me to joy.

For five months, from October through February, I prayed to the God whose shape was unclear. I wrestled with Jesus, and felt my resistance crack.

I prayed to know something about where to go and what to do.

Now, after months of praying for guidance, in the winter of 2000, the little voice spoke up. *"I need to go back to church."*

I had come as far on the spiritual journey as I could on my own. I needed a praying community, to be with others. And, if my language was Christian, I needed that community to be Christian.

This was scary to me: where can an "obvious" lesbian go and be welcome? I knew about the Metropolitan Community Church, a church founded explicitly to welcome lesbians and gays, but I didn't want to go to a church where I was defined as a lesbian. I just wanted to be welcome as I met God. I was raised Episcopalian, and I had seen that they'd become more progressive than when I was a kid. Plus, I had an Episcopal prayer book from my early days in recovery. So, like a pigeon circling to get its bearings, I headed there.

I went to the cathedral, wanting the anonymity and the beauty of a large space. I called ahead to ask about service times. The person who answered asked my name.

When I arrived, I paused before venturing in. The cathedral was large, designed to induce reverence. Stained-glass windows threw filtered color over the pews. It smelled of candle wax and, faintly, of incense. People were there, but it was quiet; some prayed, some spoke in hushed tones.

Everyone seemed to be dressed in pretty traditional clothes, women in skirts and men in suits. I was in my best clothes, but they didn't help me blend in; they were all from the men's section. I sat in the back, grateful for the quiet.

I have no idea who preached that day or what they said. I was acutely self-conscious, unsure of my welcome. I followed along in the prayer book and found my way through the hymns. I don't know if I actually sang.

When it was time for Communion I went forward, trying to look like I knew what I was doing. I knelt at the altar rail and put out my hands for the wafer.

The man with the bread came to me and said, "Shane, the body of Christ." Somehow, he knew I was the one who had called earlier. I was stunned, bowled over by being addressed so intimately. I had been seen, and welcomed. Just as I was.

Then came the chalice with the wine. I hadn't had a drop of alcohol for over 14 years. But the chalice came to me. Deep red wine filled it. I put my nose into it before I could think.

The smell was overwhelming, but it didn't smell of wine. It smelled of blood. Not repulsive blood, with that metallic scent, but nourishing, life-giving blood. Love in a cup—not the false love of my drunken past, but something real and true.

I took a tiny sip. It burned a path down my throat to my soul. I felt it slide down my spine, leaving peace and wonder behind it. It didn't make me want more wine; instead, it fired me with desire for more mystery, more presence. I stumbled back to my seat and buried my face in my hands. I prayed as I hadn't for years, if ever. I prayed to be received, I gave thanks for this gift.

I had met Jesus. This was no longer a matter of what language I spoke; it was a new place from which to stand, a source of new life. I felt God's love for me, and I felt my love rise up in return. I'd been seen, and I'd been fed. Jesus was becoming real to me, not as a historical person but as a living presence in my life. I had no idea what had happened or how or what it meant. But I knew I would keep coming.

But how would this help me know what to do next? Being a Christian is not a career. Well, not usually.

After five months of praying for direction, I knew: "I want to pray!"

I wanted to pray with other people, and help others pray. I didn't know much about prayer, but I knew I wanted it, and I wanted to share it. I knew I wouldn't develop more in isolation. And going to the cathedral was not enough, even when I went for weekday Eucharist with one or two other people.

I wanted to pray and make God the center of my life. But how?

One day the previous fall, I was sitting with one of my sponsees in my living room. I sat on the brown leather couch, and Chloe sat on the matching love seat. As she talked, I realized that she was saying something really key to her life, but she didn't know it. It just seemed to slip out of her mouth, getting lost in all the words right after it.

I stopped her and said, "Do you know that you just said this?" She paused. She stared at me. She said, "Wow, I did." We both knew we had hit on something big, something she needed for her marriage and her life.

At that moment, I felt a flow of air run through the room. Not a storm, but a definite movement. It was as though the room had been holding its breath, and now it was breathing in something new. I thought, "I want to do this. I want to listen like this, to hear what people don't know they're saying, to help them see what God is up to in them."

But sponsoring people is not a career, either. What would let me pray, and listen, and feel the Spirit move—and somehow get bills paid?

March 15, 2000. I'm in Santa Clara, California, for the annual meeting of the Western Political Science Association. I've spent days with colleagues I enjoyed, amidst hordes of political scientists with whom I had nothing in common. We came and went from breakfast to panels to coffee to panels to lunch to panels to dinner and more conversation. Now I need some quiet time, and not the kind you might get in a hotel room.

I step outside during the lunch hour. Downtown Santa Clara is bustling. The sun is shining, and the flowers are turning their bright heads toward it. I'm looking for a place where I can relax—a park or a lunch place.

Then I see the bell tower. It isn't huge, but its shape is distinctive in this cityscape of modest buildings and business signs. It promises peace, a cool repose in a busy world. And sure enough, when I follow the tower downwards, it's part of a church. It reeks of California mission history; adobe outside, a big wooden front door. Outside, a sign says, "Open for prayer. Mass at 12:15."

I enter through the huge wooden door. Before me is another door, woodframed with windows, which opens into the church itself. I hold my breath as I pull on the door.

Inside, the street noise vanishes. The scent is no longer gasoline and lunch carts, but candle wax and the residue of incense. The church is two stories high, with a balcony running along the left side of the sanctuary. Down below, the light is filtered, dark after coming in from the glaring sun outside. A dozen people are sitting in pews, praying or thinking. Off to the side is a statue of Mary, with rows of votive candles for people to light and say a prayer.

I know I don't fit here. I'm not Catholic. I have very short hair. I'm wearing a purple silk shirt and a gold men's jacket with the sleeves rolled up, very

Miami Vice, with jeans and black cross-trainers. I don't fit, but I want to be here. I go up to the balcony, where I can watch and pray in privacy.

Upstairs, the light is brighter, though still filtered through stained glass windows behind me. I sit looking down at the altar, with its snowy-white fair linen and brass candlesticks gleaming from the lit candles.

A bell rings in the tower. The priest enters, and the liturgy begins. I watch from the distance of another tradition as well as from the balcony.

I barely listen as the priest moves through the readings, the homily, and into the Communion proper. My eyes are hungry for this, my soul aches, but I do not plan to come down to receive Communion. The Roman Catholic Church asks that only Catholics receive Communion, and I have no desire to push in where I'm not welcome. I lower the kneeler down onto the floor and fold myself into a posture of prayer.

I don't go down to receive, but the sacrament comes up to me. I'm filled with a gentle light, neither the bright light of outside nor the light within the church, but a light in which I see myself differently. I realize that I am a beloved child of God. I'm invited to the banquet of love. This is my true identity, deeper than any profession or relationship. God is present, and so am I, in a way I have not known before. I've been gifted, struck by a ray of pure love. I feel something in me give way, opening me to a path I don't yet know.

The service is over, but I'm not ready to leave this place and return to my colleagues. Still dazed, I stumble down from the balcony and find my way through another door to the bookstore. It's a tight space, brightly lit, shelves packed full of books. Two people are chatting with the woman at the register, but I don't notice what they're saying. I'm searching for something, though I'm not sure what. I'll know it when I find it—or it finds me.

I see a row of books by someone named Thomas Merton. He was a prolific writer, clearly. The sheer volume of titles tells me this is someone with a lot to share.

One of the books catches my eye. The Seven-Storey Mountain *is his autobiography. I learn from the back cover that he, too, had been an academic. He left to enter a Trappist monastery when he was 26.*

I buy the book that will change my life, and I return to the convention.

Merton was born in 1915 to two artist parents, and he grew up without much religion. His family went to church, but it was not central to their lives. Through a literature professor and some of his new friends, he began to think and talk about faith. Eventually, he had a conversion experience. He started going to daily Mass and to Benediction.

And then he went on retreat to Gethsemani Abbey, a Trappist monastery in Kentucky. He fell in love with it. It felt right, righter than anything he'd known before. He had tried to enter the Franciscan order, but their advisors told him that his past disqualified him from the priesthood and from monastic life. Then, when it seemed there was no hope and he would have to settle for less than his dream, he told the Brothers at Gethsemani about his dilemma and got a very different response. Just like that, he was encouraged to come and "try his vocation." He arrived just after Pearl Harbor at the end of 1941, and he stayed until his death in 1968 (ironically, on his first trip outside the monastery).

Now, Merton's language about God was far from my own. He was writing in the 1940s, steeped in the Catholicism of his time. But his fervor, his love of God, his sense of having been saved from himself and freed from the culture of his time—all this spoke to me. In Merton, I saw someone who did not settle for the easy road. He sought experience with a hunger that matched my own. He showed me that monastic life was not bland or proper, but passionate. In Merton, I found a soul who could speak to my soul.

Oh, I'm embarrassed to tell you about this! Over the decades, thousands of people have read this book and entered monasteries and convents as a result. They heard his joy, and they wanted it. I hate to be one of a crowd, to be a cliche. But really, even if I was the only one, I'd be embarrassed. I fell for this guy as I never let myself fall for any lover.

I didn't exactly fall in love with Merton, though. Rather, I wanted to be him. I fell in love with his passionate devotion. I wanted to live that wholeheartedly, to give myself to God, to live for prayer with others. I wanted to be on fire. Reading him, I was.

One day, a few weeks later, I was praying at home. The little voice spoke up.

"You should be a nun."

Oh, no. That can't be right.

For once, I questioned the little voice.

"I'm a lesbian, feminist, postmodernist theorist. I'm barely a Christian. Tell me something that makes sense."

"You should be a nun."

I thought, "That is crazy. I've had my share of daring adventures and risky choices, but this is not daring. This is just crazy. I'm just inspired by reading Merton."

But there it was. Nothing else had been coming.

I said to the voice: "God, if this is you, show me what to do with Max."

Max was my Lhasa Apso. He was, to put it plainly, 20 pounds of bossy. Lhasa Apsos were bred to be guard dogs in Tibetan monasteries and palaces, and Max was a prize specimen. He may not kill you, but you weren't going to have an easy time getting by him. Max had always been the leader of our pack of dogs. The others had died over the years, but Max was 11 and healthy. He was not going to be disposed of for my comfort. It was never part of my plan that Max would have to be left behind. The little voice had opened up a can of worms I couldn't imagine sorting.

Still, I was intrigued by this crazy, queer turn of possibility. Something in me delighted in the unlikeliness of the idea.

I drew a line: If I'm going to leave Max eventually, he needs a good home. God will have to put up or shut up.

I walked down to the coffee shop for breakfast. As usual, the place was packed. Jim and Lloryn, friends from down the street, were there. Their three miniature Schnauzers had been friends with Max and Pepper pretty much all their lives.

I told them what had just happened. "I had the craziest experience this morning. I'm thinking of joining a—of becoming a—"

The words were too big. But they got the picture.

"Well, if you need to leave Max, we'd take him." That was amazing, and sweet.

Then I went to work. In the hall outside the writing center I ran into Peggy, one of the counselors there. I barely knew her. She asked, "What's new?" I found myself telling her this strange story. I mentioned the Max factor. "I would take your dog," she said.

What? She didn't even know Max! She barely knew me. But there she was.

Later that day, I visited a local antique shop. As I caught up with Diane, the owner, I told her the story. She, too, offered to take Max.

Max, it seemed, had an entree into all of Albuquerque. I wondered if my friends would take me in so readily? Maybe if I was small and furry and round-eyed, and easy to feed.

I said, "Okay, God, I get the point. I'll take a look." What did I have to lose, other than my identity and communities and career?

I had learned growing up that there are Episcopal nuns and monks. I found a website for their association and ordered their catalog of communities.

When the catalog came, I had to face another, bigger challenge. It wasn't about being so religious. I was on fire for God. It wasn't the vows of poverty, chastity, and obedience. I'd been celibate for three years at that point, and the other two vows felt like a great challenge, one I was up for. Through Merton, I'd heard the freedom of letting go and letting oneself be one among many, of trusting the community. I heard the undertone of love that makes letting go possible.

It wasn't the challenge of wearing a uniform. I thought I'd like the simplicity of that. No habit, though! The habit spoke to me of women's oppression, of stale respectability, of the rejection of women's bodies. No habit, but simple clothes sounded okay.

Actually, the big stumbling block was something else.

The whole nun thing was so—feminine. In order to make this shift, I would need to become a woman in a whole different way than I had been.

I was directing a Women Studies program. I was a lesbian. I was heavily identified with women, with women's issues, women's community. But I was not comfortable with femininity. I was addressed as "sir" more often than "ma'am." I did not wear women's clothes. I didn't shop in women's departments. I'd been embarrassed before when saleswomen directed me to the men's dressing rooms. Among lesbians, I wasn't any big deal; no one in that context had ever mistaken me for a man. But my sense of self was definitely not feminine. Female I could claim—anatomical truth, social identification. But not feminine. Not *that* kind of woman.

So, I was looking for a community where I wouldn't have to become "womanly."

This extended to the name given to monastic women. I could relate to being a "monk," but not a "nun." Did I want whatever was being offered enough to adopt that name?

Most of the women's communities looked like your stereotypical nuns—habits, either black or white or grey, with veils. But some were more promising than others. In two of them, the veil had vanished, so their habits just looked like a version of church vestments made simple. I wrote to them for more information. One sent me a DVD—a promising development in itself, suggesting familiarity with contemporary life. They had a commitment to women, to feminism and social justice; they looked like the best fit for me. I scheduled a visit for the fall.

The second community invited me to have a phone call with their novice director. We talked a bit about my religious history and my hopes. Then she asked me about my looks. It may have been as direct as my weight. I told her I was 6' tall and weighed about 210.

She shot back in a sprightly voice, "Well, we'll have to do something about that, won't we?" I thought: No, we won't. I'm not joining a weight-loss program, and I'm not going to be judged by my weight. I'm not going to be talked to like a little girl or a patient.

I crossed them off the list.

Then, finally, there was one community in New Jersey that had a two-week summer program for people who are curious about the religious life. They didn't look like a community I'd choose, but I could learn some basics and see if I wanted to pursue this path. I signed up for their program. I would be there for the second half of August.

Gradually, I formed a plan: If I found a place that felt right, I would proceed; if not, I would rent an apartment somewhere on the East Coast, write, and continue to explore what might be next. If nothing happened, I'd return to my job the following year.

But I had a feeling I wouldn't be back, no matter what.

As I began to tell people what I was up to, my various worlds collided. The separation I had built between my intellectual life and my personal, spiritual path manifested itself in the varying responses I received to my plan.

By now, I was going to noon Eucharist (Mass, for you Catholics; Communion, for the Protestants) at the Episcopal cathedral. I mentioned to one of the priests that I was considering entering an Episcopal community. He immediately said, "Oh, no, you shouldn't be a nun! You should be a priest." I said, "I don't want to be a priest." Being a priest looked to me like what I was doing: some writing, some teaching, some counseling, some administration. Been there, done that. The career advisors might like that, as I would be "using my gifts," but—no.

I told Sandy, a friend at the Women's Center. She said, "Oh, no! You should be a priest." I knew that for her, growing up Catholic, nuns were the subservient ones. Women should be breaking barriers, not reinforcing them. But I was clear: "I don't feel called to be a priest. I want to know God, and I want to pray with others."

I told Dennis, my best friend from graduate school. He had taught me about reading philosophy and culture through a "Jewish lens," noticing what got hidden in a philosophical culture whose roots were Christian. Together we had examined racism, sexism, anti-Semitism, heterosexism. Now, I brought him this news.

Sitting at his kitchen table, he tried to listen. He was disturbed, but not like Sandy or Byron. "I'm not upset that you're becoming a nun," he commented. "I'm unhappy that you've become a Christian." It had all been so fast, we hadn't had time to talk about that little part.

I tried to explain: "I'm not turning my back on my history or on my political commitments. But this is how I hear God. I will not break faith with you." Dennis, bless him, listened to me with the respect he had always shown me. I kept his voice, his eyes, in my heart and conscience as I searched.

My brother and sister didn't voice their opinions, but I could imagine them: this is another crazy thing Shane is up to.

My academic friends, too, were stunned. They just didn't really know what to say. I saw many of them just once or twice a year, at conferences, and there just wasn't enough time to go into it. There was some chitchat about plans and logistics, hopes that I would return, but the actual issues—Christianity, being a nun—were just too much, too difficult to broach.

Some people did get it. My recovery friends already knew the part of me that sought God, that prayed. They had seen people turn their lives around and make big changes. My sponsor was not thrilled, but she did not come out against it. She agreed I should go look.

Some of my other local friends surprised me; they weren't Christian, but they understood spiritual hunger, and they trusted that I was on a path of growth. For them, this was an exciting development.

As I prepared to leave, I told friends that this was the first truly selfish thing I'd done. I had, in fact, done a lot of self-centered stuff in my life. But what I hadn't done was to follow my bliss, to dare to do what wasn't obvious. I had known how to think and write my whole life. I used my brain to get a secure place in life. But security was not my goal now. Now, I wanted to do what would bring me joy. I was in love, and I was following the trail of that love.

In May, my friend Dorothy and I went to Greece for a conference. As we toured Greece and the islands of the Aegean, we stopped at tiny Orthodox chapels literally poured into walls between stores, with their icons and candles, I could feel the pull of silence and devotion. I could sense the mystery in those quiet, dark places.

Later, though, lying on the beach in Mykonos, I thought, "This is crazy. I'm finally at the point in my career where people are paying my way to go around the world, and I'm going to enter a convent?" But this was the only door that had opened. I knew I had to look inside.

The only thing I anticipated missing, besides Max, was my chorus. I had sung in choruses my whole life. I loved that feeling of being among 100 other people singing our hearts out. I sang first soprano, up in the rafters, so the energy we poured out and received was huge. So much of our music was religious in origin or sacred in some way. I had been singing masses all my adult life!

I expected that I wouldn't be able to join a chorus, at least for a while. Most places I'd seen wanted their novices to focus on the community. But I loved the idea of singing the daily office, learning plainchant, letting my song be prayer in a new way. I saw it as a great renunciation, giving this to God.

That's what comes of reading Merton.

In June, I took the next step toward entry. In order to join an Episcopal religious order, you have to be confirmed in the Episcopal Church or a church in the Anglican Communion. It was time, now, to take the step I'd refused when I was 12.

It's not enough to say I got confirmed in order to enter a community. It is true that I don't know if I would have done it then if not for that. The rules had changed, and I could receive Communion without confirmation. I wasn't so tied to rules and rites that confirmation meant a lot to me in that way. But it's also true that there was pleasure in being able to simply say "Yes" after all those years, to say the words and mean them.

I was coming late in the yearly cycle. I asked Rhonda, one of the priests, for help. She generously agreed to tutor me. So, after a crash course, I confirmed the promises made for me at my baptism. I felt like I belonged to something—not to the cathedral community, but to the worldwide community of Christians, the communion of saints.

I was ready to go. I was confirmed. My year of leave had begun. I'd found a couple to rent my house for a year. Since I didn't have a research or teaching agenda that summer, there was nothing more to keep me in New Mexico. I said goodbye to my friends and packed the 1991 Suburban I'd bought for the trip. I made a bed on the engine cover for Max, who would be joining me on this trip.

My 12-Step friends threw me a party, giving me small gifts to remember them and sharing memories.

I told them, "I've been learning about love for 15 years; now I'm ready for the advanced course." I look back now and laugh: I had barely walked into the classroom of love. True, given where I started, I had learned a little, but I started so far back I still hadn't caught up with most people. I lived alone, I had a few friends, but I didn't know the first thing about love. What I did know was this: I wanted to learn. I wanted to love, wholeheartedly. I was in love with Jesus, with God, and some intuition told me that this love would open me in other ways. But really, at the time, I wanted to focus on this new relationship and be with my beloved.

I didn't say goodbye to my academic colleagues. I was officially just on leave for a year, and no one just gives up tenure, so they expected me to return. It wasn't like I was retiring, or really leaving, right? I thought I was, but I wouldn't own it enough for them to respond to it. A year later, when I resigned and returned to sell my house and close up my offices, the connection had shriveled. I never really said goodbye.

Chapter Ten

The Approach

"WELCOME!" THE NUN SMILED AT ME and opened wide the huge wooden door. I tried to smile back.

I had just arrived at the convent in New Jersey. August had crested, and fall was approaching. All the leaves and bushes were still green, but the air was just a little lighter, a little thinner than it had been. I could feel the promise of autumn on the edges of my awareness.

Max and I had left Albuquerque on July 4. It seemed a bit paradoxical; on Independence Day, I was both striking out on a course I chose, and heading toward a future that might include a vow of obedience. But paradox is central to Christianity, following this guy who dies to live, tells us to lose everything to gain everything, exalts the humble and humbles the exalted. I revel in that position of fullness from which nothing is excluded and everything is held in awkward juxtaposition. July 4 seemed the perfect day to leave.

In the six weeks since departing New Mexico, I had crossed the U.S. and Canada, seeing friends and visiting national parks. I drove on secondary highways up the spine of the Rockies. I didn't play the radio. I looked at the world around me. I didn't think much. I just drove, beholding the amazing beauty of tall pines, blue sky, rivers—water for which I hungered—and glorious clouds. Max slept in his fleece-lined basket on the engine cover, waking up only for walks and meals.

Each time we crossed a river, I stopped the car and found a way to get down to the water. The Platte. The Green River. The Missouri. Every little tributary and creek. I felt life beginning to move in me every time I dipped a hand or a foot into the water. Sometimes, I took my prayer book down to the water and said a psalm or a prayer.

Psalm 40 was my favorite, though I had to rewrite it a bit to remove the masculine gender. Putting it in the second person made it not only gender-neutral, but more intimate:

"I waited patiently for you, O God; You stooped to me and heard my cry.

You lifted me out of the pit, out of the mire and clay; you set my feet upon a high cliff and made my footing sure.

You put a new song in my mouth, a song of praise to our God; many shall see, and stand in awe, and put their trust in the LORD."

Each time I read it I felt the deep truth of these words. I had been mired in alcoholism, and then in work and depression. When I reached out for help, God was there. Now I had words, a new song in my mouth. I didn't know where or with whom I would sing, but I was beginning to know the tune.

I began to see my spiritual path as a rocket launching from the earth. In the beginning, it takes a huge amount of force to lift the rocket off the platform. It seems to move so slowly. Then, at a certain point, the bottom section drops off, and new boosters push the smaller vehicle faster and farther, sending it beyond the earth's atmosphere.

For me, the initial launch was getting sober. For fifteen years, I had been letting some power gradually lift me. Now, the love of Christ was propelling me into a new space of joy. I wasn't an engineer on this project, so I didn't know what came next, but I felt the shift.

It seemed that other people saw me differently too. As I drove through Montana, people at campgrounds and stores greeted me with open eyes and warm smiles. For years, I had been accustomed to distant, polite service from people who were put off by something— my gender ambiguity? My attitude? I wasn't sure. Maybe I had been holding myself back. Whatever had been the case, it seemed that when I let myself love Jesus, people started to open up to me. I was wearing a little cross; maybe that was it.

I realized that "lesbian" and "nun" shared a number of counter-cultural qualities, but with differing valences. Both groups simplified dress, hair, makeup; both made choices other than heterosexual marriage and clustered mostly with other women. Paradoxically, "nuns" were often honored in places where "lesbians" would be least welcome—and vice versa. As I went deeper into a monastic vocation, I would find myself invisible in ways I never planned. For now, though, I was enjoying a new comfort and ease in the world.

Each time I stayed with a friend on this trip, I had to build a bridge between who they had known me to be and who I was becoming. I told them of my desire, which meant talking about God. I could tell the story of my coming to this faith and this step, but I was aware that I was usually speaking into a space where "God talk" was foreign. My friends accepted this because they cared for me, but the language I was speaking was not a shared language. I felt awkward even as we connected in our mutual care.

It wasn't only the language I spoke, and the longing I gave voice to that made the trip awkward. I realized that this might be the last time I would see some of my friends. I wasn't officially leaving UNM yet—but really, I was. I knew that some of these connections were built entirely on our shared profession and interest, and that they would not outlast such a radical shift as I was planning. Each visit was a sort of unacknowledged goodbye, with neither of us fully expressing that reality.

I—we—had driven up the Rockies into Alberta and British Columbia. After visiting friends in Edmonton, we headed back to Montana and east. Now we stayed on the interstate, in case we needed help. Across the Plains and the Midwest, we rolled along toward Ontario and another visit.

Then, one beautiful morning outside Fredonia, New York, the engine died. Just like that. It just stopped running.

I coasted to the side of the road, which was blessedly empty. My attempts to start it up again failed. I called AAA, and they towed the Suburban to a local Chevy dealer. The repair guy told me, "That engine is dead. Finished. You need a new engine." "What?" I spewed. "That car is less than ten years old!"

I had bought the Suburban as part of my plan to leave. I had walked in looking for a truck with a camper, or one I could outfit, or a van. The Suburban was like a truck with the camper built in. It had four-wheel drive. It reeked of solidity. The dealer told me, "This just came in. Some other people have been looking at it. I expect it to sell today."

I fell for it. I didn't calculate the fuel costs until my first fill-up; instead of my usual $10 fill, I was faced with a $50 charge. But still, it was solid, and it enabled me to car camp—and Max liked it.

Now Sid, the dealer in Fredonia, was apologetic. "This is the second engine this car has had in it. I don't know what's up with it, but this engine is dead. But your warranty is still good, so you're covered for the replacement and for a rental while we work on it."

"How long will that take?" I asked.

"Well, we have to order the engine, get it here, and install it. I'll have to let you know when it comes."

"Should I stay in town? I planned to visit friends in Canada."

"I think you should just go do that. It's likely to be at least a week."

A week! Maybe more. My blood pressure rose. But Sid managed the details pretty quickly. It was an unfortunate bump, but I would still get to see everyone.

The practical details were fine. I had been stuck at a safe place with a kind and competent dealer. That was great. What shook me, what shakes me when I remember it, was this: I had driven thousands of miles, hundreds of them on roads where I literally saw one car a day. The engine could have died on the road from Jasper to Edmonton, the road running next to the Saskatchewan River. With no cell phone or service, I might have sat there for days.

The engine could have died on the mountainside in British Columbia, the gravel road where I almost skidded over the side. If I had not had engine control at that point, I might well have gone over. I can still feel the vertigo rise up in me as I imagine sliding over the side of that mountain road.

I became aware for the first time how risky this trip had been. I was a 43-year-old woman traveling alone with her little dog. In my youth, I had spent a lot of time camping in the California desert, exploring old mines, and generally being away. But in those times, I had traveled with a partner—and I had been young.

What the hell was I doing?

Along with fear, I felt outrage. The dealer in Albuquerque had bamboozled me into buying this vehicle, and I bought it. I steamed when I thought of him, but I was also pretty mad at myself. How could I have fallen for this?

As Max and I headed off to Canada in my rented white Impala, the trip took on a decidedly different feel. Rather than being an adventurous lesbian, I became a woman in a sedate white car with her little dog. I felt a little older than I had a few days earlier.

For the next two weeks, Max and I visited friends in Canada. It was a quiet interlude, except for Max picking a fight with my friend Jennifer's bullmastiff. I rushed him to a vet, spurting blood. Max bit the vet. The vet swore. We returned to Jennifer's, where Max spent his time safely isolated. Then, back from Ottawa to Fredonia to pick up the Suburban. Then, back across the New York Thruway to Vermont to visit Carey and Andy, who had agreed to keep Max while I visited the first community on my schedule.

We came into Albany and the intersection with Interstate 87 around 7:30 p.m. It was not yet fully dark, but everyone had their lights on.

I looked out at the procession of lights leading north and south, and suddenly, I saw them as luminous lines of streaming energy. They were not "traffic"; they were sparks of God running out in every direction, dancing in the dusk. God filled the landscape with light and beauty.

I probably should have pulled over, but I couldn't even think of that. I just gaped at the sight and tried to keep driving while my heart pumped joy through my veins.

We went through the interchange and joined the procession of light heading north. Like the pillar of fire guiding the Israelites through the desert, the lights ahead led me on.

When we arrived, Carey gave me a book to read. *In This House of Brede*, by Rumer Godden, tells the story of a widow, a highly placed professional in the British government, who enters an enclosed Benedictine convent in the years after World War II. I loved following the ups and downs, not only of Philippa as she grew into her vocation, but of the whole community. The personalities and their foibles, the faith that enabled them to persevere and to risk new challenges, all grabbed me and gave me grist for my own discernment. Did I really think I was up for this huge shift? Was I really able, or willing, to let others define my choices of everything from food and clothing to ministry? Would I be able to make the leap from one identity to another? I didn't know if I could, but reading Philippa's story made me want to try.

Primed with dreams of contemplative life, I left Carey and Andy, their warm and peaceful household, and Max for my initial encounter with nuns, with convent life, and hopefully with God.

Now, I had arrived. I drove down the half-mile-long driveway to the convent. The leaves on the trees in the dense woods shimmered in the sunlight as I followed the road dipping and winding past the convent cemetery. Birds sang to the sisters lying there.

Then, past the cemetery, the woods gave way to what looked like a medieval French convent, with leaded windows and quietly crumbling white stucco. Across the lawn was the retreat house, a red-brick former orphanage that now hosted groups on the weekends. Beyond these stretched more woods, 80 acres in all, adjoining a nature preserve.

It was lovely—and terrifying. This place was way too quiet, too holy, for me.

I could feel the sweat on my hands and arms, sweat coming not just from the seasonal heat but from my nervousness. I approached the big wooden door and rang the bell. It opened.

This was my first time meeting a Sister who looked like "a nun." She was wearing a long black habit and a veil. She was small, maybe 5'3", which made me more nervous. I felt like a tank next to her.

"I'm Sister Phyllis," she offered.

I blurted, "I'm Shane Phelan." Thank God, she took it from there. "Come on in," she invited, acting like everything was normal.

As I entered, we began our small talk. Sister Phyllis asked about the drive and whether I'd been to New Jersey before. I tried to keep up my side, but inwardly I thought: "Oh my God, I'm in a convent!" The drive? The landscape? My spiritual rocket seemed to have shot me to Mars! I could have gotten there by spaceship, and it wouldn't have felt much stranger.

As we talked, Sister Phyllis showed me around. The parlor, the refectory, the pantry with coffee and tea. The main kitchen was down one floor in the basement. Food came up on a dumbwaiter, pulled with a rope. I loved that; somehow, every archaic touch seemed to add to the monastic glamour of the place. Brown tile floors and illuminated manuscripts on the walls added to the otherworldly vibe.

Stairs led up to the second floor and the modest chapel, a space big enough for 20 Sisters and a few rows of guests. The afternoon light streamed through the leaded windows. Light-colored wooden choir stalls reflected the light.

I loved the size, the intimacy, the simplicity, the light. This room was why I had come. I looked forward to praying here.

Down the opposite hall from the chapel was "enclosure"—space not open to guests, unless they were specifically invited. The Sisters' cells ran down the hall to the left.

"Why are your rooms called cells?" I asked.

"It is a traditional term for monastic sleeping areas. The first monks and nuns each had their own space for sleeping and prayer. But we also call them cells because they are too small for the fire code; if we called them rooms, we'd have to tear down walls and make everything larger. They are only meant to be used for sleeping and private prayer, so they don't need to be any bigger."

Visions of simplicity filled my mind.

We stepped into the library. Oh, the library! A vaulted ceiling opened up two floors, with windows running all the way up the far end and looking out over a back garden area. The upper floor had more bookshelves, with a narrow balcony for getting to them. The main floor held books, books, books; books that pertained to prayer, religious life, church history and theology, general history. There were printed volumes from as far back as 1587, and a vellum book of plain-chant, created in the days when everything was done by hand. There was a world in this library, a world I wanted to know. I could imagine reading for years in this library.

A beautiful gray stone fireplace, about six feet wide and four feet tall, hearkened back to the days before central heating. Circled around the fireplace were eight green fabric-covered chairs. The library was where the Sisters gathered each night for "recreation," a time of relaxed conversations, handwork, or board games.

Now it was time to go to my room. Sister Phyllis showed me one of the unused cells, just outside the enclosure. It was about 7x10 feet, with a single bed, a night table, a straight-backed chair with a woven seat, and a World War I army locker painted white. The locker had a long side for habits and a side with shelves for everything else.

I loved it. I've always loved small spaces and felt safe in them. Those places let me hide from the chaos of my family. They gave me a sense of privacy. This space was small, and its size demanded simplicity—another thing that felt soothing. After my too-large, too-full house, this was what I sought.

But I wouldn't be staying there for my visit. I had a small but plush guest room, with a flouncy bed cover, pillows, a desk and chair. The cell would have to wait.

I loved the whole feel of it, but I felt certain I didn't belong there. For sure I'd break something, or fart, or laugh too loud, or—something. I was just too big, too queer. But then, I didn't expect to actually stay there; this was just a two-week visit to see if some version of monastic life was right for me. And I did love the grounds and the building; they were archetypal, evocative of holiness. I felt the solidity of the place. But come here? No way.

Soon I met the two other "inquirers," and that helped to put me at ease. Like me, Julia was a lesbian in her 40s who wanted a deeper relationship with God. Margaret was not really seeking religious life, but she was encouraged to come by one of the Sisters. So, I had some companions. The Sisters may have been a foreign country, but I had two fellow travelers who still spoke my language.

At 4:50, the bell rang for Vespers, the evening service. I headed down the stairs to the chapel, where they seated us in the back. I felt eager, and nervous. The chapel Sister gave me pieces of paper to help me follow the service.

At 5:00, the second bell rang. Sister Phyllis, who turned out to be the Superior, stood, and we followed. She opened the prayers, singing in a clear, strong voice: "Oh God, make speed to save us," while crossing herself. The others responded, "Oh Lord, make haste to help us," and plunged into prayer—singing the "Phos Hilaron," an ancient evening hymn, followed by psalms, readings, another hymn, the "Magnificat" (Mary's song), and closing prayers. The Sisters sang antiphonally, one side singing one verse of a psalm and the other side answering.

Suddenly, all my fears fell aside. I knew I wanted to do this. I wanted to sing to God, to sing plainchant. I could feel the breeze, the flow of energy in the room as the Sisters sent the sound back and forth. I could hear them listening for each other, listening for when to begin and what pace to follow. It felt like tall grass moved by the wind, like lying in a field under a tree with the breeze gently blowing back and forth. It wasn't Merton, it wasn't a Trappist monastery, it was a little place in exurban New Jersey. No matter—God was here, breathing peace and devotion.

The half-hour between Vespers and dinner was quiet. I sat in the chapel and tried to take in this beauty.

At dinner that night we talked a bit, though I learned that most meals are taken in silence. After dinner, we met with the Sisters. They told us their stories of how they came to be there and what their lives were like now. What I learned surprised me. Two Sisters were born Jewish, one to Holocaust survivors. One had been in a Vedanta convent for years before becoming a Christian. One was raised a Quaker, one a Presbyterian. By a variety of routes, they had all landed here.

They talked of "vocation," of sensing God moving in their lives, in a way that no one else I knew spoke of these things. God was a regular, basic presence in their lives, whether they were in chapel or the refectory or working. I could talk of my desire here and be understood.

The other thing I noticed that night was that they laughed. They were loud sometimes. They wore these habits, but they wore them as clothes, not like little starched outfits. They were human. I didn't exactly feel I belonged, but I could see similarities in our journeys that gave me hope that I might be on the right track. It may be a crazy desire that was driving me, but it seemed that others shared that crazy desire, and some acted on it. I wanted to know more.

The following day, the bell rang at 6. Three bells were rung three times, followed by nine. The bells rang at 6 a.m., 12 noon, and 6 p.m. on an electric-powered bell that was so loud it could take off the top of your head if you were standing beneath it.

That first morning, I got up, washed, got coffee, and sat to pray. I mostly stared out the window, trying to take it all in. I was in a convent. With nuns, dressed head to toe in black, praying with others, on a schedule. I felt called to monastic life. But here? With habits? I couldn't imagine it.

When the bell rang for Lauds, the first service of the day, I went down to the chapel. As on the night before, the chapel Sister gave me papers to help me follow the "office." Opening, psalms, reading, hymn, canticle, prayers: the same structure as Vespers. It was a quieter service than Vespers, mostly said rather than sung, but it still embodied that collective flow of breath and prayer. I managed to follow it, and to join in some of the words.

When Lauds was done, the chapel Sister went out and rang the hall bell once. The Superior left her seat. It was time for Eucharist. By now, I knew my way around the prayer book. I could participate in the Eucharist with assurance.

Then, when everyone else was settled, the Superior returned.

She entered in a green chasuble, the poncho-like garment that marks the presider at Eucharist. The chasuble had been cut for a larger person, a man, and it almost reached the floor. She still wore her black veil. She entered at the front, bowed to the altar, and turned to face us.

I don't know if I had realized that she was also ordained a priest. Now it hit me like a giant wave carrying me to some new shore. Wearing the veil and the chasuble together, this small woman seemed to embody all the power of the feminine divine. Rather than clashing with the vestments traditionally worn by men, the veil heightened their impact. It seemed I was standing in Avalon, watching something ancient—primal. My nostrils contracted as I breathed in.

I began to see that my lines between "traditional" and "contemporary" were too simple to capture the enormous reality I had begun to touch. Something older than "the tradition" was here, brought to light by contemporary women fighting for inclusion. In her role as priest, Sister Phyllis smashed the division I had been presented with in New Mexico—priest or nun, feminist or conservative, traditional or radical. There was a wholeness here that I had not dreamed of.

I don't know when I began to imagine myself belonging there. I loved the prayer, the chant, the grounds, even the tiled floor. Everything in me that cried out for peace and serenity, and the hunger for the moist eastern climate that had sent me from New Mexico, seemed to sigh in relief when I came up the driveway through the woods. The arches on the cloister spoke to me of grace and beauty.

But really. Is that enough reason to leave a tenured position, a secure life, and take a chance on a tiny community of strangers who seem to be living in another century?

The night before we left, the novice director took us out for Chinese food. My fortune cookie read: "You will soon have a change of clothing."

We all raised our eyebrows.

On the last day, as we were getting ready to leave, Sister Helen was sitting in her wheelchair in the hall by the front door. She was the exception to the general relaxed feel of the place: 95 years old, arthritic, with a severe expression usually on her face, you couldn't imagine Sister Helen giggling. She had been Mother Superior for 30 years, and now, long after she had stepped down, she was the matriarch. She didn't need a full name; if someone said, "Sister," everyone knew who was meant.

We had hardly talked on this visit, so I still didn't know what to make of this imposing figure. As I paused to say goodbye, however, she grabbed my arm, looked at me intently through her Coke-bottle glasses, and said, "Come back."

Inside me, some sleeping animal woke up and stretched and looked around. I looked into her eyes and let her see me—and I saw her. I saw years of service and struggle and love, and I felt her desire to share those with me. I wanted to know her more. I wanted to know what she saw in me.

I mumbled something and stumbled out the door.

When I left, I headed back to Vermont to catch my breath and get Max. I knew I had made some sort of passage. I was no longer simply "exploring"; I felt really drawn into this life, and particularly, to this surprising community. But I needed to not just jump. I needed to at least try to do some more research.

After two weeks in Vermont, Max and I headed back south, this time to upstate New York. Max would have to stay in a kennel for this visit. I felt uneasy when I dropped him off; my baby, in a kennel with people I didn't know? Slightly on edge, I headed for my next visit.

This was the place I had expected to land in. They had sent me the DVD, signaling their comfort with contemporary technology. They still had habits for public events, but they had abandoned the veil.

They looked like monks without hoods. They only wore the habits on Sundays and feast days; the rest of the time, they dressed in clothes of their choosing.

They did not have an official inquirers' week. I was coming on my own and staying for a week. They welcomed me, but I stayed in the guest wing, alone. There were no real classes and no companions. Mostly, I was on my own.

Sister Gloria welcomed me. We sat in her modern, slightly cluttered office as she told me about the ministries of the Sisters. They were actively involved in a number of feminist and peace-oriented ministries. Members expressed themselves in poetry, in writing plainchant, in serving the poor. Three of the Sisters lived in New York City, with full-time work there.

I admired their accomplishments and commitments, but really all this activity scared me. "You all seem awfully busy," I said.

Sister Gloria looked me straight in the eye. "This is a place of work and prayer," she said. "We share our gifts as we are called."

I squirmed inwardly. I approved of that. Then why was I intimidated? Was I just looking to lounge around? Maybe. But honestly, I didn't know what gifts I had to share. I hadn't thought of ministry. I just wanted to pray and be with others praying.

Sister Gloria showed me around the building. The chapel, the heartbeat of any monastery or convent, was radically different from that in New Jersey. Like the rest of the building, it was modern, somewhat stark, made of gray concrete blocks. It was circular, rising in the center. In the middle, a huge wooden-carved crucifix hung above the altar. The chapel had been designed for a larger community than the one currently living there, so rather than being intimate, it was spacious. Well, maybe "spacious" isn't the word. It just felt big and sort of empty. As at the other convent, the choir stalls were aligned to face one another, but the space between the sides felt like a chasm.

I was seated in a choir stall with the Sisters. I appreciated that sense of invitation and inclusion; here, I would be not a spectator, but a participant.

That was helpful, but disturbing. From my place close in, I could sense disharmony among the Sisters. It was an energetic awareness rather than a rational knowing. There was trouble here. There may well have been clashes at the other community as well, but from the back pew, I didn't notice it. I had been entranced by the office itself, by the prayer.

Once I had tuned in to it, I felt tension in other places. We ate lunch in silence, though we talked at dinner. And here's a thing about silence: when words aren't dominating everything and crowding your awareness, other senses can open up. Just like closing your eyes can help you smell and hear and taste, so silence can help you notice more subtle movements. And that sense beyond the senses, our intuition or energy awareness, can wake up and show you things that the left brain might censor.

In the silence of not speaking, I could hear not only the occasional dropped fork and the beep of the microwave, but the sighs of frustration, the rustling of restless bodies. Discord swirled around like a serpent slithering through. It wasn't huge, but it was noticeable. I ate quickly.

Then I learned that they were not only more up-to-date than other communities about feminism and technology. They were also more "contemporary" in ways I wasn't so happy with. Specifically, they drank alcohol. We visited the convent in the city, and after Vespers, the Sisters gathered for beer or wine. I was stunned. As a recovering alcoholic and aspiring saint, it had not occurred to me that some communities allowed alcohol.

I showed up measuring everything against my experience in New Jersey, and of course, this place failed. I must have driven those Sisters crazy, noticing and mentioning comparisons. I was an old hand now, with my two weeks of experience.

I learned on this visit that my heart did not always match up with my head. In this transformation that was unfolding in me, the things that had mattered to me, the non-negotiables, mattered no longer. If I had asked my left brain what mattered, I would have tried this community. Their feminist and social justice commitments aligned with mine. I respected the work done by the Sisters in the city, and the creativity I saw in Sisters writing poetry and plainchant. They were actively creating their monastic community, trying to bridge the past and the present.

But my stupid heart wanted to go to a place where women still wore black floor-length habits and veils, where God was masculine and "Father, Son, and Holy Spirit" was in everyday use. My silly soul wanted to pray in that little chapel and wander those grounds.

I ended my visit clear that I wanted to return to New Jersey.

I may not have been destined to join those Sisters, but I had a powerful mystical experience at the convent there, an experience that really ushered me into this new life.

I sat in an alcove just off the hallway between the guest wing and the dining room. There was a simple cross on the wall, not for prayer so much as decoration, or to keep you company while you sit.

I sit, looking at the cross. Then, suddenly, I'm standing at the foot of the cross, and Jesus is hanging above me. He's suffering, as the Romans intend their victims to suffer—not only from the pain of the nails, but the pain of suffocation as he can no longer hold himself up. I feel an overpowering need to take him down. I want to do what I can to ease the pain of my beloved.

Jesus demurs. "If you try to help me, they will crucify you too," he says. "They will nail you up, and it won't save you in the end."

"I don't care. How can I just watch you die?"

I have to try; not to do so would be a failure of love. How could I leave him there? How could I not try? I approach and begin to pull at the nails.

And sure enough, the soldiers catch me and crucify me next to him. I hang on a much smaller cross, helpless to save myself, but somehow content. I don't want to die, but I couldn't have left him there alone.

I didn't tell anyone about this incident, but it stayed with me. That moment of love, in which love was bigger than my fear and pain, has stayed with me through all the years since. I began to see what loving might cost. I began to imagine being willing to pay the price.

By now, I knew I wanted to try religious life, specifically with the convent in New Jersey. Julia and I had begun to consider returning for the next step—a month-long visit with physical and psychological exams. This stage is called "aspirancy." This was a big commitment, not least because we had to pay for (and undergo) physical and psychological exams, and trust others with the results. But I wouldn't be alone. We would come at the same time, for the month of October. We had it all planned out, and we told the Superior what we wanted to do. She said yes.

Max would need to return to New Mexico before I made my month's visit. I couldn't ask Carey and Andy to keep him again, and I wouldn't consider putting him in a kennel. Jim and Lloryn, his long-time friends, had agreed to take him. But first, a little time to reflect.

After picking up Max from the kennel, I headed to a cottage on Cape Cod. It was perfect timing: after Labor Day the crowds had thinned, the Summer Olympics were on TV, the beach was still warm enough to enjoy. Max finally got the hang of water, running on the beach and into the smallest of the waves. It was almost perfect, dimmed only by my awareness that after this, we would fly west, and I would leave him.

At the end of two weeks, we got on a plane. I had bought him a little cloth carrier so he could fit under my seat and not have to travel in with the luggage. We made it back, and I delivered him to my friends. I told myself this was fine, that he would have a good life there, but I hadn't thought about how I would feel. When I returned to New Jersey, I carried a bundle of grief that took a long time to surface and release. But at that point, I didn't know whether this separation was permanent; I might spend a month and decide not to enter, or they might turn me away. This was just the next step in a long process. I didn't have to feel it all now.

During October in New Jersey the sky is blue, the trees are showing their colors, the weather is warm during the day and crisp at night. I discovered one of the joys of not teaching: I could take vacation in October!

This month was meant for me to experience living in the community, and for them to know me more. We had classes and lots of free time. Julia and I both began to work outside, something that Sisters did not do (except when Sister Maria tended her garden). We began cleaning vines and moss off old walls. It was a glorious time to be outside. I shoveled, I hauled, I scraped.

As I did, my hands and wrists began to really complain. They had already been sore from all the driving I had done. Now, the trouble became noticeable. I dropped things in the pantry. Then I needed help cutting my meat. I couldn't really hold up the prayer book; I needed to use my little one or hold it in my lap.

I went off to the community's local doctor, who sent me for nerve tests. They couldn't see anything clearly, but they were pretty sure I had carpal tunnel syndrome from all the driving and scraping and shoveling and hauling. They recommended surgery.

I was not about to have surgery here, during this year, away from my own doctors, during this month. Terrified that they wouldn't let me join the community because my hands didn't work, I gave up scraping and hauling.

That wasn't the only cost to my body of that stint of manual labor. I had spent most of my life in places where poison ivy was not a problem, and I didn't recognize it when I saw it. So, as I scraped and cleaned the garden walls, I grabbed vines and tore them out.

I found out about poison ivy. I learned about Tech-nu, a wash that is supposed to clean the oil off your skin, but I learned too late; putting it on already-inflamed skin just made it worse. By the time I left at the end of October, I had to stop in an emergency room. Chills ran through me as my ravaged skin flamed red.

The doctor asked me what I had been doing.

"I've been at a convent. I'm thinking of becoming a nun."

He looked at me sharply. "Why would you throw your life away? Isn't that selfish?"

"It isn't throwing away my life. It's giving myself a life. And it's not selfish. I believe in the power of prayer."

He shrugged, disgust and incomprehension mingling in the gesture. I felt angry with him, and uneasy. Was that how it looked to people? Was this a real call, or was I just abandoning ship?

At month's end, after we left, the Sisters would decide whether we could enter. I asked to return at the end of November, to witness Sister Frances making her first profession of vows. After a month of visiting friends up and down the East Coast, I returned, still unsure as to whether and when I might come.

On the day of the profession, the main chapel filled with guests. This was the first time I had seen the large chapel in use. The rows of straight-backed chairs faced steps leading up to a rood screen, beyond which were the choir stalls for the Sisters. Up more steps, the altar was dressed with a breathtakingly beautiful frontal, embroidered decades ago by the Sisters. The frontal matched the gold vestments worn by the bishop who would preside at the service. Candelabras on the altar were flanked by standing pillar candles. Two Sisters lit the candles as a team, synchronizing their movements. As guests filed in, I had a glimpse of what this community had once been, and what it still was for some. This was a place soaked in prayer and devotion, a refuge for many.

As Sister Frances left behind the white veil marking her novitiate and received the black veil of the professed Sisters, I saw her being absorbed into the body of the community. She was taller than the others by several inches, but she was no longer as distinct as she had been. It was a visible sign of her formation and incorporation into this particular part of the larger body of Christ. It was everything I longed for; belonging not only to these other persons but to the mystical body. For years I had been writing about belonging, but I had never, really, named my own hunger for this deep form of it. Now I was witnessing it, and I wanted it.

That evening, the Sisters met for recreation and a meeting. I sat in the darkened chapel and prayed. Just before Compline, Sister Phyllis entered. "Oh, there you are," she said. "We've been looking all over for you." With her shy smile, she said, "I'm happy to say that we have accepted you as a postulant."

I let go of my breath. Ready or not, I was going in.

Chapter Eleven

Big Queer Postulant

"BELOVED IN CHRIST, WHAT DO YOU DESIRE?" The ancient question asked of all who seek entry into monastic life.

"I desire to love God and serve God, and to learn about the religious life in this community."

"Do you believe you are called to this life?"

"I do." (Well, I hope I am.)

In the Catholic Church, December 12 is the Feast of Our Lady of Guadalupe, patron saint of the Americas. In the calendar of the community, it was a minor feast, remembering Jane Frances de Chantal. On that day, I would be received as a postulant, the first step toward becoming a Sister. I would be assigned a cell in the enclosure and given space in the novitiate office. I would move from the pew in the back of the chapel to a stall in the choir. I would join the community. Although I had worn my "postulant clothes" before, the white shirt and black jumper and sweater, now they would become my only clothes for six days of the week.

The clothes had been an issue for me. During my return to New Mexico, I had shopped for the black and white (just in case they approved me for postulancy). I moved resolutely through stores full of lively colors in search of what I needed. Finally, I found a skirt and a jumper and some white shirts.

When I returned to the convent, I complained to Sister Helen.

Most afternoons she came down for tea around 4, and I joined her. I poured out my frustration: "All these beautiful clothes, Sister, and I had to choose black and white!"

She gave me that look that only she could deliver, and shot back lovingly but firmly: "Honey, you can still enjoy those beautiful things; you just can't have them."

Oh! I didn't have to own it to enjoy it. I could enjoy seeing those flamboyant colors on others; in fact, I might enjoy it more, as I would see them more than I would see them on myself. I liked that thought.

There was another layer to my struggle, though, that I didn't feel I could share with any of the Sisters. I had not shopped in a women's store or a women's department in years. It wasn't just that the clothes didn't suit me (though I was definitely too tall for their pants); it was the awkwardness of not fitting in, of being stared at, of being told I was in the wrong section when someone mistook me for a man. Once I put them on, the strangeness increased. Somehow, these clothes were more confusing than the habit. The habit was so obviously not part of a contemporary fashion statement—its femininity was so archaic that it felt remote from my struggles with gender. But these clothes put me in a borderland, a much stranger place than what I had occupied as a fairly butch lesbian. My lesbian space was familiar and felt right to me; this felt like unsuccessful transvestitism. In trying to "be a woman," I felt myself less one than before.

And yet, I couldn't wait to don this outfit and belong. This strange territory was where I hoped to give myself to God, to let go of my ideas and see what might be waiting for me. I hoped that humbling myself, letting myself be strange to myself, would open me to—something. I could sense it like the promise of a favorite meal. These clothes would lead me beyond who I had been, toward who God intended me to be.

Now the day had come. I spent it in silent retreat while the business of the community went on around me. I sat in the little chapel, and walked up and down the driveway. This was a day to reflect and prepare for an unknown future as well as I could.

When the bell rang for Vespers, I came down the stairs from the guest wing. I went to my usual place in the back, and knelt and prayed. After the second bell, the Superior went forward and stood on the step of the sanctuary. The novice director came and got me from the pew and led me to face the Superior. I held a sheet of paper with questions and answers.

"What do you desire?"

I desire to know Jesus, to follow, to give my life. Those weren't the words on the sheet, but they were the ones in my heart.

I read the words I had been given, brief and to the point.

After the questions and answers, Sr. Phyllis welcomed me as a postulant. I would learn about religious life and this particular community, and over the next six months, we would discern together whether I should go forward here.

The novice director led me to my new place in choir. At my seat I found a card, bookmark-sized. It was made of robin's-egg blue cardboard, laminated. On it was an icon sticker of The Virgin Mary, with her hands upraised in the orans (prayer) position. A medal of Jesus hung around her neck, but the effect was to put him in her center, as though we could look into her womb. Beside the picture, in gold ink, were the words attributed to her when the angel told her she would bear this improbable, impossibly glorious son: "Behold the handmaid of the Lord." On the back was simply printed: "Shane Phelan, Postulant. December 12, 2000." I gazed at the card with a kind of awe.

Me—the handmaid of the Lord!

The regular Vespers service began. I tried to concentrate and chant with everyone else, but I kept looking at the card. "Behold the handmaid of the Lord!" I wanted to be that. I wanted to give my life in whatever way I was asked to do it. I had no idea what I was in for or who I might become. But I knew I wanted to try.

After Vespers, the Superior took me by the hand and led me, with all the other Sisters, to the novitiate office. With no other postulants or novices at that point, I had this lovely space all to myself. The office was roughly the size of two cells together, maybe 14 feet by 10. It held a simple wooden table with three chairs and two glassed-in bookcases.

There were no computer wires or terminals, no phone, no desks. It was in the middle of the house, at the top of those mysterious stairs I had not been able to use before, just above the house clock that chimed every quarter hour. The leaded windows looked out over the driveway circle and the retreat house across the way.

The Superior said, "This is your space. We will not violate your space or enter without your permission." Trying for solemnity, but radiating a sort of girlish glee, she gazed up with a delighted smile and reached to hug me.

After a few more hugs and smiles, everyone left, and I sat by myself and tried to absorb what had just happened.

I felt like a precious child, a little girl who is welcomed into a new family, as though I had been an orphan who had found a home. My older, more cynical self could look at all this as antiquated or sickly sweet, but a younger part of me began to wake up and look around. I didn't really know a thing about her, but I could feel her stirring.

After dinner, I went to recreation. Into the library, not as a guest but as a member! Conversation moved from the controversy over the Presidential ballots in Florida, to the latest antics of Pete the dog. I sank into one of the olive-green, half-circle chairs and soaked it all in. I could come to this room whenever I wished. I could join the others! In fact, attendance at recreation and community times was required.

Sister Helen beckoned to me to sit next to her. During my month's visit I had grown to deeply respect and admire this woman. I loved her stories, and her stubborn devotion to the Rule—not the version written by the community in 1997, but the 1907 Rule, in its leather binding, worn and cracked from use. This was the real thing to her, the Rule that specified how to do everything from praying while putting on the habit to cleaning the sacred vessels of the chapel to how to address another Sister. No generalities, no "laxity" for her! She knew who she was, and she knew who God was, and she was rocklike in that faith.

"How are you?" She asked.

"I'm awesome, Sister," I said.

"How is your cell?"

"It's perfect."

It was perfect. In fact, it was like all the others, other than being a bit starker than most since I had just moved in. I now had my own 7x10 domain, with a bed, nightstand, chair, and locker. A cross on the wall over my bed. I would eventually find a small table to put next to the chair for a book. My coffee cup didn't need a table; our rooms were heated by pipes filled with hot water, and the pipe made a perfect warming niche for my cup. My love of small spaces served me here; I felt held and safe.

"You come and see me whenever you want to talk." She patted my hand with her own, twisted and gnarled with arthritis, but smooth. I felt like a little girl again, but now with a loving grandmother. I looked around the circle at my new Sisters, and relaxed into the green embrace of the chair.

Soon after I entered the convent, I had my first meeting with a spiritual director. I don't mean my new director; I mean my first ever. I had come this far, including thinking I wanted to be a director, without ever actually having been in direction. Now I would find out how it felt to be vulnerable in this way.

The Superior had found me a director, and I looked forward to knowing her better. Susan was a local Episcopal priest. I had met her, and liked her. She was a lesbian, and she was full of energy and a passion for social justice. We had never talked about faith before, so I had no idea how this conversation might go.

We met in her office at her church, a typical 1960s big barn of a place. Her office was large and full of furniture, with books lining bookshelves and spilling out onto tables and, a few of them, on the floor. Posters of Óscar Romero, Martin Luther King, and Pauli Murray decorated the walls. It felt like a place full of purpose.

After a few pleasantries, she leaned back in her chair and looked at me.

"Who is Jesus for you?"

I thought, what a place to start! Let's go for the big stuff right away.

Even in my shock, though, I realized I could answer. Almost without pausing I responded, "Jesus is the great integrator."

I thought of the passage in the letter to the Colossians where the author writes, "He himself is before all things, and in him all things hold together." I loved—I love—that line. That's exactly how I think of him. Like a Celtic cross where all the arms are of equal length, Jesus seemed to unify everything: not only the world, but me, myself.

Christ Jesus is the great integrator, the strange attractor who holds my center.

I have no idea what else we talked about, where the conversation went after that. I know that Susan was not my director very long; she got busy, and I didn't really feel an affinity after all. I began seeing someone else. Still, in fifteen short minutes, she gave me a huge gift. She led me to the central truth of my new life, a truth waiting for me to name it.

That was the feeling I had sponsoring people. That was exactly what I wanted to do for others. I knew I didn't know how yet, but I determined that I would find out.

Five times a day, we prayed together in the chapel. Now I joined in the wave I had sensed on my first visit, part of the listening for pitch and pace, hearing my Sisters' intake of breath before each half-verse. My new seat in choir was closer to the altar and the tabernacle. I had a place for my own prayer book and office book and Bible; I had a home in the house of God.

I found that closing my eyes enabled me to feel closer to God, and even to my Sisters. With my eyes closed, my vision stopped, I could notice the flow of energy and sounds and the whisper of breezes. I could aim my intention at God, and speak directly. When we prayed the Lord's Prayer or made petitions, I didn't bow my head. If anything, I lifted it. It felt like basking in sunshine, in a radiance of love. I closed my eyes as one does when the sun is too bright. Like a beachgoer on a hot day, I wanted to be exposed to this light, but I knew it was too much to look on directly. I stood, and lifted my face, and prayed.

Sitting in the same place, surrounded by the same voices, day after day, the rhythm of the church year became part of my life. We had seasons and feast days of varying levels of importance. The feasts offered variety during years of saying the same psalms and canticles, but they also taught me church history. Who knew the patron saint of Oxford was a 7th-century nun named Frideswide? Who knew Oxford had a patron saint?

Then there were the seasonal changes. I came in Advent when the vestments were violet, then we celebrated Christmastide with gold and white, and Epiphany's green, before entering into the forty days of Lent. During Lent, the tone was repentance. Every day we sang hymns about fasting, sleeping less, laughing less, cleansing our hearts to return to God. The tradition of "Lenten reading," of following a meditation book or study volume through the season, also marked this time.

And then, finally, it was time for Holy Week, the apex of the year. More silence, prayer in the chapel in place of recreation. Maundy Thursday, with its transition from a shared meal and foot-washing to stripping the altar and following Jesus into the hours of darkness. Overnight vigil, time alone with Jesus in the garden of Gethsemane. A cell off to the side of the chapel hallway, usually our incense room, had been converted into a beautiful prayer space. It held a tiny altar to hold the tabernacle, the "house" for the consecrated host, and two chairs. Around the altar were flowers—tulips, lilies, with palm fronds. It was a garden in which to sit with Jesus as he awaited the time of his arrest and passion.

I sat for my appointed hour, 1 a.m. to 2. When the hour ended, the next Sister came for her turn. I returned to my cell, sleepy but also looking forward to more time in that place of prayer.

The next day, Good Friday. We did the Stations of the Cross, shuffling down the second-floor hall to each picture, reading, praying, chanting. At 12, we said Noonday prayers, then we moved into the Good Friday service.

Afterwards, I headed to the cemetery. It was partway down the driveway, at its lowest point. There, beyond the rows of graves for departed Sisters (and some Associates), was a huge crucifix, its copper leaving turquoise streaks down the sides. On either side stood 5-foot-tall statues of Mary and John the Evangelist, looking on with sorrow and wonder at this figure on the cross.

I entered through the little gate with its bell tower, long unused. The whole cemetery was a bit neglected; the block walls were covered with moss that was gradually eroding the stucco and the mortar between the blocks. It seemed right for this day, for the melancholy I felt.

The headstones, simple stone crosses with each Sister's name and dates, were worn but clear. I walked through the field of stones, thanking the Sisters for creating and maintaining this place and way of life until I could come. I then went to the tableau at the end. I gazed at Jesus and tried to imagine what that day had been like for him. I wasn't sure I wanted to know how it felt to be crucified, but I wanted to know him. What had he thought as he carried his own death down the road? Had he thought anything, or had he settled into that numb place of moving one foot before the other? What, if anything, did he think as the nails were being driven in and he was hoisted skyward? Can one even think in the face of such pain?

This wondering didn't feel morbid to me. It felt like love with its own sweet pain. I said to the figure, to the one the figure imaged, "I'm so sorry. I'm so sorry you had to die this way. Thank you for loving the world enough to not back down from what you saw before you. Teach me that courage and love."

He didn't answer; he didn't look at me. His work was done.

I turned and walked back to the convent.

On Easter morning, we began the service at 6 a.m., at the beginning of dawn. We gathered in the dark on the cloister. The priest lit the new fire and the very tall, decorated Paschal candle that would be lit throughout Easter season. Holding small candles, we processed into the convent and up the stairs to the chapel, where the lights remained off. We paused three times to sing: "The light of Christ"; "Thanks be to God." By the third time we had entered the chapel. The priest brought the Paschal candle to its holder, and then turned and sang the ancient hymn, *the Exsultet.* "Rejoice now, heavenly hosts and choirs of angels." I soared with the joy and beauty of this story of God's love. It was still new to me; this was only my second Easter as an adult Christian.

After the 50 days of Easter season, we returned to the simpler services of "Ordinary Time," the long season between Pentecost and Advent, before the cycle began again.

I became a postulant in Advent, two weeks before Christmas. Through these weeks, I began to glimpse the challenge before me, the challenge of becoming "a monastic." For Christmas, we had a large creche at the entrance to the chapel, a wooden stable about 3 feet wide and 2 feet tall, that we filled with hay. On Christmas Eve, the postulants and novices (read: me) got to put in all the figures except the baby Jesus, who would go in during the Christmas midnight Mass, and the wise men, who would arrive on Epiphany. I delighted at the chance to exercise my creativity, until I learned that there was a certain way the figures were to be arranged; putting them in became less a creative offering than a job.

One of the chapel Sisters helped me. After we put in the ceramic figures, the ox and the ass and the lambs, I considered. I thought my little stuffed lamb Agnes Day, given to me on my postulant day, should be in the creche too. After all, she was a lamb. She'd want to be at this party. "What do you think?" I asked the Sister who was supervising me. "Yes!" No question. Agnes belonged here. So that afternoon, in time for Vespers, Agnes appeared. She sat in front of the creche. A tiny stuffed lamb, about 3 inches tall, with her legs sticking out in front of her, adoring the scene before her.

Sisters filed in for Vespers. Some didn't see her. Some did, and smiled. No one said anything, we were in silence—but reactions were visible on their faces.

During the next few days, a strange thing happened. Some other animals began to appear next to Agnes. Mostly they were Beanie Babies: a bird, a little dog, a bear. By the end of Christmastide, Agnes had a dozen friends watching with her.

I had no idea that I had landed in Beanie Baby heaven. In our little cells, Beanie Babies brought miniature companions. Sister Helen had at least 30. I loved the color and the vibrancy that the Babies brought. I thought they made the scene more devotional, somehow; all these animals jostling to look at Jesus!

The Superior did not agree. She let the show run until Epiphany, and then she announced, "We will have no more additions to the creche in the future. This was fun, but it does not lend itself to devotion." I removed the animals, feeling chastened. It appeared that, here at least, "devotion" was a serious matter, to be entered into with decorum. Decorum had never been my strong point.

This wasn't my only dash of cold water. In other areas, too, I gradually got the message that some of my energy needed reining in. One evening, I came zipping around a corner, heading for the pantry stairs, and almost ran into Sister Fiona. She jumped back and squealed, "Slow down!" Later I learned that moving quickly was "not monastic." Nuns were to move slowly and carefully.

"But what about Sister Laura?" I asked the Superior when she told me this. "She races down the corridors."

"Yes, she always has. But we want to start you off right."

I thought to myself, the difference was that Laura was 4'10" and weighed maybe 90 pounds. The Superior herself had been known to hustle sometimes, but she, too, was small. When I came at you, it was a different thing—more like a small tractor.

It wasn't just movements and creches that were rated on the "monastic" scale. At Vespers each evening we sang the "Magnificat" in plainchant, with different tones for each day. I would leave the chapel and go down to the pantry to set up for dinner. There, I'd keep singing the "Magnificat," but I'd jazz it up a bit, syncopating the tone. "My *soul* proclaims the greatness of the *Lord,*" looping the solemn tone's dips and rises. The words of joy called me to dance. Then, one day, a senior Sister heard me. I learned that my singing was disrespectful, not monastic.

So, "monastic" meant serious, serene, quiet, slow. I could be all of these things (well, serene not so much), but I could also be irreverent, goofy, vocal, energetic. I wanted the virtues the community labelled monastic, but not only them. I wanted to express my passionate love for God across the whole register of attitudes and expressions. Over time, I did learn how to slow down, how to be quiet (at least outwardly), but I also found other places to let out that rowdier, more playful self. My compartmentalized life had not ended with entrance into the convent; it would just shift dimensions.

Julia arrived three weeks after me, entering on January 6. Together we had planned to come, and we had become friends. But something shifted when she came.

We shared this bond, this being new. And sometimes that bond came to the fore as we shared our experience. We had lots of time to complain to one another about the silly ways things were done, or about Sister So-and-So, or whatever. And we could laugh together.

But we also had a lot of tension. Our good times now had a lot of bad times mixed in.

Julia entered with the same ceremony I had had, complete with being led to the novitiate. Unlike my experience, though, she was not the queen of her tiny domain. Already there for three whole weeks, I had made the place mine. This chair, this side of the table facing the door, was *mine.* She got the other side. We didn't negotiate.

I didn't mean to be bossy. It just came so naturally!

We now had classes together, something every day. We studied the history of religious life and the Rule, we practiced plainchant, we learned community history.

I reveled in this sea of information. Learning was my thing! I was hungry to know about the life I was entering, eager to read and study. I soaked up the history and reflection on the religious life.

I loved to sing, so plainchant was a joy for me. Our teacher was the sort of person who liked to really dig into the details. We sat at the piano with her as she played tunes and told us the history and theory behind the tones. I asked questions, and she answered. I was intrigued and eager, the perfect student.

Julia didn't have the same background in music as I did, and singing was not something she was really comfortable with. Pretty quickly, our teacher started aiming her remarks at me, and Julia began to simmer with—impatience? Boredom? She never said, exactly, but I knew she was not on board.

That pattern repeated itself in other classes. I read quickly, and study was familiar to me. I'd show up for classes full of ideas and questions. Again, I became the focal point.

Gradually, our paths diverged. Julia became close with one of the Sisters. I spent more time with our novice director, going on hikes and the occasional meal on Sabbath days. When we spent time in the office together, we shifted back and forth between partnership and hostility. Mostly, we bonded through complaint. We agreed that a lot of the practices and attitudes we saw were messed up: why did they do this, or not do that? We agreed that some Sisters were pains in the butt, always seeming to put us in our place. But then something would crop up in conversation, and we'd be pitted against one another. We were competing, somehow, for something I couldn't name.

These months were filled with drama, not only with Julia but with others—and most basically, with myself. They say that entering religious community often involves regression, that people unravel a bit before they grow into a new identity. Initiation includes replaying and confronting old family patterns before developing new ways of being. Given my family history, this was not an easy path. I truly wanted to be an open vessel, to learn humility and love and patience, but mostly in those months I struggled.

Poverty and chastity weren't difficult. It was that obedience thing, living with others, that got to me.

As I prepared to graduate from high school, I had briefly considered joining the Army. My older brother Dal, who was an Army lifer, had advised against it. "Someone would tell you to do something you thought was stupid, and you'd last about a week," he said. At 17, I knew he was right; but surely now, at 44, I could let go? I wanted to let go.

But no. Every correction, every snide remark or rebuke, every "stupid" thing someone told me to do just because "we do it that way," seized me with fury and frustration. Personal rebukes stung too. Sister Cecily dismissing my singing; Sister Fiona telling me that her vacation plans were none of my business; all the little indignities of living with other flawed people hit me hard. Criticism and correction hit me like a baseball bat.

I had spent my life either striving to be perfect, leaving no room for criticism, or rejecting goals and norms entirely so as not to be measured and found wanting. My teenage years had been about rejecting the expectations of my parents and teachers. Once I decided to rejoin the world, I worked for perfection. I had had a pretty perfect time in graduate school (until I almost lost it all) and a pretty perfect path to tenure and beyond.

Here, there was no way to be perfect. No longer measured by my intelligence or by a checklist of publications and teaching evaluations, I was sharing a life, bathrooms, work spaces, recreation, with people who brought their own issues and perceptions. Any desire I felt for unequivocal affirmation was frustrated. Each little slight or correction hit me like a door swinging in my face.

Personalities weren't the only rub. New information angered me when things didn't line up with my picture of monastic life. These women were not saints; they weren't living like Thomas Merton's description. (As a friend later pointed out, even Merton didn't always live like the ideal I cherished.) It didn't match my picture, and I didn't like it.

As the newest of the new, I had no voice in how things were done. I couldn't expect to have a voice for years. But I had opinions! I wanted to learn humility and obedience and trust, but I kept stopping before the actual realities of our life together: "Surely, I'm not supposed to trust her! Or accept that! I see a better way!" Gratitude and judgment fought within me every hour.

During these first months, my life began to center around the rhythm of prayer I had longed for. We prayed together five times a day, but the Rule also called for private prayer on a schedule that worked for each of us. I quickly got into a pattern. I rose at six when the Angelus was rung. I'd go get coffee and bring it up to my cell. There, I had a table with room for a candle and a small icon. I had begun to read the day's lessons each morning, using an outdated but basic commentary. For me, every day was a revelation. I had never read the Bible in this way, in short bits with commentary and time to reflect. Each sentence dripped with meaning for me, drawing me more deeply into a relationship with God and Jesus. After reading, I'd wash and get dressed and be in the chapel by 7. That gave me a half hour to just sit, to let whatever thoughts and feelings float up that wanted to, and to talk to God directly.

As I struggled with my expectations and frustration, the time before Lauds was when it all poured out. I cried, I railed at God. Somehow, most of the time, I got put back together by the time others began to show up, but sometimes I cried my way through Lauds as well. No one checked on me; they seemed to think it was normal.

Each evening after Vespers, I stayed in the chapel and sat at the base of the step leading up to the sanctuary. I had a little rug and a prayer bench, three boards nailed together, to enable me to sit kneeling on the floor. I tried to empty my mind and be present to Jesus in the tabernacle. I sat with the crucifix above it, just trying to take in the presence. I sat with the two statues of Mary and John, statues I had never liked.

Over the next months, as I sat with the little silver crucifix, I began to see meaning behind images I had abhorred. The Book of Revelation talks of martyrs "washed in the blood of the Lamb." I had found this not only queasy-making, but morally offensive—turning these people's deaths into a cleansing somehow. I didn't want the blood, or the sacrifice.

Now, though, as I sat with Jesus, I began to see for myself the power of that image. I saw that, through the holes in his hands, his feet, his side, Jesus' love flowed out like—like blood, flowing over the whole world. His piercing, it seemed to me, was a sign of his radical openness to us and to all creation. He had allowed himself to be pierced by evil in order to let goodness flow. What had been embodied in him during his lifetime, contained in his body, was now freed to be everywhere.

The Holy Spirit was in all of us, released through his willing undergoing. I still didn't want to be washed in blood literally, but I could feel the love pouring out of that crucifix, and out of the tabernacle it sat on.

The statues changed too. As the Forerunner of Jesus, John had been known to excoriate others, to call them to repentance. He was fierce. Now, in his raised arm and finger pointing up, I saw humility. It wasn't self-hatred or humiliation; this was a bold claim of what mattered more than his stature or even his life. John knew he wasn't the center of his own life. He was pointing to another; as he told his disciples when they asked about Jesus, "He must increase; I must decrease." He was just a part of a much larger story about God's work in the world. His knowledge and acceptance of his role in things freed him to proclaim the message he had been given, rather than fight for supremacy of a movement. This humility led to strength.

This was what I saw in people growing in recovery. This was what I wanted for myself—to let myself be the little toenail of the body of Christ, to do my part without the bondage of ego. As I cried over the slights and corrections I experienced in community, I turned to John to teach me about keeping my eyes on the prize.

As my understanding of John evolved, so did my relationship to Mary. Her statue portrayed her as lily white, stereotypically submissive, with downcast eyes and folded hands. As I sat, I began to see the courage she needed to say yes and to keep going. Whether I believed the Gospel story of the Holy Spirit "overshadowing" her, or the historically more likely story of sex before marriage, whether consensual sex or rape, this woman went through a lot. Her neighbors would talk about her, likely as long as she lived there. She narrowly escaped stoning or total rejection. And yet, she raised Jesus to be an amazing human being. That doesn't come, I thought, from resentment and regret, or submission. I saw that this woman didn't just submit, she didn't just resign herself to what she was facing. Mary's "Let it be unto me" was an affirmation, an act of agency. Mary took this circumstance and made a life of it. She raised a man who could face down demons.

Over time, the statue began to look to me like all the women who are seen as delicate, who are valued for their silence, while their hearts are full of fierce love. The Holy Spirit did indeed fill this woman, and would fill me if I let it.

I got to watch the interplay of courage and humility, not only in a statue or a story, but in a living, breathing person. I took Sister Helen up on her offer to talk to me when I needed it. She was born in 1904 on the plains of South Dakota. She entered the community in 1932, and she had been Mother Superior for thirty years. Her shadow was everywhere in the community; generations of schoolgirls and local priests had known her as their authority figure. The current leaders of the community were all her "daughters," still watching for her approval or disdain. She had no trouble expressing her opinion, but over time, she had worked to learn obedience as well as leadership. She was not happy with the changes that had come to the community over the years. "Sister" saw the changes as laxity, falling away from the rigor of the 1907 Rule and active ministry. She despaired over the lack of new vocations. The present was not a kindly time for her. Still, she did her best to be faithful, to let others govern. Her strength now manifested in her effort to accept how things were, how she was.

On the surface, we couldn't have been more different. One day, as we sat in the front hall, she in her wheelchair and me on the bench next to her, she told me that she was a lifelong Republican, "and you'd better be too."

"Sister, I'm a socialist feminist," I replied.

"Oh," she said. "Alright." You could almost hear her shrug.

Underneath any differences in point of view or background, we recognized each other. I no longer feared her. I loved her strength, her certainty, her vitality. Even in her wheelchair, barely able to write, she commanded attention.

Her memory and love for what had been met my curiosity and desire to enter into the community. During our community history lessons, we read the old Rule and some histories of the community written by friends of the community. Then we found some photo albums, and began looking at pictures of Sisters long dead, in houses we no longer served in. She knew all the names and faces, from the first American Sister to the most recently dead. When she spoke of them, her eyes glowed a bit, as though she was seeing them with an inner eye.

Through her, I met a whole host of ancestors. Places I had never been to became part of my history: the first house in England, the gigantic complex they built at the peak of the order, the convent in New York City; the refuges for prostitutes, convalescent homes, and branch houses attached to local churches. I read the reports from these places. I saw the beautiful vestments they made for churches all over the country. These women had done all this work on top of praying the traditional seven offices a day! I saw why they didn't need big rooms; they were never in them, except to sleep. I didn't want to try to keep that schedule, but I felt proud to have them as foremothers. "Sister" was my link to them.

I started coming to Sister Helen when I had trouble dealing with other Sisters or constraints of the new life.

First, though, I had to get to her.

She had the last cell at the end of the second floor, the hall where the senior Sisters lived. The first time I came through the door to that wing, the infirmarian met me in the hall. "Can I help you?" she asked. She was, after all, the infirmarian, and she might well have thought I had need of aspirin or a bandage. Her tone, however, didn't offer help. Her tone said, "What are you doing here?"

It was a fair question. In the good old days, postulants and novices would never have come through that door.

I had, however, been invited by the most senior of Sisters. I answered: "Sister Helen invited me to visit."

She paused. "Let me see if she is awake." She padded down the hall to the end, where Sister Helen lived. After a moment, she came out and said, "Sister will see you now."

I came in and sat down. My neck itched with the certainty that someone was listening. In keeping with monastic practice, the door stayed open. So, I sat, and talked politely about what I was learning. Nothing deeply personal, just getting started on a new relationship.

Really, I wanted to ask: Sister, am I on the right track, following God? Or am I just here for a time before returning to my orderly life? Or is there something else waiting for me? How will I know? I bobbed on a sea of uncertainty.

As time went on, I became able to confide in her more. Once, I stalked down the hall to her room and told her of my anger at another Sister. Hanging my head, tears streaming down, I cried out my confusion and frustration.

She sat in her wheelchair while I sat at the end of her white-covered single bed, facing her rows of Beanie Babies. She listened patiently.

Then she said, "Don't you just want to break their kneecaps?"

I stared at her. What did she say?

Through my tears I said, "Yes, I do." I couldn't help but laugh a little. She smiled, a little smile that hinted at real laughter underneath. I smiled back.

Then she gently coached me toward accepting that the others were how they were, and that life in community sometimes meant putting up with things that seemed just plain wrong to me. She didn't tell me the others were right, or to see things from their point of view; she didn't try to talk me out of my perception. She just laid it out. I was a newbie; nothing was going to change just because I wanted it to.

If the time before Lauds was my time to pour out my feelings to God, my time with Sister Helen gave me a human being who was not afraid of my feelings. I needed that companionship. My novice director was calm, too, but I felt her more as a colleague than a mentor. In Sister Helen, I had found someone as fierce and strong-willed as myself, who somehow had found something I wanted.

In spite of all the drama, I stayed. I found that God was there. I felt nourished by the prayer life, the daily round of prayer, what I called my "prayer leash," leading me back if my mind wandered. I would always get another chance to connect.

I loved what I was learning. More than learning, I found myself immersed in a whole world, a world of passionate service, of music and beauty of a different sort than I had known. I was gradually taking in what I was learning, letting it settle into my understanding of myself. I loved the bones of the life, the point of it, even when our daily reality didn't measure up to my ideal. My yearning was met here, not perfectly, but enough. I was with others who wanted to know God more, who prayed and read and thought about God.

Above all, I stayed because I didn't hear God saying I should leave. When my bones were wracked with frustration, I'd sit in the chapel and shake my fists and silently yell at Jesus on the cross. "What are you thinking? What am I doing here? If you want me to do something else, show me." Then I'd listen.

My little voice was silent. It usually speaks up when there's a problem, and apparently, my frustration didn't rise to that level. Whenever I tried to think about an alternative life, nothing came.

I asked to become a novice, and they accepted me. I resigned my position at UNM, knowing there was no re-entry to another tenured position. That door was closed. I would have to wait for God to open another door, if She chose. Until then, I would stay where I was.

I'll confess, God. As I've grown older, without the funds that I would have had if I had stayed, I've sometimes wondered what my life would have been like had I remained at the university. But a few minutes of reflection tells me: I'd be financially secure, but to no purpose. I can't imagine how I could have stayed. I know you can breathe new life anywhere, but really. Thank you for calling me beyond security to the fullness I now know.

Chapter Twelve

Opening to Love

"Oh, Sister, I'm so sorry!"

The clerk in the toll booth was distraught. Just as I drove up to her booth, the power on the skyway had gone out. All the lights were down, the toll booths weren't functioning. The clerk said the first thing that came into her mind: "Shit!" Then she saw me looking at her from my window.

Well, actually, I don't think she saw me; she saw a nun in a black habit with a white veil.

When the lights had gone out, she cussed like anyone would. And then she saw me, and her reaction was spontaneous. "Oh, Sister, I'm so sorry!"

I said, "That's alright," paid the toll, and drove through.

Next to me, my brother Dave was laughing his head off. "Oh my God, I can't believe it!" he chortled. He practically slid onto the floor of the car.

"That was amazing," I replied.

"You! 'Oh, Sister!' That was worth the whole trip."

I was driving Dave back to our cousin's apartment near Jersey City after he had attended my novice clothing earlier that day. This was day one of my life in a habit.

Dave repeated in a sing-song voice, "Oh, Sister, I'm so sorry!" We both cracked up.

In another, hidden part of me, though, I loved hearing that clerk's response. After I dropped Dave off, I had a long drive home to savor what had happened that day. I might laugh with Dave at other people's responses, at the unlikeliness of me being a nun. It did seem as bizarre to me as it might have to others. Still, I knew I wanted all this. I wanted to be clothed in a way that joined me to others. I wanted to declare my intention to live a life devoted to God. I didn't know how to talk about those things to people outside the convent, but my clothes seemed to say it for me, and to me. My discomfort with being separated out was mingled with the desire for precisely that, for a statement of my devotion to God in Christ.

I had been with the community for six months. Julia and I had both asked to go forward to the next stage, to become novices. We would be "clothed" on the same day, June 30, 2001. On that day, we would wear habits for the first time. I would shift from a lightweight shirt and skirt to three layers of dress and a cap and veil. I would look like "a nun."

The retreat days leading up to the clothing didn't go quite as planned. I came down with Lyme disease. My only symptom was a migraine, my first and only. After I began vomiting, the Sisters took me to the doctor and got me on antibiotics. I felt better with each dose but still a bit unsteady as the day approached.

On the day of our clothing, the temperature was 90 degrees by 10 a.m. After breakfast, Julia and I went to our rooms to dress. We put on the layers and the cap. I began to feel the heat.

The heat wasn't all I felt, though. At 6 feet tall and 210 pounds, I did not feel especially elegant in these clothes. The dress and scapular might flow, and they helped to hide tummies, but still—I was big. I also felt silly in the cap without the veil, like a super-sized little Dutch girl, or a big black whale, wearing a silly little white cap.

And, again, I felt *hot.*

Just before 10:30, the Superior knocked. "It's time." She saw us and said, "You look beautiful." We looked at each other and tried not to laugh. Then she led us from our rooms to the main chapel.

The chapel was packed. All the friends and associates of the community had been invited, and many had come.

When the music began, the Sisters walked in two by two in order of seniority. We came at the end, with the Superior accompanying us. As we walked up the long center aisle, with smiling faces turned to watch us, I felt the gravity of the moment. Beneath my illness and my awkwardness was the powerful lure of a life lived with God, in God. Every step brought me closer to—something.

We all stood in our places in the choir and joined in the singing. The Presiding Minister of the community led the service.

Flowers, red and white, graced the altar and the sides of the chapel. The enormous candelabras were gleaming with reflected light. The music of the organ, the incense, all created an atmosphere of reverent celebration.

I saw and heard and felt the beauty, but I couldn't really take it in. For one thing, it was approaching 100 degrees in the chapel. I sweated pools of water into my new habit. I could barely breathe; I thought I might faint.

It helped to look at the priest. He had on his street clothes, and over them all the vestments for a big service. They were gorgeous, and they must have weighed five pounds. I gazed at him and thought, "If he can do it, I can do it."

And then, a second later, it hit me: when the service was over, he would get to take those extra layers off! I would still be wearing three layers and a veil.

I kept breathing.

The heat was distracting, but it wasn't the main event. I was crossing a line into a territory I knew so little about, really. I had turned in my resignation at the university. I knew what I had left behind, but I had no idea of my future. What was I promising? What was I hoping? Was I up to it? This service, elaborate and beautiful as it was, could not begin to express the immensity of the change this entailed.

When the time came, the Presiding Minister stood. The Superior and the novice director led us to stand before him. He asked us the questions:

"Beloved in the Lord, what do you desire?"

We each replied:

"I desire to devote my life to God, and admission to the Religious Life in this Community."

"Do you believe that you are called by God to this estate, and not moved by self-will or whim?"

"I do so believe."

"Do you promise to observe faithfully the Rule and Constitutions of the Community during the time of probation?"

"By God's help I will do so."

"Is it your desire that you be found worthy to persevere to the end of this calling?"

"I do so desire."

We knelt on the step before him while he said a prayer. Then he turned to the altar and blessed the veils and the crosses we would wear. The Superior and the novice director helped us put them on. With the veil on, I felt better; my silly little Dutch girl cap was now anchoring a flowing white sheet, draping gracefully down my back. The cross was much bigger than what I had been wearing, but it was light and simple. I felt more complete somehow.

The clothes and the cross felt like they might come to fit, but something else didn't fit so well. For the first time, I heard my new name: "Sister Shane Margaret."

Each novice was encouraged to retain her baptismal name, but to add the name of a saint as well. Shane was not my baptismal name, but it was my confirmation name; that was not going to change. But now, Shane was not enough; I needed a saint attached.

The second name was chosen by the Superior, out of three choices offered by the postulant. My first choice was Augustine; I still felt a kinship with that passionate lover of God. The community had had a Sister Augustine, long ago, so I thought that might work. But no.

My second choice was Madeleine, in honor of Mary Magdalene. Luke's Gospel says she was "healed of seven demons." Whatever those demons were, I could relate: in my recovery from alcoholism and now in my growth through encountering Jesus, I felt myself healed of a lot. I had learned that her feast day is July 22, which happened to be the day I walked into the rooms of recovery.

I also related to Mary's wild devotion to Jesus. She was the first to go to Jesus' tomb and meet the risen Christ. She ran and told the other disciples. She's known in the Eastern churches (Eastern Orthodox, not East Coast) as "the apostle to the apostles" (Greek *apostolo*) because she was sent to tell the good news. She was a symbol of women's authority, authority that has been overlooked and erased but keeps rising again.

But no. "Shane Madeleine" did not appeal to the Superior.

My distant third choice was Margaret. I needed a third name. Margaret was an important name in the history of the community, so I thought I could continue the line.

The Superior chose Margaret. It didn't occur to me to argue.

Now, as I heard the name pronounced, I felt somehow constrained. This was not a name I could see growing into. I had fought, years ago, to claim my real name. Now, Shane was being covered up, or gently smeared over, with a name given to me.

I told myself this was a part of obedience and humility.

I had entered the chapel as a 43-year-old Associate Professor of Political Science and Director of the Women Studies Program, author and editor, specializing in LGBT politics. I emerged an hour later as Sister Shane Margaret, novice.

Something had shifted, something bigger than a change of clothes. I didn't have words, but I knew it inside. I returned to my seat, now with a beautiful booklet of the service made for me by the novice director. As the Sisters sang "the Te Deum", I sat in shock. What had happened?

Later, I got hugs and smiles from the Sisters and congratulations from the guests. I laughed with my brother, I ate some lunch. I longed for air conditioning. I drove my brother back to my cousin's house and finally returned to my cell. Later, I would have chances to digest. For now, it was enough to peel off my new layers and let in an evening breeze.

Two weeks after the clothing ceremony, I left the convent.

Not for good. I had to return to New Mexico and close out my life there. As a professor on leave, I still had two offices full of books and papers. I had a three-bedroom house, fully furnished, with more books. I had a lot to let go of.

Returning was another disorientation. So much had happened, I had undergone such change in the year since leaving. My friends respected my choice, but they couldn't understand it. Even my friends in recovery, even the few who went to church, couldn't relate to my hunger and my choice.

I finalized the sale of my house, packed the things I planned to take back to the convent, petted Max goodbye for real this time, and left.

After four days of driving across the country with one of the Sisters, I returned to the convent. I went to my cell and emerged in habit once again. I looked at myself, from my black cross-trainers, to my long black dress, the scapular over it and the black wooden cross at my chest, and finally to the long white veil over my short hair. I wasn't used to this look yet, especially the white veil. I looked sallow in white, and more noticeably fat than in my jeans. "Oh well," I thought; "Vanity, get behind me!" My mind filled with the romance of renunciation.

I headed toward the chapel for Vespers and sank into my stall. The sun shone on my back, and through the open window, I could hear the birds singing in the woods. Across from me, Sisters were drifting in and taking their places. My prayer book and notebook welcomed me, calling me to pray.

I could feel myself sigh as I sat. I felt my muscles relax in this upright box. This was my stall, where I belonged. It received me like a mother waiting for her child to return.

I had been here for six months. I had been clothed, prayed here, argued and fought with people. It was at this moment, though, this stall receiving me, that showed me I had indeed begun to become a nun. I was at home, in this simple space, with these women. This was where I belonged.

Now, the time came to dig into my new status and the changes it entailed. As a novice, my primary job area shifted from the pantry to the chapel. Julia and I became "chapel novices," assigned to work under the direction of the chapel Sister. I joined the team that made the services happen for others.

I loved everything about working in the chapel. I loved the beauty, the order. Over the years, I would become the chapel Sister, in charge of "the team," standing on my feet for long hours to prepare for holy days and weeks. But for now, as a novice, it was enough to learn to notice whether everything was in place.

My other new job was self-appointed. I had more time than I needed for study and work, and my energy needed an outlet. I explored the library, and as I did so, I raised clouds of dust. I learned that the books had not been dusted since the last librarian had died 25 years ago. There was no librarian per se. Sometimes Sisters bought books, and somehow they got shelved. I decided to dust the library.

The downstairs was dusty, but not too bad. Upstairs was another story.

Forget 25 years. Those books hadn't seen a dust rag since World War II.

I set to work. I found a long black apron, and I commandeered it for this project. We could remove our veils (not our caps) within the enclosure, so I would unsnap the veil and set it aside. Soon I realized I needed a dust mask, so I headed off to Lowe's. My hands were drying out from the dust. In the summer heat, on the upper floor where the hot air rose up, I sweated my way through hours of dusting.

Soon I had a project emerging. I began to read up on basic archival methods, and I got permission to order some supplies: gloves, special pencils, some covers to protect the most vulnerable and valuable books. I had always loved clearing out and organizing spaces. I aimed to make room for something new, some breath of fresh air to run through the library and the community.

I kept dusting. I dusted each day for five months. Along the way, the books I found taught me the history of Anglo-Catholicism in England and the United States. It was a fascinating story, and I felt myself swimming within this small but fervent sea. I learned the names, the dates, the issues. The Anglo-Catholic movement brought back candles and incense and fancy vestments, all the "smells and bells" repudiated by the more Protestant Anglican tradition. Religious communities were seen as "Popish," and the backlash was strong. Lurid stories of kidnapped daughters and avaricious abbesses led to riots. Our community had been one of the first to be founded in this new wave, and I gained respect for their courage.

When dusting was done, I turned to other frontiers. I poked into cupboards set in the walls, and I found piles of old photos and notebooks. Each week, I brought photos to our community history class. Sister Helen remembered every face from the last 70 years, and she knew some by photos she had seen when she was younger. Every photo prompted a story about the Sisters in it.

In Sister Helen's stories, I learned the difference between a contemplative order and a community that simply no longer had the ministries that had given it birth. Ours was not founded as a monastic community, but as an active one—praying, yes, but focused on ministry. Now, the community had the DNA of those who served, but the shape of the ministry had changed beyond recognition. Who were they now? Who were we now? Who was I in this?

Unlike those earlier Sisters, I had no thoughts of ministry. I had come to pray. I had come to a place that seemed centered on prayer, but I began to sense that another fire burned in the ashes—in the community, and in me.

Two and a half months after my clothing, on September 11, 2001, five of us took a walk between breakfast and Terce. Tuesday was our regular "community day," when we met in the morning for conversations around various topics, and then, in the afternoon, those on councils or boards had their meetings. But that wasn't how this day went.

As we walked the long driveway, Sister Miriam returned from dropping Sister Elaine at the airport. She pulled up and told us, "A plane just crashed into the Twin Towers." Her eyes were wide, and she seemed to be panting. "It's a terrorist attack," she added.

Inwardly, I rolled my eyes: It was just like her to get excited and see plots and malice. Why did she have to get so dramatic? It might have been a tragic accident. Either way, though, the situation was horrible.

We all went back to the convent and turned on the TV. There, we watched in shock and disbelief as the second plane plowed into the second tower. Miriam had been right.

We began to pray, to cry, to watch the scene on television over and over. We went to village prayer services, lamenting for those we knew and those we didn't.

The feeling of helpless grief was everywhere. No one could sleep. In the convent, we prayed for the dead, for those still trapped in the rubble, for the workers.

I tried to sleep and go on as though things were normal. We continued our daily round of prayers and worship, five times a day in the chapel. We ate our meals and did our work. It helped to ground me, but it wasn't enough to shut out the horror.

As the work began to find survivors and remove the dead with dignity, it seemed that everyone, everywhere wanted to help. People drove across the country to bring supplies for the workers and to pray nearby. Religious leaders of all faiths enlisted. I saw God at work in all the love. I wanted to be part of it. I wanted to help, but I couldn't see how. I had no training, no experience. I was a new nun, barely used to my clothes.

One day, a priest, a friend of the community, came to see us. He'd been working at Ground Zero with the Red Cross. They had organized a program of chaplaincy for the respite centers. Several large hotels right by the site had become centers for the workers to eat and rest between shifts. He told us stories about the horrible, powerful work going on there.

"They're looking for more chaplains," he said. Chaplains with certification were given a brief training on this crisis and sent to those who wanted to talk and pray.

I had no training as a chaplain, no experience. But I wanted to serve.

I went to the Superior.

"You're just a novice," she told me. "You have no training. Besides, we don't send Sisters out alone."

"Sister Frances wants to go too. I can go with her," I said. "She hasn't been trained either. They'll train us there."

She looked at me. She had a powerful pull toward service herself. I had no doubt she would have volunteered if she weren't Superior.

"Okay," she said. "Go see if this is something you should do."

That was it.

Seeing a nun in habit, the Red Cross trainer assumed I had prior training. Off I went with Frances for our one-day course. At the end of the day, I was assigned to one of the respite centers once a week. I received a hard hat in case I needed to go into "the pit." We had our pictures taken with our veils and hard hats.

The next week, I took the train into the city toward Ground Zero. As we rumbled across the Meadowlands of New Jersey, the absence of the Twin Towers was disorienting. Then, the train dove under the Hudson River and moved into Penn Station. I caught the subway south as far as it could go. It wasn't as far as it had been before the attack; the subway had been destroyed at the stop I would have taken.

When I came up from the subway, the smell was everywhere. Long before I saw the destruction, I smelled it. It was partly smoke, partly dust, but there was something else: the smell of burning, rotting flesh. Deep below ground, the fires still raged, and bodies were being consumed. Everyone knew what it was, though we didn't talk about it. I didn't even admit it to myself, though I knew.

Everywhere, people looked stunned, their faces shuttered against the grief. I looked at them as I passed. Some looked at me. Seeing my habit, they would try to smile. I'd smile back, my eyes sending a different message: I hurt with you. I love you. Then I'd keep going on my way.

I passed St. Paul's Chapel, which was being used as another respite center. On the wrought-iron fence, people wrote on sheets volunteers had hung out for them. Below on the sidewalk were piles of flowers and photos of loved ones either missing or known dead. Teddy bears and candles bore testimony and kept vigil. All around the fence, people stood reading flyers, hoping to see a familiar face. It was October by now, and no one really expected to find lost ones. They stood in longing and grief, hanging on to those smiling faces on the flyers.

My heart opened. I felt the grief I had stopped-up in the past weeks. Rather than locking me in, as it had in the past, pain now opened me to the love that defined this place.

Finally, I arrived at the Downtown Marriott, right by Ground Zero. Three thousand people died across the street, and the hotel windows were still intact? It felt unreal.

Entering was a relief of sorts, a mirage of normalcy. The air conditioning system reduced the smell, even with the gathering workers. But as I went up the escalator, the veneer of normal gave way to dislocation. The hotel ballroom was set up as a rest area, with rows of recliners facing TV screens. In the hallway outside the ballroom, a kitchen crew dispensed breakfast. On other floors, stocks of supplies waited for the men: soap, cloths, shoes to replace those whose soles burned through working on the still-hot site.

The first thing I noticed was the trauma and exhaustion that hung in the air. The love at St. Paul's seemed absent; in its place was numbness, people slogging through a hellish job. The sheer masculinity of the place hit me. The only women were hotel staff and chaplains. The men were not conventioneers in suits or tourists in comfortable clothes; they were men who went down to hell with shovels and picks and drills.

I went into the chaplains' area and read the briefing book of any incidents. Then I headed out to—what? Be with people? How do I do that? I could smile at people, I could make small talk if anyone cared (few did), but I had no clue how to open a conversation about what these men were experiencing. I felt unsure. If it were me, would I rather talk or sit in front of a TV? I'd probably go for the TV.

I joined the breakfast line. The hotel chef was serving in the hall, standing behind mountains of eggs, sausage, potatoes, and fruit. The chef was short and broad with brown hair trimmed neatly. Like me, he was of the place but not in the direct line of fire.

Make conversation! Reach out somehow. I did my best with him.

"Your scrambled eggs are so creamy. I love them! How do you do that?"

"Here's the secret," he told me; "you cook them over very low heat and keep stirring all the time."

Okay, we've begun. Then I ventured, "How are you?"

"I'm hanging in there, thanks." Then he turned to the next person.

After a solitary breakfast, I wandered the halls, making eye contact but rarely speaking beyond smiling and saying "hello." What do you say to someone who has spent the day, or the night, or both, digging body parts out of rubble?

In the absence of conversation, I smiled. I smiled at men who likely hadn't seen a smile for a while. I said hello, and occasionally I got a response. It didn't feel like much. I felt certain the trained chaplains were having deep conversations; I could see signs of it in the log. Everyone else knew something I didn't. I felt awkward, but I needed to be there. All I had was a habit and a hard hat and a heart that needed to connect.

At the end of the day, I returned to the convent. Back to quiet time in the chapel, sitting after dinner, and making conversation. Sisters asked, "How did it go?" I didn't know what to say. Overwhelming? Awkwardly wonderful? Surreal? "Okay," I answered.

After a few weeks at the Marriott, I moved to St. Paul's Chapel. The respite work was the same, but instead of recliners in a ballroom, the men used the pews of the chapel to rest. There were live concerts at noon and hot food I helped serve.

My real work at St. Paul's turned out to be with the visitors outside. I stood by the sheet-draped fence, holding colored felt pens.

I watched for people who seemed trapped in a feeling. Then, I'd approach. "Would you like to write something?" Most did.

The writing began a conversation. I'd ask, "Did you lose someone?" Whether they had lost a specific person or not, this opened the floodgates. These people were not exhausted by the physical work of Ground Zero, but by the emotional labor of waiting and watching and wondering if their loved ones would be found. Some didn't have a particular person they were waiting for, but they felt the pain of the whole thing. They were drawn there to be with others who grieved. The sorrow was a magnet, calling us to be there. My job was simply to listen, to help lance the emotional abscess.

I served at St. Paul's until winter hit. They had more than enough volunteers, and my community wanted me home. I turned in my hard hat and took the train back home a final time, toward our daily routine of prayer and meals and work. I had been a tiny part of a defining moment in my country's history. I felt an opening toward service that hadn't been there before, that would blossom in the following year. I knew my life was never going to be the same.

"Okay, send me to the rehab."

By the spring of 2002, I had been at the convent for 14 months, and I had become restless. The initial bloom of learning and exploring was over, and now I faced long days without enough to occupy my restless mind and body. There was only so much dusting to be done.

But restlessness alone didn't drive me to make this request. I had spent the past year praying in the chapel, sitting with Jesus alone twice a day. Over the days, I had felt myself filling up with love and gratitude. I had seen that the love I received was not for me to hoard, but for me to share, to be part of a larger river of healing. My time at Ground Zero had opened me to the joy of seeking to serve and to love in ways I didn't know.

Sister Phyllis had encouraged me to go to the rehab when I visited as an aspirant. I had turned her down, saying I don't like teenagers. Now, though, I began to see some possibility.

As a novice, there were not many places I would be allowed to go on my own to minister (Ground Zero was a huge, unprecedented exception). But I could go to the rehab. This facility for teenagers was located in the old convent school building, just down our drive.

And I fit. I had been a teenage alcoholic and addict. I had been to some of the places these kids had been: sleeping outside, juvenile detention, locked wards. Now 16 years sober, I had something to share and a need to be with others who knew that experience.

The Superior looked at me. "I thought you didn't want to go there."

"I changed my mind."

"What would you do there?"

"I don't know. I could always lead a 12-step meeting."

"Okay. I'll call them and see what they say."

They said to come visit.

The next day, I met the director and senior staff. I learned that it had been founded by a Catholic priest, though it was not affiliated with the Catholic Church. They served both females and males, unlike many places that were male-only. They were what is called a "therapeutic community," a distinct sort of animal in the recovery world. Along with personal and group therapy, therapeutic communities incorporate community meetings, work, and hierarchy to teach responsibility and belonging. Each day began with a community meeting, mostly led by the residents, including a thought for the day, announcements, and "pull-ups," where members called the community to attention. For example, someone might notice that people are coming to meetings late; they urge everyone to come on time to focus on their recovery. The community offers a structure to learn some qualities that are lacking in the lives of most addicts.

Because of this ethos, volunteers were not routinely welcomed. Those who worked there had to undergo days of intensive training in their principles and practices and to revisit those periodically. So, even though I would only be leading one meeting a week, I went through the training. I learned about why they did what they did, about mistakes not to make, and how to handle problems as they arose. I was daunted by how much there was to learn, but also excited and curious.

The first week I went to lead a meeting, all 60 residents were gathered in the gym in chairs lined up in rows. I asked that we form a circle; now we took up the whole space, with lots of open space in the middle. The kids were restless, as always; they didn't want to be sitting in a chair, or to be at anything required. Many of them were looking at me, in my habit and veil, but no one said hello.

I sat in the circle until it was time to start. Then I stood. I opened it like a regular meeting. I introduced myself, and told them my story—my "qualification" for membership. I could see eyebrows go up and heads tilt toward me. This was not what they expected to hear from a nun. After I shared, I opened it for their shares. Not many had much to say that night, but when we announced that next week's meeting would be voluntary and people could sign up, about 15 of them did. There were some there who wanted something.

After a few months, as I started to get to know some of the residents, I asked them about their lives and what they needed. They told me, and a seed formed. I could lead a group for those who were spiritually hungry. Because the rehab received federal funding, their programs were all non-religious, but that was no problem. Between my own history with a generic higher power, I knew I could do that.

I went to Jim, the clinical director, to ask if I could do a spirituality group.

He leaned back in his chair. "What would you do?" he asked.

I outlined a simple program of meditation and conversation, fostering gratitude and hope.

"Well, the residents like you. When would you do it?"

"Friday afternoon. Then I could stay for dinner and talk with whoever wants to talk, before the meeting."

He barely paused before he sat up and leaned forward. "Okay, let's do it."

Each week we had a signup sheet to keep the group size manageable. We met in a cozy room at the north end of the dorms, the quietest place in the house, filled with ratty old sofas and chairs. I got to know the residents (never "kids"), and they got to know me.

I had a new identity. At the convent, my name was Sister Shane Margaret, but that was too big a mouthful for a place like that. From my second week there, one of the kids called me "Sister Shane," and that felt really right. At those meetings, I became "Sister Shane," a more relaxed, more complete being.

Each Friday, I left the convent, walked up the long driveway through the woods, and emerged into the large open playing field. Sometimes some of the residents would be outside, playing softball or football, and I would pause to watch and say hi. Sometimes I'd meet one of them running an errand, and we'd chat for a minute. At other times, I'd arrive and find someone sitting on the bench outside, waiting to talk to me. I had become the unofficial chaplain of the place, the one adult who was not entirely within the umbrella, the one who wouldn't immediately put them into a therapeutic box. I was like a visiting aunt, related but not the parental, disciplinary figure.

In that space, something grew in me. "Sister Shane!" someone would call as I approached. And they would rush to tell me something good and something new. I felt loved, and I felt my love for them. "Hi hon," I'd say; words I never would have spoken before. To me, these young people were sweet and vulnerable and bruised and battered, and still full of life.

The upside was the warmth of enjoying them and being in that circuit of love. The downside was the pain of loving addicts. Although many residents completed the program and seemed ready to stand on their own, too many returned to the same situations they had left: Parents who were alcoholics or addicts themselves, dangerous neighborhoods, friends "from before," all worked to send them back to old patterns.

Some of them returned and tried again. Some of them never got the chance.

One night I came in. I'd had another meeting that afternoon, so I had missed the spirituality group and dinner. It was a rainy night in November, and I had driven up the driveway instead of walking. I entered through the main door and approached the desk.

Jim came out of his office. "Hey, Sister Shane," he called, "Can you come in here for a minute?"

I came in and closed the door. "What's up?" I asked.

Jim said, "We won't be having the meeting tonight. We're having a house meeting at 7."

"You need to know. Colleen and Sertac both died of overdoses this week."

Oh my God. Colleen, blonde, beautiful, 16. She had been looking shaky, but she had been trying.

Sertac, 17, as dark as Colleen was light. He had looked strong and sure when he graduated just last week.

Two glorious young people, each with gifts to share, who could not stand against the demon. I had spent enough time with them to know how much they wanted a decent life, and to glimpse how far they had to go. And now they were dead.

I stood in the back for the house meeting while Jim and Willie told the residents. I hugged some of them, holding them while they cried.

Then I went to the car I had checked out for the evening. I sat in the parking lot and watched the rain pour down the windshield. And I sobbed. I cried for these beautiful lives lost, and all the others I'd known. I scrambled for a pack of Kleenex that someone had left in the car.

As the tears flowed, I realized something new. I had no desire to stop coming, or to shield myself from this pain. I loved these children. I didn't just enjoy them or feel good about myself doing the work. I loved them. The love I had found in the chapel, the love of God poured out on the world, had entered me and opened me. I became part of the flow of God's love.

It's not that I hadn't loved before or cried over someone. I think, though, that I had never consciously chosen to put myself in the path of suffering. I had loved Karen, I had loved Blake, I had loved my family, but my love was shot through with wanting something from them—that particular neediness that our culture calls "love." I had not chosen to stand in the hurricane of another's pain.

Here, I saw, was part of what my "vision" at the New York convent meant—to hang there with Jesus, powerless to change the situation but willing to suffer with another. The love that was growing in me was cracking hard soil and planting seeds, watering them with tears. Jesus' costly love was gradually taking root in me.

Chapter Thirteen

A Nun—And a Priest?

"Beloved in Christ, what do you desire?"

"I desire to know and serve God with all my being."

After two years of novitiate, I wanted to make my initial vows. I was still on fire for the promise of living the life fully, of dedicating myself to God. The next step was taking vows, but for a period of one year at a time, testing if I could really live them before making life profession.

The road to making my first vows had not been easy. While my ministry was beginning to take shape, and was bringing me joy (and pain), life in the convent was still hard. I huffed and I puffed as the changes I hoped for did not emerge. I lobbied to end wearing the veil, but no one was convinced by my arguments about women's subordination. I wanted to move toward gender-neutral language in worship, but the majority felt that keeping the traditional words would be more welcoming to visitors—and more comfortable for them. I seethed.

So, things weren't idyllic in the community—where are they? It was a truism in religious life that the hard part was living with others. I had come to engage that challenge, to learn more about loving. My recovery program told me that I didn't have to be controlled by my environment, that I could choose my attitude. So, I kept working on letting go of judgments, releasing the frustration and tension I felt. I wanted to stay. I felt ready, and the community agreed.

I had an eight-day retreat to prepare, with questions and Scripture passages to reflect on. What did I desire? To give my life to God. To know God, to see God, to feel God pulsing through me and the universe. Then, meditations on the vows: how did Jesus model obedience? Poverty? Chastity? What is God calling me to be and do? I reflected while walking in the woods, sitting in the chapel, in my room. I reread our Rule and some community history. I heard the Sisters pray for me each day. I felt enfolded in the community's love.

The day came: June 28, 2003, the feast of St. Irenaeus. Irenaeus was a pillar of orthodoxy, not someone I'd want to be taught by, but he is known now mostly for his great declaration: "The glory of God is the human being fully alive." That's exactly how I felt: I was coming alive, bit by bit, through my life in this place.

All that summer and fall, the aliveness grew. In a strange paradox, I felt more empowered, more outgoing, more joyful in my habit and black veil. I had lost 50 pounds, and I had begun to run again. I felt comfortable, even attractive, in my body. I felt beautiful, in mind and spirit as well as body. I could see from others' looks that they saw it too.

The vow, and the habit, did not build a wall. The habit provided an enclosure, analogous to the enclosure of the convent, within which I could choose my level of relationship. Within the contours of this garment, my body could move freely; I could sit on the floor with modesty, I could dance, I could hike.

Within my black cocoon, I was growing. My erotic energy, energy that had only known sexual expressions, was beginning to flow into easy soul intimacy with others. I had never known how to draw boundaries without pushing people away; now I could give myself more freely.

As the days and months went on, I realized that I was indeed being "formed" in a new way of life. I had decades of rock and roll lyrics in my head. Now they were sharing space with psalms and hymns and Scripture. I found myself singing the "Benedictus" or the "Magnificat," or some office hymn. I knew whole psalms by heart and phrases from the Bible. My inner landscape was becoming more aware of God's love and power, not so much by conscious choice as by immersion in the language of prayer. Whenever I said the opening of Psalm 63—"O God, you are my God; eagerly I seek you"—I felt my breath slow and my heart open. I didn't become more "holy," whatever that means, but I began to have a different inner vocabulary. Vocabularies make worlds; and so, gradually, I had begun to enter a new world.

By that fall, it was clear that Sister Helen was dying. She no longer left her bed. Through the month of October, the parade moved down the hall to the cell on the end: priests she had mentored over the years, some of them now bishops, came to see her, to thank her, to bless her, and to receive her blessing. I didn't get to see her much anymore. That hurt, but I knew it wasn't a rejection; it was just an ache, as I watched my mentor let go of the attachments of a lifetime. She needed to let go, and I needed to let go of her. Still, I feared: what would I do without her? I, like those many visitors, had no one else like her to turn to.

Finally, on the morning of October 30, 2003, Sister Helen went gently, pulled on the tide of old age, without great pain. She was simply used up, her work and life complete. Sister Laura rang the big chapel bell 33 times, slowly, to signal the death. We gathered in the chapel for prayers and then dispersed to our various tasks and griefs.

I lay on my bed and cried. "Oh, God, Sister, I can't do this without you." My spiritual grandmother had died, the one who had raised me thus far in religious life. I felt orphaned, more profoundly than when my parents died. I ached over the next weeks and months.

"You should be a priest!"

Rick, one of our regular visiting priests, told me that after a service one day in 2003. We had become friends over the time he had been coming each Wednesday morning. After Mass, I cleaned the sacred vessels and laid the vestments for the next day. It gave us time to chat a little.

Morning light streamed through the windows, bathing the tiled floor and the white walls.

"I don't want to be a priest."

"Well, you'd be great."

"Thanks."

End of that.

It's not that I wanted not to be a priest; I just didn't want it. Not enough to go back to school. I had spent forty years in school one way or another; I did not want to return. I could take vacation in October, when the eastern skies are a brilliant azure blue and the days are warm enough to go to the beach. I could read what I wanted, when I wanted. I could serve in the ways I did already without going through that.

I knew the community could use another priest. Another Sister was in "the process," but you never knew who would actually get ordained.

Maybe we could use another priest, but that wasn't enough to get me to enter a multi-year process. That wasn't a call; that was strategic thinking.

I didn't know it when I entered, but my sedate little convent was located in one of the most progressive dioceses of the Episcopal Church. The church in the next town, moreover, was the most experimental church in the diocese. They called themselves "A Christian Liberation Community in the Episcopal Tradition." There were people of varying shapes and sizes and colors, dressed in everything from suits to shorts, coupled in various ways. The first transgendered member had just joined, early in her transition, with her wife and son.

I had gradually become involved in the congregation. I attended Sunday worship occasionally, and I had been welcomed like everyone was. Then, in 2003, I spoke at their Recovery Sunday service. I told my story, and Phillip, the rector, realized I was not just a prim and proper nun. I began leading some parish retreat days, and I joined the healing prayer group. I sold shirts and bags from Cameroon to raise money for an orphanage the community was supporting, and I got to let out my inner clown.

I loved this community. I loved Phillip, and Larry, a former Methodist minister who'd been thrown out for being gay, who now served as a lay pastoral assistant. I loved Dennie. She had come as a seminarian and stayed through her ordination as a deacon and then a priest.

Now, in the spring of 2004, it was time for Dennie to go elsewhere and grow her own ministry. Throughout the church there was a tone of sadness.

One day, Dennie and Phillip came to the convent and spent the morning in private conversation, talking about her plans and considering the future.

That afternoon, Phillip called me into the room where they'd been talking.

"Dennie and Larry and I have talked, and we think you would be a great addition to our staff. We'd like you to become a lay pastoral assistant."

"Me?" Something rustled in my soul.

"You have a presence and an ease that calms everyone. You're a great listener. You bring a deeper spirituality to us. You connect with people, and you can speak."

(Really? Me?)

He outlined a plan. On Sundays, I would share leading worship. I would convene a women's group, and I'd offer parish retreats and group series with Phillip.

Hmmm. It was true, I loved to lead retreats and to teach informally. I hadn't preached yet, other than my Recovery Sunday talk, but I had spoken a lot. I felt I could do this. And, I loved these people. I wanted to be there.

The next week, I went to the church to meet with the team there. After the staff meeting, Phillip and I got comfortable in his office. I sat on the sofa on one side of the old fireplace, and he sat in one of the wingback chairs on the other side. Just chatting, getting to know one another. Then he threw in:

"You know, you'd be a great priest."

There it was again.

"I don't need to be a priest. I've got a great ministry now, without going through all that."

"Yes," he said, "but you have more inside you. And being at the altar, feeding the people, that's special. You should be a priest."

"Thanks," I said. Flattered, my ego played with this a bit. People saw me as a priest! But still—I didn't want to go through all that. Just to say some words at the altar?

My heart was set on being a spiritual director. The community had said I couldn't receive training until after I made final vows, but I had pushed, and I had been approved to go to a program the following winter. And I did have a great ministry, at the rehab and now, I hoped, at this church. Go back to school for years? Just to say some words with the authority of the Church?

The whole thing was a stew in my mind. For the next two months I played with it, mostly warding it off. I didn't want to go through all that, but I couldn't just drop it either.

That summer, I went on a silent five-day retreat, part of my preparation for direction training.

As soon as I arrived, I headed to the main chapel.

Unlike the rest of the house, with its ambiance of quiet, shadowed old-fashioned elegance, the main chapel was all sharp surfaces: marble floors without rugs, a marble altar, heavy wooden pews bolted to the floor, patterned windows that let in light without allowing you to see outside. I sat in one of the pews, alone in this large and cold place.

I felt excited to begin the retreat that would prepare me, or at least qualify me, to begin training in spiritual direction, but right then, what I noticed most was the cold. The chapel must have been air-conditioned, as well as shut off from the weather outside; it went beyond refreshing.

I knelt and closed my eyes.

As I knelt, I heard my little voice. The voice that had saved me time and time again, moving me toward fullness of life.

"You should be a priest."

Oh, my God, no.

I started to sob. Please, no.

I remembered saying to Byron, "It's too much like my old job." I remembered standing with Rick in the sacristy and just saying no. I remembered telling Phillip that I didn't need ordination in order to have meaningful ministry. I had put my foot down. I would not go back to school or grind through an exhausting and dispiriting ordination process, just to stand at an altar and say some words. For years, I'd said no: No, I do not want this. I do not need this. I am not called to this. I am on retreat to prepare to be a spiritual director.

But there was the voice.

I couldn't pretend that I didn't hear that voice. I didn't have a theology around it, but I knew it when I heard it.

"You should be a priest."

I cried for several minutes, a lifetime. I cried a river of fear, a burst dam of desire that I did not know was there.

All my defenses crumbled. I kept looking at the crucifix. Really? Is this you, God? Oh shit. Somehow, this new whisper terrified me in a way that the call to religious life had not.

No more words came. The statement just sat there. I kept crying, grateful no one else was in the chapel.

"I don't want to go through all that!"

No answer, no argument. Just the one sentence.

Finally, I said, "Okay."

I'll look at this.

I won't run anymore.

Go ahead, ruin my life.

I stopped crying. I sat in some kind of shock. I had done my best to ignore this prompt from other people. I had toyed with it and then pushed it aside when it appeared in my mind. But this was different. The voice cut through my rationalizations and my denials. It just said what it said. I didn't just jump on board, but I had a new place to stand. I would look.

On the next morning, I met with my retreat director. I wasn't sure what a Roman Catholic male priest would make of this, but I needed to tell him. My retreat was now about exploring and discerning this call, not making any decisions, but letting God speak to me without my usual obstructions.

Over the week I spent most of the days, and part of some nights, on a cushion on the floor of a tiny chapel, a chapel named "Christ the Priest" (God's sense of humor at work), trying to assimilate this new possibility. My director gave me readings and prayers to guide me in discernment.

I returned home after five days, still overwhelmed. I sat with a friend of the community on a bench by the convent garage and told him what had happened. It was still so raw I could hardly say the words at all, and I couldn't say them without crying.

Ron said, "Of course you have this in you. It's clear. You have to look at this."

I told a friend who was visiting the convent that I had this idea. Trying to dismiss it, I said, "I'm too old to start this long process." She looked at me with the wisdom of 70 years and replied, "You are if you think you are."

Oh. What did I think I should be doing at this age? Did I see this life as retirement, somehow? Did I think my life was complete?

I kept practicing talking about it. I couldn't say a lot yet, but gradually I got used to the idea enough to say it without crying.

I kept listening, to the voices inside and outside. Most people were cautious, knowing that there's a long road between an initial sense of vocation and its manifestation.

Two months later, I began to serve at the church. I learned a new pattern for Sunday mornings: into the convent chapel at 7:00 for Sunday Lauds and Eucharist, done at 8:30, into the car with a peanut butter and banana sandwich and coffee. Drive to church, wipe off the crumbs, and go get more coffee for me and Phillip before Adult Forum began at 9.

On this day, my first day, the main service began at 10:30. We processed in from the back of the church. Standing in the aisle, I led the opening call and response. I looked at the people in the pews, looking up at me, smiling, looking expectant.

Then, I went behind the altar and raised my arms to pray the opening prayer.

The energy of the universe shoots through that room, running across the altar and zooming through the big church like a beam of light bouncing from wall to wall to ceiling to floor, moving through bodies and spirits, lifting us all while our feet remained on the ground.

I know that energy. That's the current I felt in the orange grove behind our house in California when I was 16. I didn't know what it was then, I didn't know if it was safe, but I knew it was real. Now I know it's more than safe. It is life itself, humming and thrumming all around us all the time.

I want to tell the congregation: "The fact that you rose this morning and dressed and began to face the day, your day, is a miracle. Do not take this for granted. You have received a gift, the gift of being part of creation. You are a gift in turn, as you make the coffee and kiss your children and take care of what needs taking care of.

"I know your pain. I know your struggles, your frustrations. I know because I have them too. I love you, you who share this world. I give thanks for the gift of sharing this world with you."

I didn't say any of that out loud. I followed the service bulletin.

"The Lord be with you," I said.

"And also with you," they answered.

"Let us pray."

And we did.

Over the next months, I found that I loved my ministry there. This was leadership in a situation of partnership, and I flourished. I had things to study and people with whom to share what I learned in a context of worship. I felt new waves of energy and joy pouring into me, and through me to others.

At the church, as at the rehab, I found my message, the message God gave me to share with others.

You are a beloved child of God. I am too.

I got the message in a flash one Sunday morning during a sermon. I'd heard it before, but now I knew: this is what I am supposed to live into, and to help others live into.

We are beloved children. Period.

Here; I pass it to you. Pass it on.

Finally, in January of 2005, it was time for me to begin training in spiritual direction. I had pushed to be trained before final vows and had finally won this prize. I headed off for a two-week intensive. Yet, now that I had it, my energies were really focused on my current ministry, and my mind was on ordination. My ministry was leading elsewhere. I became less certain that I could, or should, or wanted to be directing people. Coyote rumbled, but didn't quite laugh out loud.

Paradoxically, my family life was changing in ways I hadn't anticipated. I had been prepared to loosen my ties with them as I entered the convent; instead, we were gradually growing closer. I was able to make amends for some of my past behavior, and my brother and sister affirmed that I had grown through my time in religious life. I became eager to be a part of my family.

I had entered the convent with romantic ideas about "leaving the world behind," but instead, I found a bigger world. I was blooming, and happier than I ever had been—when I wasn't sobbing over some half-articulated pain about convent life. I had my family and ministry and people I loved in both places. Submerging my uneasiness about my community relationships, I shrugged and kept moving.

Chapter Fourteen

Inside/Out

By the summer of 2006, as the time for life profession approached, I was torn. Yes, I was growing. Yes, I had many friends; I had grown closer to my family. My ministry was meaningful and satisfying.

But.

There was no romantic glow about life in community anymore. The convent culture of complaint and passive aggression wore on me, even as I participated in it. The slow pace of change frustrated me. The effort to not feel the feelings I had, my fear of other Sisters' anger, my own anger, exhausted me. I had a wider world now, and I enjoyed the people "out there" much more than those "inside."

At the same time, I had begun pursuit of the priesthood. I had entered Drew Theological School in the fall of 2005, and I was flourishing there. The students and faculty were the most diverse group I'd ever been with, flowing across nationalities, races, sexualities, denominations. These were people I could enjoy and learn from. The faculty were doing interesting work, work that drew on similar sources from my earlier life: postmodernist, feminist, queer, postcolonial. Writing papers, reading, thinking: It was like putting on a familiar garment and rediscovering how much I loved it.

If my academic garment fit comfortably, my habit was wearing thin. Not the physical habit, although my original one was now five years old. No, my spiritual life was taking a hit. Even as I grew in "equipment" for ministry, the base that had led me to it was erod-ing. Between school, church, and study, I missed a lot of our daily services. I sometimes read for class instead of doing spiritual reading before Lauds or after Vespers. I no longer ran in the mornings because church meetings kept me out late. I showed up for the basic business of the house, but I was not as connected to the life there, or to my rea-son for being there, as I had been in my first years. My eyes were on my "career" again, using my intellect and avoiding my feelings. From that place, it was easy to push my way through life as I had done in the past.

I attended seminary, but I wasn't yet in the official ordination pro-cess. That would not get underway until I made life profession; just as many committees turn down people in the midst of divorce or big life changes, any uncertainty about my future in community would put me on pause.

I hate to be on pause.

I kept moving. I asked to make my life vows, and the community voted to accept me. So, I had some doubts. Who doesn't have doubts?

Well, maybe more than doubts.

Four months after my life profession, in October of 2006, I had my first panic attack.

Driving to my cousin Amie's wedding in Queens, I had to take a long bridge into the Holland Tunnel. It was a tedious drive, but not a difficult one.

I passed through the toll booth and began the long drive toward Bayonne. The bridge was long, longer than I expected.

Suddenly, I felt out of breath. I needed air, more air than I could get. My heart started pounding. I thought I might pass out. I opened all the car windows and breathed as deeply as I could while I continued to keep up with the traffic.

"That was weird," I thought, as the bridge ended. Then, into the tunnel. I still felt a little light-headed, but at least I could breathe.

Then, up out of the tunnel and onto another bridge. Again, I lost my breath. Again, my heart pounded. What the hell was the matter with me? I felt relieved that my brother Dave would be at the wedding; as a doctor, he'd have an idea of what I should do.

Finally, I arrived at the wedding venue, a refurbished warehouse in Queens. I sat in the car for a few minutes, trying to compose myself. I had never had such a thing happen to me. Strong and healthy, if a bit overweight again (all those free meals at seminary!), I had no physical problems I knew of.

When I could breathe, I entered and looked for Dave.

"The weirdest thing happened to me on the way," I said. I described my symptoms to him. Dave looked at me intently, as he always does when he's talking about symptoms. Then he said, "It sounds like a panic attack."

I'd never had such a thing. I only remotely knew there was such a thing. Other people had panic attacks. I am a rock, steady in all weather. I don't get panic attacks.

Somehow, I got over the bridges going home. I opened all the windows, I turned on the radio for distraction, and I breathed as slowly and deeply as I could. I prayed to God to keep me driving at a good pace, instead of the 10 miles an hour I wanted. Really, I wanted to walk. But I had to drive. I got home.

When I told the Superior of my panic attack, she went online and looked up the symbolism of bridges. Transitions were at the top of the list. We agreed the fear was likely attached to my life profession. She filed it away as something that would pass. I filed it under "inconvenient but manageable."

It wasn't just inconvenient, though. It made my life unmanageable. Where bridges had been connectors, they now were barriers. Every time I approached even a little bridge, I doubted its ability to stand. I doubted my ability to keep driving and not go over the side. I imagined the car heading toward the side and bouncing off the (too low) wall. I wanted to crawl across the bridges, but I also wanted to go as fast as possible, to get over. Mostly, I wanted to not have to face a bridge. I learned alternate routes to get to some of the places I needed to go to. I added on travel time to accommodate these detours. I subtly constrained my life to fit inside my fear. When my cousin Suki was dying of lung cancer at a hospice in the Bronx, I had to get another Sister to drive me. For all my love and desire to be there, I could not drive across the George Washington Bridge. Fear paralyzed me.

Life profession brought with it new responsibilities and new awareness. I had been elected to the Superior's Consultative Council and the Board of Directors. I thought I knew the underbelly of convent life, but now I was privy to all the conflict that brewed among us.

I wanted to run away. But I had made a vow, and I intended to keep it. And, of course, there was the ordination process.

My ordination process had begun, with "discernment committees" both at church and at the convent, to listen and see if I should go forward toward ordination. Eventually, both committees said yes, and I went forward. I didn't talk about my discontent or my fears.

As part of the preparation for priesthood, I had spent the previous summer working full-time as a chaplain intern at a local hospital. Called "clinical pastoral education" or CPE, it combined working with patients with intensive group work designed to teach you about yourself and help remove blockages to your ministry. Five full days a week, and sometimes overnight, I was working at the hospital.

Part of the time, I visited rooms, meeting strangers. I felt like a fraud at first, knowing nothing, entering rooms where people were hooked up to all sorts of machines. Some of them took one look at me and sent me away, either as a ghost from some old experience with Catholic nuns, or as an invader into a non-Christian space. Some of them wanted to talk about God, which could be harder. I met people who believed that God caused every illness, every disaster, and they wanted to know why God had done this. I tried to answer, but the gap between us sometimes yawned as large as the George Washington Bridge.

My time at the hospital brought me some precious gifts, wrapped in rough paper. Some patients became friends, and some friends needed, eventually, to be buried. This is a painful, beautiful honor.

The biggest gift, though, came as a horrible surprise. They warn you that, in chaplaincy, you will get to revisit all your old stuff. I didn't think much about it, until one night.

I got called to the ER, where a mother had brought in her infant son. He died of SIDS just days before his scheduled baptism. Her husband was in London, and her family was due to come over the weekend for the blessed event. She would not leave the baby, and she couldn't take him with her, so she was prepared to stay in the ER until her husband returned. The nurses called me.

"You need to get her to leave," she said.

"Let me see what's going on," I replied.

After a few minutes with Sharon, I saw she was going to stay—she needed to stay with her baby. Her husband was on a plane. The whole family was converging, moving their plans to get there immediately. Sharon, and her baby Colin, needed to wait for them.

I channeled the fierceness I had seen my mother use.

"She's not going anywhere," I told the nurses. "I'm staying with her until her husband comes."

"But that will be hours!"

"I know. But you can't make her leave this way. She needs to see this through."

Sharon and I sat for six hours. Other people came and went on the other side of the curtain, but we stayed put except for bathroom breaks. Once the nurses accepted that we weren't going to leave, they brought us snacks.

Sharon lay on the hospital bed with Colin in her arms. She rocked him and stroked his wispy blond hair. His body slowly cooled, but he was wrapped in a white blanket and looked peaceful. I held on to his spirit, and hers.

Sharon wanted her baby baptized. They were good Catholics, but the Catholic priests weren't going near this one. She wanted me to baptize Colin.

The Episcopal Church is quite clear: we don't baptize dead people. But her need was also clear. No death certificate had been issued; last rites had not been offered.

Gradually, everyone arrived. I led the service of baptism that any baptized person can perform. Then I said the prayers for the dead. We prayed for Sharon and Jim. Colin was laid to rest. We all cried.

I called the nurse, who took Colin from Sharon's arms. She looked incomplete without him. But it wasn't only Sharon who was different; the room was changed. Colin had been with us, in his way. In his absence, the room was "normal," orderly, but empty. Sometimes neat and normal are just pain swept under the rug.

Out in the corridor, I talked to family members who wanted to know why God allowed this to happen, or, even worse, made it happen. I stumbled over answers. Finally, everyone drifted out the door.

That night after work, I went home and sobbed for my unborn daughter. I had never forgotten my miscarriage, or that baby that might have been. As the years passed, I would calculate: how old would she be now? What would she be doing? I thought of her as "she," though I didn't really know. I saw her through grammar and high school, through college, law school. Then it got vague. The thought was there sometimes, but it was just a thought, a reminder. I didn't talk about it any more than my mother had.

I knew that I, like Sharon, needed to name my child and lay her to rest. I prayed to know her name, and heard "Angela." That is not a name I've had an affinity with, and it seemed too easy, a cliche. But there it was. Angela.

I asked Don, my confessor, to help me release her. A few weeks later, 35 years after she died, I let Angela go. She lives now in my heart, claimed and loved and cried for, like all the children whose parents grieve over them.

———

As new thresholds beckoned, I had to leave some old beloved places.

After five years, I said goodbye to the rehab. I had learned so much about loving there, and now, I learned more about letting my heart ache as I said goodbye.

I also had to leave my church. The ordination process required me to leave the congregation that was sponsoring me and learn in another setting. The diocesan commission on ministry wanted me to go to a smaller church, one more conventional than mine. And so, in the fall of 2007, I said goodbye to the kids and my beloved friends. I cried and hugged, and I headed north.

I lived in the car. Seminary was 30 minutes southeast from the convent; church was 45 minutes northeast. Rarely did I go directly from seminary to church. Sunday mornings, a bagel and cream cheese in the car took over from my earlier peanut butter banana sandwich. I got my only speeding ticket heading to church.

During my second year at the new church, my last in seminary, my life got more complicated. The diocesan Commission on Ministry had decreed that I needed to go to the General Theological Seminary in New York City for one semester, to get "Anglicized"—to take the courses that would prepare me specifically for Episcopal priesthood.

I needed to stay in New York for the three days of classes each week. My community had opened a branch house at an Anglo-Catholic parish with an apartment for a convent. There was no room for me in the apartment, but they made a room for me one floor down. I could share Sunday supper and worship with them. Between my school schedule and their commitments, I was basically on my own from Sunday night until I returned to New Jersey on Thursday.

When I first arrived at the church in September of 2008, I saw several men sitting on the church steps. I said hello and entered the church and joined my Sisters.

The next morning, I came pounding down the stairs and opened the front door. There before me was a man, asleep on the step, on a broken-down cardboard box. I almost stepped on him in my haste.

I gingerly stepped over him, trying to keep my long skirt from brushing his face. I whispered, "Excuse me," but he didn't seem to wake up. I scooted down the remaining steps and tried not to run down the street.

A man was sleeping on the steps where I lived! Each morning, I would be faced with this. What on earth should I do, or not do?

I realized that I would be afraid of this man, and any others hanging around, until I got to know them.

The next morning, I brought an apple (and here's a tip: don't give hard foods to people who don't have regular access to dental care). He was asleep, but I put the apple next to him. In the evening, when I returned, he was sitting on the steps with two friends.

"Hi. I'm Sister Shane," I said. "I'm going to be staying here this fall. I guess we'll be neighbors."

Immediately, one of the trio spoke up. He looked to be about 40, but he could have been younger. He was a White guy, dark hair, slight build, with an open face. "Hi, Shane. I'm Tony. This is Mark, and that one is Andrew." Mark, a rounded African-American, and Andrew, another youngish White guy, nodded. Mark stuck out his hand, and I shook it.

"Glad to meet you," I said. "Are you guys here all the time?"

"Usually, during the day the rector lets us sleep in the back pews. We have to go outside during services and after the evening service."

And so, I found my peeps in the city. Tony, Mark, and Andrew were around more than my Sisters. I found that I related to them more easily than to the Sisters living there. They spoke to my inner outcast, to the teenager who slept in parks and panhandled money. With the Sisters, in their small apartment, I felt like an intruder.

Each Sunday afternoon, I arrived in time for Evensong, but I spent it on the steps with the guys rather than praying with my Sisters and the other parishioners.

As the fall went on, I felt safer. But more, I had companions. I looked forward to seeing them each week. I had a posse, people I looked forward to seeing and who seemed to like me, even if it wasn't the posse I was officially connected to.

Thank you, guys, for giving me a seat on your steps. It wasn't much, and it wasn't long, but you were my community more than the seminarians, with their own little world, or the Sisters, with theirs. Thank you, God, for teaching me to reach out rather than run away. I pray that these men found their way home, whatever that means for them. Be with all the unhoused people, until we can end this scandal of indifference.

By now, two years after life profession, my relationship with the community felt like nothing but obligation. If there was companionship to be had there, I wasn't there to find it. When I did look for it, others seemed to be as busy as me. And, truly, I wasn't exactly someone they might want to spend time with.

I realized that I not only lived different lives in and out of the convent; I was two different people. "Outside," where I felt safe and welcome, I was genuinely loving and patient and bold. When I stepped in the doors of the convent, I pulled a shield down. I did not feel safe or welcome, and I acted accordingly. I complained with the other newer members. I alternately strove to support the Superior, and harangued her when my frustration was up. I avoided those I perceived as a threat, and met them with a stony politeness.

I didn't want to live like this anymore, so I turned to what I knew. I began to do some 12-Step work on my resentments toward the Sisters. The premise of the Steps is that I am the only one I can change, with God's help. The resentments I have are my problem, not something for others to fix by giving me what I want. I need to look for my part, where I have put myself in the position I'm in.

As I moved through the Steps, I began to see: there was nothing wrong with the Sisters. They wanted to live a life that didn't fit me. I had been trying to make them into the sort of community that would meet my desires and needs, but they weren't going to do that. Given that, I had to ask: Do I still belong here? Did I ever?

One day, as I walked in the woods, I heard my little voice. *"I need to leave."* The voice that had guided me into the convent, the one I had waited to hear but didn't all these years, spoke with simple clarity.

I had made a life vow, and I had a life here. I felt sure that the vows were real and important—crucial—to my being, but I felt increasingly certain that I couldn't live them out and flourish there. The aliveness I had felt in 2003 had shriveled. I told the Superior about my feelings, and I asked to start seeing a therapist.

My new therapist was also an Episcopal priest. She listened to me and my struggles, both the current ones and those around my family history. She heard my pain and my fear of leaving. Gradually, she began to prepare me to leave the community and become a priest.

As my seminary years drew to a close, I knew I stood at a turning point. The Sisters expected me to center my life on the community after ordination. The prospect of returning full-time to the convent filled me with dread. I had shoved my feelings aside, and I had managed to be out of the house for these years, but now I had to confront the truth. I did not feel loved there, and I didn't feel much love. I was using them, settling for a simulacrum of monastic life. I had learned and grown there, but I no longer belonged there.

Slowly, over that year, I came to see how much about the community echoed my family, and how I reacted to that as I had when young. In the face of anger or attack, I withdrew to my room (now my cell, or the woods). I had learned to put up with loneliness and to find refuge in work. I had made myself blind to the cost of living with hostility. I had told myself it didn't have to get to me, but now I saw that it did.

The ministry I loved enabled me to avoid being "at home." As much as I loved the common prayer life and the structure of our days (days I often missed as I drove to seminary or church), I needed to acknowledge my misery. It had been there for years, and I poured out my tears to God and sometimes to another person, but I hadn't been able to face leaving. Now, it seemed, I couldn't face staying for much longer.

I didn't want to leave religious life; but I knew I couldn't graduate from seminary, get ordained, and live full-time in the community. Was there some way for me to maintain my membership and my vows without living in a place that brought me pain? And if not, where would I go? What would I do?

Everyone around me, outside of the community, told me I would be a great parish priest. I wasn't so sure. I had spent enough time with priests to know what their job was like, and I doubted that the people who liked me so much as an assistant would feel the same if I were their rector.

On the other hand, curiosity unfurled in me. Could I do it? I certainly found more life in my parish ministry than at "home." Still, I knew community life, vowed life, was essential for my spiritual health.

My life was on a collision course. I was due to be ordained in 2009. The Sisters, and the diocese, had assumed I would exercise my priestly ministry mostly in the convent, presiding at Eucharist in my turn. Now, it looked like I would need to serve in a parish simply to support myself—assuming the bishop approved me for ordination! I needed to tell my bishop what was going on.

Before they are ordained to the priesthood, Episcopal candidates are ordained to the diaconate. As the date for my diaconal ordination approached, I went to talk to my bishop. This was meant to be a general last conversation before ordination, but I had a surprise for him.

The bishop welcomed me as we settled into chairs in his sunlit office. My chest was tight, but I tried to look calm.

"Good morning, Bishop. I need to tell you something."

He looked at me more closely and waited.

"I need you to know, before you ordain me, that I may not remain with my community. I know that we are ordained to serve the Church rather than one particular place, but everyone has expected me to be in the community. There's a good chance I will be looking for a call to a parish. You may decide not to ordain me, or to wait, but I can't go forward without you knowing this."

Is it possible to release your breath and hold it at the same time? I felt glad it was out on the table, but terrified of his response. My future rested with his decision.

The bishop sat for a minute. Then he began:

"Thank you for telling me. This must be very hard for you."

After a pause, he said amazing, magic words, words much bigger than yes or no.

"I trust your process. I trust your discernment. Of course, I will still ordain you."

I tried not to burst into tears. I dribbled a bit, but he didn't seem to mind. I began to breathe again. After we went through the details of my diaconal ordination, he reassured me again: I was called to serve not only my little community, but the wider Church.

In June, I was ordained a deacon. It's a huge deal. Members of the sponsoring congregations come, clergy come, friends come to witness this moment. People came from both my churches.

For most candidates, ordination day is special because it marks the first time they wear a clerical collar. On my ordination day, though, under my alb and my new deacon's stole, I wore my habit.

This had become a point of contention between me and my therapist. She felt strongly that I needed to claim a clerical identity, and that meant dressing the part. She pushed me to start wearing a clerical collar once I became a deacon—something neither of our other ordained Sisters had done.

I pushed back. I knew, somehow, that taking this step would seal my separation from the community. Even as I edged toward the door, I clung to my membership. I didn't want to rock the boat, but that boat was rocking. I knew, in some part of me, that I had outgrown that habit. I just didn't want to make it real yet.

Finally, I asked to buy some clerical clothes to wear at church. I argued that male monastic priests often wore "clericals" when they served in churches. The Superior agreed, dubiously. On Sunday mornings, I put on my habit for our morning services, then I ran to my cell to change and snuck out the back door so I didn't scandalize anyone (or myself). I'd come home and change before I joined the others. I could feel the widening gap.

———

I needed a plan. If I were to leave, I needed to let some people know my intention and seek their help.

I sat at Pat and Colleen's kitchen table, sharing a cup of tea. I told them, "I need you to know something. I have to leave the convent. I don't know whether it's temporary or permanent, but I need to get away and find out whether parish life is right for me."

Instantly Colleen said, "You can come here if you need to." Pat nodded.

What? I had not been telling them in order to ask for a place. I told them because I needed them to know. Maybe Colleen had spoken too soon. Maybe Pat wasn't really on board. Maybe—but for now, they were showing me that "way would open," as the Quakers say, when the time is right.

God, it seemed, had decided to open the door.

In mid-July, I went to the Superior and asked for a leave of absence. I knew it would be a big request, but I thought it would be okay. Another Sister had just had five months of sabbatical, living in a cabin in the New Jersey hills.

We had also spent the last year hosting a Sister from another order. Like me, she had made her life vows in 2006. Like me, she was unhappy and needed time away. She still wanted to live the life, but she wasn't sure if that was the right community for her. When she asked for a year's leave, her community shut her out. She was granted the leave but ordered to have no contact with them. She received no support from them. As the full story of her separation came out, all of us were horrified. "How could they do that?" we cried. "Where is the love?" Now, almost a year later, she was considering joining us.

When I went to ask for leave, then, I thought it would be upsetting but manageable. So much for my plans.

The first time I told the Superior, she asked if I was certain I wanted to do this. I said yes, I needed to explore parish ministry on my own. I hoped that maybe someday we would have a branch house, with me as the priest and other Sisters sharing in ministry. I had been invited by the bishop of another diocese to talk about ministry opportunities there, and another Sister and I played with the idea that we could go serve in a parish, as other Sisters had, but now one of us would be the parish priest. For now, though, I just needed to try living "outside."

I waited two weeks, and heard nothing.

Our community chaplain was coming for a visit in August, and I knew his calm, good sense would be needed as we talked about this. So, at the end of July, I asked again. The Superior said she would bring it up to the community.

Finally, as mid-August approached with no mention of my plans, I forced the issue.

"What's the holdup?" I asked.

It turned out that our visiting Sister had just decided not to join but to leave religious life and return to teaching. Sr. Phyllis had not yet told the community, and she felt they needed to digest this disappointment before facing my request.

I needed to move.

"There's not going to be a good time," I said. "If you won't tell them, I will." (So obedient! So patient!)

And so, that evening at recreation, Sister Phyllis announced that I had made a request. She turned to me. I explained to everyone that I needed a leave to discern my future.

Everyone sat in silence. The knitting speeded up in people's hands.

Finally, one of the quiet but perceptive Sisters asked, "Is it because we're so unhappy?"

She never did mince words.

"No," I said, but inside I knew that answer wasn't entirely true. They *were* unhappy, as a group, if not each person, each day. I felt that staying, especially after ordination, would sink me into depression and despair. That was not what God wanted for me.

"No, it's not your unhappiness; it's my need."

"Where will you go?"

I explained that Pat and Colleen would house me until I could get a clerical job.

No one said another word. They knitted in silence.

The next day was Monday, our Sabbath day. Sisters usually dispersed, though some might gather for a TV show or a meal. I didn't see anyone that day; no one talked to me about my request.

The following day, we had community time in the morning. Sister Phyllis asked me not to come so that others might share their feelings and thoughts. It didn't occur to me to say that perhaps I should hear them directly; that was not how things were done. In the afternoon, the Consultative Council met to discuss how to proceed.

That evening, the Superior called me to her office. The Assistant Superior joined us.

"We are not going to approve a leave of absence," Sister Phyllis said. "This is not like Sister Fiona's leave. This is a serious breach."

"Why?" I asked.

"This is not about a rest or time to pray. You are leaving us."

I didn't know what to say.

"We will offer you exclaustration for a year."

I hadn't really heard that word before. She explained.

"You will still officially belong to the order, and your vows are still binding. However, you will not participate in community business, or wear the habit or cross. We will need you to call before you visit to prepare for your presence."

As much as I had thought I wanted to leave, this was a blow.

There was more, though.

"The Sisters are furious with you. You need to leave tonight."

"Tonight?"

"Well, you could stay overnight, but you need to be gone by morning."

I had no words. They were so angry that they couldn't have me in the building. Even the Sister I had dreamed about ministry with was too angry to speak to me. Apparently, it was one thing to blow off some steam and to daydream; it was another to actually take action.

I called Pat and Colleen. They came and picked me up, me and my "Sabbath clothes" and clericals. Anything else would come later.

I left my habit hanging in the closet. My big silver cross on its red cord, my black crocheted cincture with the three knots for the three vows, had to stay. I still had my ring. A simple gold band on the ring finger of my right hand was all the sign I had of my vows and my vocation, my identity.

From now on, I would have to inhabit my vows in a new way, a way I didn't yet see.

O my Sisters, I am so sorry. I do believe God was at work sending me to you, and I also believe I had to leave. I wish I could have done so without hurting you. I almost wrote that I wish I hadn't had to leave, but that's not true. Leaving opened the door to so much new life. Still, the price for us all was high. I pray that you are thriving and joyful. May we all give glory to God in our own way.

Chapter Fifteen

Fish Out of Water

THE NEXT SEVERAL MONTHS were a blur. I don't know what my friends had envisioned when they made their offer, but I knew I would not have a paying position until after my priestly ordination—if it was approved! In the meantime, they adopted me into their household. Their seven rescue pugs adopted me too. Baxter, the eldest, had a sense of who needed love, and he pressed his old, heavy body next to mine on the sofa.

In the space of an hour, I migrated to another world. The house was huge; my bedroom was at least twice the size of my cell. I slept in a double bed with nice soft sheets. I prayed alone, in my room. Each night Pat and I ate ice cream or some sweet treat. I fought my weight on a treadmill in the basement, but I never said no to that bowl.

My duties at church were a blessed distraction. David, the rector, had gone on sabbatical, and I had become "deacon in charge" for three months. This gave me an opportunity to go to the church several days a week, to write a weekly reflection, and to preach every other week. I visited sick and elderly parishioners. Most things ran smoothly, so I didn't have a lot to do, but I did get to be a pastoral presence.

I gradually got used to my clerical collar. I still wore my ring, on my right ring finger as the community did, but it gradually felt more and more alien. I drifted into a state of limbo, still a "religious" but without any of the usual signs and supports. Now I was "Deacon Shane"; "Sister Shane" was invisible in this strange new world.

The one place I made sense, to myself and maybe to others, was the monastery. I first went there as part of my visit to the New York convent. It was right on the Hudson. On that first visit, I entered through the main door and followed the corridors to the chapel. This was a large, airy space, with windows high up on either side of the long building. Simple white walls, hardwood floors, cushioned straight chairs for guests, and long wooden choir stalls for the Brothers. It was simple, but not stark. It felt spacious. Open. Lovely.

When I arrived there, I thought to myself, "This is where I belong." I could feel the peace and ordered simplicity of this space. Of course, they didn't accept women, so I had gone on my way. Over the following years, though, I had come up for private retreat time and sometimes just for vacation. I could go there and pray with others, following patterns that were now in my bones.

Now, I sat in the chapel and cried. I prayed to God: "Show me how to live the life I still believe You have called me to. Show me how to live my vows if I'm not in the convent or in any of the established women's Episcopal communities. Send me companions. I can't live this life; I can't be faithful, alone."

One day, as I prayed and cried, Brother Andrew passed through the back of the chapel. He was a crusty Scotsman, a priest, a gay man, and a recovering alcoholic. He could be stubborn and arrogant and judgmental, but also loving and generous and wise.

Andrew heard me crying and came and sat with me as I sniffled. "Ah, lass, what's the matter?" he asked.

I suddenly knew what I needed. "Would you hear my confession?" I asked.

"Of course." We arranged to meet that afternoon in the small parlor reserved for private conversations.

When I arrived, Andrew had arranged two wingback chairs to face one another, and laid out prayer books for us to follow the form. I began, and when it got to the specifics, I put aside the book and told him my struggle.

"I made life vows three years ago, and now I'm out. I'm fickle and unreliable. I've let down these women who trusted me. I need God's forgiveness."

Andrew was typically direct. "You don't need forgiveness. This is not a sin."

"It's not?"

"I've watched you struggle with your vocation, with the community. I know how hard you've tried. It's not the place for you. It's not a sin to leave now."

"But I vowed!"

"Yes, you did. And you're still under vows, even though you aren't living there. But if it becomes clear that you need to leave for good, you will know that is God's will. You're being dramatic. Just let it be."

This was the Andrew I loved. I knew that his blunt speech could sound dismissive or insulting, but it came from love. He would not dance around, or try to gentle his words. But he would love me.

The next day, he caught up to me on the way into lunch. "You know," he said, "You should talk to Elizabeth."

I knew Elizabeth Broyles, a tiny bit. She had lived at the monastery for several years, working in the guesthouse and the bookstore. She was a priest and sometimes presided at the Eucharist there. She was hard to miss: her fiery red hair, thick and wavy, reached down to her waist.

Somehow, we had never connected. Why would Andrew want me to talk to her?

"She's been longing for religious life for years but never found a community that fit. You might have something in common."

Later, I found out that he told Elizabeth, "You should talk to Shane about starting a community."

Somehow, we managed to schedule a time to talk on my next visit. I learned that Elizabeth had visited a community nearby, but she didn't feel a fit. None of the other communities looked promising to her. I spoke of my pain and disappointment, but also about my hope for a way to continue living "the life." At the end of our time, we knew one another better, but I didn't feel a special resonance.

My reluctance to talk more had another reason besides "resonance." I felt like a newly divorced person. I wasn't even "divorced," for God's sake; it was more like a legal separation at that point. I needed to let the dust settle, to grieve and find my feet. I needed to explore priesthood and parish ministry before jumping into anything else.

For now, I would remain a fish out of water.

Finally, the day came for my priestly ordination. On December 12, nine years to the day from my entry into the convent, I stood again before a bishop and answered questions. Then I knelt before the bishop. The other priests gathered around me. The bishop pressed his hands down on my head while the others reached for my back, shoulders, arms. Everyone chanted "Veni Sancte Spiritus," which means "Come, Holy Spirit." I struggled to stay erect under the pressure of the many hands. I felt surrounded in a cocoon of love and power from which I would emerge a priest.

Perhaps, though, it had already happened.

Three weeks before this day, I had taken a walk. I entered the woods on a trail I had never walked before. From the parking lot, a single path wound up a slight hill and curved out of sight. I got out of the car and bent over to tie my laces tighter. I slammed the door and pocketed my keys.

I began up the path, noticing the faded reds and golds on the fall leaves underfoot. As I crunched along on them, I could smell the beginnings of their mold rise up. I loved that smell, the decay that would become new soil come spring. One lone crow hovered, but the squirrels and chipmunks seemed to have taken to their burrows. In the distance, Canada geese who had come for the winter were making their claim to the high school playing field, but here it was just me and the crow and my prayer book. I had come here to "practice" the Eucharistic prayer I would say as a priest.

I reached a rise and looked out over the lumpy hills of northern New Jersey. It was as close to a mountaintop as I would get here.

I stood and looked out at the barren trees, the leaves freshly fallen and awaiting their winter blanket, the old stumps hewn out by water and wind and covered now with moss. I felt the beauty and the power of this place, this perfectly ordinary suburban woods.

Suddenly, the words of the prayer came to me, and I began to say them: not just to recite them, but to pray them from my heart. They became my words, my blessing on the world and its gifts, my prayer to God to bless us all. I turned around, a full circle. I blessed it all. I gave thanks for it all. I cried out my love. I stood there and blessed the sleeping chipmunks and the cautious crow. I blessed the geese who would drive us crazy by February. I saw, and everything I saw was part of the body of Christ. Tears flowed as I stood in the center of the swirl of beauty.

I found a tissue in my jacket pocket and blew my nose. I turned back the way I had come. I heard my feet shuffle through the leaves, I felt the fullness of my sinuses, but mostly I walked in a daze of love and gratitude.

Now, at my ordination service, what I had felt on that hill was being affirmed by the wider Church. My sister and brother, who had traveled far for this moment, brought up my new vestments. Colleen was not only a good friend; she was a gifted maker of silk vestments, specializing in vestments that tell a story. My stole featured my priestly "medicine animals," based on cards I had drawn with this intention. Running along a stream of water and various grasses were a whale, a spider, an owl, an elk, a wolf, a frog, and a coyote—my old friend the trickster. At the top, where it would surround my neck, was a butterfly, symbol of transformation. Because my ordination was on the Feast of Our Lady of Guadalupe, Colleen had found a butterfly named "Mexican Sister," and that was the one she put around my neck.

And, in the corner, barely visible, was the tail of a pug.

I turned and looked at the church, packed to the gills. Dave and Jan; I got to give Communion to my brother and sister! My former church's choir had joined in with the current one to make this beautiful music. Several of the Sisters had come. For that one moment, the strands of my life threaded together.

I had finally been ordained a priest, but being ordained is distinct from having a position in a church. I didn't have a prospect yet. For now, I would remain where I was, without pay.

One day in January, I got a call from the canon, the lead assistant to the bishop. He had a possibility for me. It was in the far northeast corner of New Jersey. I had never heard of this town. I knew it was suburban—my least favorite environment—but it was a prospect! A full-time job! He put me in touch with their senior warden (the lay leader of the congregation). We arranged an interview for the following Tuesday evening.

My first challenge was finding the place. I set out to explore a whole new part of New Jersey. In the dark, in the rain, without GPS, I looked for signs and turns. To my surprise, I arrived. The church was set back on a side road that became dirt several blocks further down; it would be easy to miss.

I parked and scooted through the rain. Carol, the parish leader, met me there and took me through into the church. As we joined the group, I looked at the faces gathered around the table. They were mostly White, and mostly older. Like many of our churches, women were the majority. They didn't look particularly friendly, but neither were they hostile.

They asked me questions: how would I grow the church? Did I have experience with young people? They knew I had been in a convent, but no one asked about that. Maybe that was a blessing: I didn't have to explain that I still technically belonged to that community.

Finally, we got to the question that, I later learned, was foremost on their minds: "Would you be willing to live in the rectory, on the grounds?" For me this was a no-brainer: I needed a place to live. "Of course," I said.

In the church we talk about "vocation" and "discernment." Clergy shouldn't look on their position as a job, but as a call from God. Clergy and congregations should be discerning God's will for them.

None of us really did that, though. I later learned that they had turned down another candidate, an experienced priest, because she and her partner refused to live in the rectory. I was their last chance; the diocese would not send them another candidate.

And me? I needed a job and a place to live. I wanted it to be a call, I wanted to serve, but I knew that if they offered me the position, I would take it. I prayed that it would indeed be a call, I treated it as such, but really, I didn't discern any more than they did.

It was still raining as I began my journey home in the dark.

They offered me the position, and I took it.

I began to get a sense of how things might be when the senior warden couldn't print the contract. After weeks of waiting, I drove out and printed it and filled it out for her. I wanted to be there in time for Easter, and I pushed to make it happen.

Little bells rang for me, subtle warnings about leadership or partnership in the parish. I plowed ahead, full of dreams about how we would restart this church, how we would attract new people by witnessing God's goodness in our lives. I felt confident I could get something going.

Oh God, was I in the dark! Driving home in the rain was the least of it. Not knowing either my own capacity or theirs, not sure of my vocation(s), grieving. I believe that you carried me, you provided for me and, I suppose, for them. But I wanted so much more! I wanted the shared commitment and desire to follow Jesus, I wanted to be in a community of seekers. I didn't really know about the varied reasons people come to church; I had gone straight from conversion to monastic life. I didn't realize, either, how much I needed affirmation and welcome in order to be the person who welcomed others. I didn't know how much I judged others, how distant I still held myself. All this was in the shadows, waiting to come to light.

I left Colleen and Pat's house on a Saturday in March 2010. It was not an ideal day for moving: a nor'easter had blown in overnight, and rain and wind were making a mess of roads. But I was due to start my new ministry the next day, and I had no intention of waiting. My moving team, Pat and Steve, was willing, so that morning, they showed up with a U-Haul, which we filled with my new furnishings, donations from Pat and Colleen, and my friends at church.

I had a lot. The women at my church had decided I needed more than I could afford, so they threw me a shower. I went to Bed Bath & Beyond, and their bridal registration agent took me through the store choosing items. On my last Sunday at the church, they sat me down in an over-stuffed chair and presented me with everything from cutlery to pillows. They gifted me with the beginnings of a household, and their love.

After years divesting myself of things, I felt embarrassed. What was I doing with all this? In my heart, I hoped to find a monastic community, but I still needed all this stuff to be "in the world" for the time being.

Along with the awkwardness, though, I felt loved. I could look at the quilt that Joan made for me and think of her. I could give thanks for Joanne and Steve when I used the pots and pans; Ginny and Brian were there in the dishes. John and David had blessed me with sheets and blankets for the futon couch that would become the guest bed. The list went on and on.

I hugged Colleen about seventeen times, petted the dogs, and we headed out into the storm. We plowed our way east on I-80, fighting through the storm.

When we arrived, several of my new parishioners greeted us. They all pitched in and unloaded. It didn't take long: what felt like a pile of riches to me was still pretty stark. If it hadn't been for the couch left behind by the previous priest, we wouldn't have been able to sit more than four people.

Soon they left, and I began to explore this new space. It was huge. There was an office, with a separate outdoor entrance, to ensure privacy for priestly conversations. There was no office in the church; this had been where priests saw their people. But now the world had changed. I was a woman, living alone. The Church had begun to realize that situations like this were unsafe for parishioners, who might be preyed upon by their priest, but no one had really begun talking about the risk for female clergy, especially single women. I didn't really get it either. Vulnerability wasn't something I was good at noticing. I was grateful for an office with a computer and a laser printer, with bookshelves and even a few books, a desk, chairs.

Then I went upstairs. My bed was in one of the two huge bedrooms, looking a bit lost in the big space. The other bedroom was just empty, except for a cheap desk someone had left behind. I had brought my single futon from the convent—no one there wanted it—and I threw it down in a corner for meditating. The desk would become my jigsaw puzzle center while I listened to classical radio.

The walls were that flat off-white that people use when they have no idea about the preferences of the next people. There was nothing on them. In its own weird way, it was "monastic"—simple, uncluttered for sure, nearly barren. I was fine with that; I already possessed way more than I had anticipated!

After seven solid months with Pat and Colleen, the quiet was extreme, broken only by the storm outside, lashing the trees and the side of the house.

I was excited, thinking about the next day. I was in a new place, starting a new job. My sermon was ready. Others would make sure the church was open, the choir rehearsed, and the coffeepot was ready to go.

This Sunday, the Gospel was about the prodigal son, the one who wastes his inheritance and then comes home. His father welcomes him back with joy. The older son, who's worked so hard and been so obedient, is furious that his father has welcomed this wastrel. It's a story about God's crazy love, a love that welcomes us back no matter what we've done, that doesn't rank people's achievements and failings but wants us all.

For me, it's Jesus' big challenge: do I identify with the older brother, the (self-) righteous one simmering with resentment, or do I really get my own need for forgiveness? For years, I focused on my gratitude for being saved, but eventually, I saw just how often I'm the older brother, judging those poor shlebs who just won't get with my program.

I had a job, a call to serve, a roof over my head, food in the fridge.

None of this seemed like my doing; it was all gift. In that moment, I was the younger son, receiving beyond any measurement of worth.

I ate dinner early. I looked forward to an evening listening to the radio and relaxing.

At 6:00, the power went out. I had a candle, and somewhere in the car I knew there was a flashlight. I lit the candle, found the flashlight, and waited. Surely the power would be back soon; I was in the middle of suburbia.

By 7:00, there was still no power. No one called. They likely didn't have power either.

8:00. I had a cell phone with just enough power to call for help, but I didn't want to waste that power on anything non-essential. Surely the power would return soon.

Now it was dark, and my one candle wasn't enough for me to read by. I decided to treat this as a retreat, a chance to prepare for my new position. I brushed my teeth by candlelight, found my nightclothes in the jumble in my room, and got into bed. Then I prayed—for those without power, for the workers. I gave thanks for my safe arrival and my new companions. I asked to be shown how to serve these people and how to live my vows in this new place.

I slept.

The next morning, I woke up to watery sunshine. We still didn't have power, but I could see my way. I couldn't cook or use the microwave, but I could at least wash my body and eat some bread and milk. An adventure! Just enough hardship to make me feel alive, not enough to overwhelm me.

The church didn't have power either. The main worship area was too dim for us; its stained-glass windows cut out the light. I decided that we would worship in the parish hall, where they usually had cof-fee hour. Claudia, the choir director, arrived, and together we set up a table and covered it to make an altar. We had candles for the altar, which also helped illuminate the area a bit.

People began to drift in. As they gathered, they introduced themselves. The storm gave us lots to talk about—a sort of icebreaker.

As the service began, everyone clustered around circular tables and the worn, brown couches. We read the readings, and I preached my sermon. Finally, we came to the Eucharist. I said the familiar words, and blessed and broke the bread. People came up and received and showed me their faces and souls one by one.

I looked out and loved them. They were my new flock, my new family. They were there, being faithful in the midst of a power outage. They were not deterred by our less-than-elegant worship; somehow, being in the parish hall made it more authentic. The storm had stripped us down (almost) to essentials: people gathered to hear the word of God, to break bread, to pray together.

I cleared the table as well as I could and said the closing prayers. But the words I felt, the ones I wanted to communicate to them, were silent:

"We have no electricity, but we have lots of power. We are the people of God, gathered together in the light of day. We've come through a long, hard night, and we've found our way here together.

"I wouldn't have us meet any other way."

It turned out that this was just the beginning. Over the next two-and-a-half years, five storms cut power for more than four days at a time. Hurricane Irene, Superstorm Sandy, and other nameless freak events tore a swath through our part of Bergen County.

That area hasn't had a storm like those since I left.

I haven't had such an experience, such an extended disaster, since then.

Make of that what you will.

On that first Sunday, the senior warden and her husband invited me to stay overnight with them. It was awkward, we didn't talk a lot, but I was very grateful to spend time with them and not in my cold house.

During my last storm, in the fall of 2012, I got to stay with another family and spend time with their young children—a rare delight!

But in between, there was a lot of time on my own.

The church couldn't afford a secretary, and they hired a cleaning service in lieu of a sexton. I learned that I was expected to take out the garbage. The parishes that had prepared me for ordination all had parish administrators, sextons to care for the grounds, active vestry members making sure things worked. Now, I was a one-woman band. I learned that I was seen less as a spiritual resource and more as an employee.

There was a notable lack of interest or curiosity about me. (Only much later did I learn how uncomfortable some members were with a female priest, much less one who had been a nun.) The senior lay leader was facing cancer, but she didn't want to talk to me. Another member's husband was dying, and she wanted me to visit him, but he didn't want anything to do with clergy. After I had reached out to a couple of long-time parishioners to visit them and had been rebuffed, I began to get a complex. Every visit with my members began to feel excruciating.

I really didn't "get" this suburban corner of the world, and they didn't get me. I was lonely, grieving, and underemployed. I was reading a lot about parish ministry and learning about adult education programs and stewardship programs, and I was writing a sermon every week, but I was also watching a lot of TV. So, I didn't feel overwhelmed; if anything, I was underwhelmed! My head was full of ideas, but I didn't have the partners I'd need to see them bear fruit. And, I was still officially a member of my community. I didn't feel I belonged anywhere. Subtly, depression seeped into my bones.

I prayed the morning service from the St. Helena Breviary each day, with coffee at my side. In the evenings, I went to the church to say Vespers. I hoped others might join me. One or two people came for a while, but they didn't stay. I learned that not many people felt drawn to pray in that way, that often. After a few months, I moved my Vespers observance back to the rectory. Within a year, I had stopped saying it myself, watching afternoon TV instead. I knew Compline by heart, so I could say it in bed.

My favorite part of ministry there was the Wednesday night healing prayer service. Each Wednesday, I entered the darkened church, lit only by the sanctuary lamp by the front altar. I came a half hour early, to pray and gather energy. I held out my hands toward the altar, palms open toward the Blessed Sacrament in the tabernacle, and said the beginning of the St. Francis Prayer: "Lord, make me an instrument of your peace." After a minute, I could feel the palms of my hands receiving energy and warming up. I sat in silence, half-kneeling, and let myself be enfolded in that circuit. Later in the service, when I laid hands on people, I felt the energy move between us. For me, that time was more precious, Christ was more present, than in the Sunday Eucharist with its ritual choreographies. I loved that too, I gave thanks for it, but it was Wednesday that really sang for me.

Soon, my situation got more complicated—and richer.

A year before I came, the church had entered into an extraordinary adventure. A nearby Lutheran (ELCA) congregation had finally faced that their dwindling population did not have the resources to maintain their buildings. They still had a pastor, though she had moved out of state; she commuted on alternate weekends.

When the previous priest heard of their dilemma, he had spontaneously offered: "You can come here!" The ELCA church agreed to pay half the expenses for the Episcopal one. Everybody won. Each week, the two congregations worshipped together, alternating between the Episcopal Prayer Book and the Lutheran Book of Worship.

When they had begun, they had expressed the intention to become one blended congregation. At this point, though, the two congregations were still independent, each with their own governing body (the Lutheran Council and the Episcopal Vestry). I was intrigued by the arrangement and eager to move them along toward a real union. I looked up churches that had already become one blended church. I started by blending worship so we didn't have to use two sets of books. Both our denominations had actually produced more recent worship materials, and they had done much of it together, so the new words were identical and more gender-neutral. Using those resources, I made worship booklets, one for each season of the church year.

Then, two months after I arrived, the Lutheran pastor announced that she would be retiring in October—five months away. The original deal struck by the two churches presumed that their two clergy would be in place to oversee the transition to one congregation. Now what?

I was the only clergyperson left. I'd been ordained for five months, and I was alone in my first job. I had plenty of time on my hands, and I liked the Lutheran parishioners. So, when the Lutheran council approached me and asked if I would be their pastor as well as the priest, I said yes.

It would mean learning a lot. I'd have to learn about Lutheran theology and worship and governance; I'd have to answer to two bishops and work with two church councils. I'd get to create something new. It sounded like fun, something I could sink my teeth into.

My theme song became, "What an adventure we're on!" Gradually, I learned that not everyone wants an adventure.

I had come back to church out of a passionate desire to follow Jesus and to know God. I knew the churches were diminishing, but I saw that as fruitful ground for new ways of following Christ. But many people, I learned, came to church for the comfort of the familiar, and they wanted things to stay the same. They wanted to return to the time when the pews were full, there were lots of children and young families, without any changes in worship or theology. My job, it appeared, was to make that happen. That was not the adventure I had in mind, or in my heart. Really, leading a parish was not the adventure I had in my heart; I just didn't know what else to do, yet.

By the summer of 2010, I'd been living outside community for a year. I hadn't yet officially ended my membership there, but the writing was on the wall. The Superior had given me an ultimatum: return in

August or leave the community. I knew I couldn't return. But what was next?

On a hot day in July, I sat in my car in the parking lot of the Chinese buffet. The buffet fed the workers in the surrounding stores, and travelers off the interstate, and local gluttons like myself. It was cheap, there was a lot of variety, and I could eat as much and whatever I wanted.

After lunch, I returned to my car. It was blazing hot, sitting in the summer sun, so I opened the windows and started the engine. The radio opened immediately onto the noonday show on WNYC.

Before I could begin to drive, my phone rang. I was still new to cell phones, but getting there.

Elizabeth was on the other end.

"I'm calling from South Africa." She sounded excited, or nervous—something.

I couldn't imagine what would prompt her to call from so far away. "What's up?"

"How would you like to move to South Africa and start a women's community?"

What?

I gazed out at the parking lot. Hardly anyone was there. Beyond the parking lot, brilliant green grass marched up a hill toward small trees planted to hide the interstate.

I turned off the car. Without the air conditioning, the car was heating up. I could feel the sweat beading on my forehead and neck. My T-shirt was getting damp.

I watched the dust on the dashboard. I looked down and noticed the clumps of grass and tiny rocks that had made it onto the floor of the car.

I wanted to sweep them out.

I wanted to turn on the car and drive.

I wanted to cry.

"No. I don't want to move to South Africa. I'm just starting to get close to my family. I want to get closer to them, not further away."

"Oh. Okay."

During the previous fall, when Brother Andrew had told us each to talk to the other, I knew it was too early to think about anything new. At that time, I was still a member of my community, I was still looking for my first parish call, I was in between identities, and I was grieving. Now, I was still officially in my community, though it looked like I was gone for good. I was not ready to make another commitment, even to explore.

I especially was in no condition to start something I wanted so much. I wanted community like I wanted water, like I had wanted the food in that buffet. No, more: I wanted to know God with all of my being, and I knew I needed community for that. I wanted to live full out, to give myself to God with like-minded others. And I was terrified to try again.

Now, nine months later, Elizabeth was calling with an outrageous proposal. Her signal was weak, her voice was sort of distant, but I could hear her well enough.

"What made you think of that?"

"I'm here with the Brothers. It's beautiful here, and simple. They live the life I want to live. There's no women's community here. I think there's potential."

"Oh. Well, I get that, but it's just too much for me now."

"Okay. Well, let's talk when I get back."

I gazed around the parking lot. I needed to find something to distract me, to hold my attention. I watched the sunlight glint off the silver Toyota two lanes over. I wanted color and motion, but nothing was moving in the heat. Not even the leaves were stirring. Maybe, like me, they were holding their breath.

Elizabeth had gone to South Africa to mark her 50th birthday. She spent three months there, our summer, their winter. For three months, she had prayed and read and dreamed. She was fired up. I was the cold water on that fire.

But I didn't drown the fire. I just slowed it down.

A few months later, on a cold November afternoon, I walked out to the mailbox. I wasn't expecting anything, but still, mail was a fixed point in my day—some possibility, something to do.

I reached in and pulled out a long, slim envelope. The return address was the Presiding Bishop's office, 815 Second Ave, New York. What did the Presiding Bishop want with me? I walked a little more quickly to get back inside and find out. I closed the door to the rectory and sat down on one of the couches I had bought with my first earnings as a priest. The room was still bare, just the couches and the TV center and a few plants, but it didn't matter. I didn't expect to be accumulating a lot of stuff.

I slid out the letter. I read the words: "In accordance with the canons of the Episcopal Church, I hereby dispense you from your vows."

I was no longer recognized as a religious, as part of a community, as someone who lived under religious vows. I was now officially a single woman.

I stared at the letter. In the pale November light, the words were faint but clear. The Presiding Bishop's signature was large and forceful.

I gazed down at my green corduroys and my fancy Coldwater Creek sweater, at my black clerical blouse and collar. I looked like a dowdy professional woman, a pudgy middle-aged priest. I slumped in my chair and read the letter again.

"No," I said to myself. "No."

Yes, it had been over a year since I had left. And yes, I had refused to return when the (new) Superior wrote me in August. Really, I had left the year before. I pretended it was a year's leave to explore, but really, I had known. I had even sat with Elizabeth and talked about a new community. But I never thought that I would be without vows, not really. We may have separated, but getting the divorce decree was another level of finality.

I grabbed for my large silver cross, but it wasn't there. I had left it in my cell. Now I had a simple, small cross, bought by me rather than given. I felt for my cincture, the rope with the three knots for the vows, but all I found was the leather belt on my corduroys. I still had my ring. I had never liked it, but now, although I didn't want to wear it, I wanted to remember it and see it. I wanted my vows.

I stared at the room. What was I doing? I knew by now, eight months in, that I didn't belong there, in that church. I was not of this suburban world, but according to the Church I was no longer of the monastic world either. I still felt the same fire in my heart that led me to the convent, but the only place I could share it was the monastery. My parishioners didn't get this part of me: they saw a single woman who didn't spend much money, who lived in an almost-empty house alone. They acknowledged neither my sexuality nor my monastic vocation, even when I spoke about them. The friends with whom I might talk about this were not that far away, but I couldn't make myself reach out. My local friends might commiserate, but they didn't get it either.

I was still a nun, but I was incognito—unrecognized by the Church, by my peers, by my parishioners. Before, living with Pat and Colleen, I had been a rescue, like their seven pugs; now I was a true fish out of water, flopping and gasping. I was present in the Church as a priest, but my monastic self was invisible to all but a few.

"No."

"You cannot take my vows from me. You do not have the power, the authority, to release me from these vows. I made them to God. I plan to keep them. Not in the way you recognize, not in the way others can see, but in a way that God will see and I will know."

But how?

Okay, more embarrassing revelations. Not only did I fall for Merton; decades earlier, I fell for Julie Andrews. I watched The Sound of Music *at least once a year; I had it on videocassette. Toward the end, when the Captain proposes to her, Maria says that the Reverend Mother of the abbey always said, "When God closes a door, somewhere He opens a window." (Yes, I'm pretty much line-perfect for this movie.)*

Still, you never force us to climb through. Is there a time limit on these openings? And what if I need a chair, or a hand, to reach the window? Do you provide that too?

Yes.

Chapter Sixteen

Doors and Windows

I MAY HAVE BELIEVED I didn't belong in my former community, but I still had nagging guilty feelings. Was I just unfaithful? I had left the convent, I had left New Mexico, I had left Karen. There was a thread here, and I didn't like what it seemed to be showing me.

The month after I received my dispensation letter, I met with my spiritual director. Jim was a not-so-gentle giant. Severe arthritis and blindness left him with two canes. He looked like a frail old tree, but he had the heart of a towering oak. He was blunt and direct, not bothering with "polite" language when a more forceful word suited him. One of my friends called him "Yoda." He was full of compassion, but he had no interest in enabling or pitying others. He told it like he saw it—and, in spite of his eyes, he saw plenty.

We hobbled up the stairs to his direction space, a sun-filled room with windows on three sides and bookshelves lined with jigsaw puzzles. I sat on the patterned futon couch, and he settled into his old blue-cushioned rocker. I told him about the letter. I started to cry, and reached for the Kleenex.

I said I was unreliable and fickle. Yoda flashed out.

"You had to leave," he said.

"Really?" I could feel my brow furrow. I wanted to hear these words, but they were hard to digest.

"You're like water. If you block its flow, it starts to stink and stagnate."

Brother Andrew had told me that leaving wasn't a sin, but it hadn't sunk in. Now, Jim's words gave me another way of seeing myself and my history. I had grown up in a culture that valued stability, in which the ideal was one (heterosexual) marriage, and one job—or at least one company—for life. I knew that academics sometimes moved around, but they never left academia. And religious? Well, they stayed forever, once they made vows, didn't they? Certainly, in my former community only one person in the last fifty years had left after making life vows.

In my family, I had watched my mother stay with my father for 49 years. For many of them she was miserable, as his drinking took him away from her and made him a hostile stranger. But she never left, even when my brother and I begged her to. She argued that without skills or experience, she couldn't support us. I suspect, though, a deeper reason. She died seven months after him, as though their lives were too tightly bound to be separated.

I had never consciously signed on to this presumption of stability, but some part of me had taken it in. It didn't govern my actions, but it turned out to be a loud voice condemning me when I violated its rules. Now, Jim just cut through the noise and gave me another story.

"I am water."

I had tried to stay still, I'd tried to settle, I'd tried to bloom where I was planted, but if the ground wasn't fertile, or worse, if it was toxic for me, I always found another channel and flowed in another direction. As I repeated the words, I began to be aware of that flow in me. The breeze in the tall grass, the whisper in my ear, the gurgling and coursing water, were all of a piece.

This new perspective didn't instantly shift my internal conversation, but now I had a response to the accusing voice, and I had permission to keep seeking a deeper relationship with God. I didn't know the shape of the container, but I could begin to imagine a future.

If Jim gave me permission to continue on my journey, his friend Bob introduced me to tools that would enable me to not only discern the path, but to create it as I went.

I went to a workshop on spiritual gifts led by two local priests. One of them was new to me. He had 50 years of experience and a desire to share what he had learned. He specialized in healing broken churches, in stabilizing them so a new priest could come into a strong place.

I had been thinking that I needed a coach to help me learn the ropes of parish ministry. Here was this guy, a fifteen-minute drive from me, with a mountain of wisdom and goodwill. He was daunting in his directness, and some found him downright rude, but I could face that. I actually relished his clarity, as I did Jim's.

After the workshop I got his number, and the next week I called him up. "Bob," I said, "I need a priest coach. Are you open to such a thing?"

"What did you have in mind?" he asked. This was the first of many times that Bob would challenge me to take the initiative and form my own agenda, rather than following in his wake.

"I don't know anything. I need to learn about attracting new members, and stewardship campaigns, and organizing things in the parish. And beyond that, I don't know what I need to know."

Those were magic words to him. "I don't know what I don't know, or what I need to know." From Bob, I began to learn the importance of knowing and owning that I don't know things—and not only knowing what I don't know, but knowing that there's a lot I don't know I don't know!

Each time we met, I brought him a particular issue. I didn't leave with a template or a ready-made solution, but I heard a lot of cryptic wisdom that I took home to mull over.

After I'd been in the parish for a year, I found myself stymied in my attempts to connect and move people forward. I was struggling with the question of how long I would stay. I knew it wasn't my home, I knew I still wanted to live in community, but I knew that these two churches were a long way from being settled.

I asked Bob, "How long is a good time to stay? How long does it usually take to prepare them for another person?"

He replied, "That's not the question you need to ask. The real question is, can you love them? If you love them, stay until they're healed. If you don't love them, get out of the way so someone else can."

Wow. As simple as that. I knew pretty soon that I wished them well, I wanted them to succeed, but I didn't really love them, not like they needed loving. And I hadn't let go of living in community. But what was I to do with that? My little voice was silent.

My life was on pause, poised for God to show me the next step.

I get it now, God. I needed more equipment, and more partners, before I could go further. Thank you for teaching me to trust you when things are not moving according to my schedule or in my planned direction. Nothing is wasted.

A few weeks later, Bob told me about a workshop he thought would help me. "It's called 'Making A Difference.' It's for clergy and laypeople engaged in ministry, across faiths. It helps people get clear about what matters to them in their ministry, to get out of their own way to do what they're fired up about. I really think it would be great for you."

Unwittingly, I stepped into a whole new world.

The workshop was not like anything I'd ever been to. We didn't learn tools for our ministry; no handy tips for increasing attendance or giving or impact. It wasn't actually about our ministry at all. It was about us, about what in us was clogging up our vocational arteries. The leaders pushed on the places where previous experience limited what we were willing to risk now, and how those limits shaped how we went about our work. They challenged us to get down to the core of our ministry, beyond plans and titles and outcomes.

At the end, we each had to stand and declare ourselves, not occupationally, as in "I'm a priest," but in words that spoke of our being more fundamentally. I stood and said, "I am a burning and shining light." I wanted to burn and shine God's light. More, in this place, I felt that burning and shining already in me; not as an aspiration or a goal, but already there as a starting place. As I said it, I felt chills, like something in me woke up and volunteered for service. I was alive, all the way down.

Afterward, my friend Mark and I got in his car and returned home. "What the hell was that?" I asked. "What was that truck that ran me over?"

Mark laughed and said, "I don't have a clue."

Over the next weeks, Bob would refer to something from the workshop as we talked about my parish. Gradually, I began to glimpse some possibility. I began to hear how I listened, what I listened for, and what I screened out. And I would return to my final declaration for inspiration. I began talking to others about what I had learned.

The next month, Elizabeth called again. In the year since our last call, a lot had shifted. I had been dispensed from my vows. I knew that parish ministry was not my long-term future, but I still wanted to make something happen at the church. I was a burning and shining light, but I didn't know how to let that light shine.

Elizabeth had gone back to South Africa, and returned.

"Do you want to start a Benedictine women's community here in the U.S.?"

"No. I'm a Jesuit."

Since I had come to the church and I had got to know other priests in the area, I saw a pattern. Every few miles there was an Episcopal Church. At one time, they had been bustling. Now, most were struggling to get by, renting their space for extra income. Their congregations were determined to stay where they were, even as the bills mounted. The largest part of many budgets was the priest: each congregation had its own priest, with pension and health insurance paid at rates determined by the diocese or the larger church. Each priest, in turn, worked alone. Some churches managed to pay a part-time administrator; in the smaller ones, like mine, the priest was the only employee. Congregations were strapped, and clergy were isolated.

What if several priests were willing to live in community, to share one rectory, and serve several churches together? That would enable their churches to do other things with the unused rectories, and the priests would have company in their ministry. The churches would have access to several clergy, so more people could find compatible pastoral care.

I likened this model to the Jesuits because of a conversation I had with the assistant to the Lutheran bishop. He talked a lot about the need to be "nimble," to adjust to the world as it changed. I saw the Jesuits as nimble, with a history of entering "foreign" places and learning how to share the Gospel in ways that resonated with the people there. They were more engaged with the world than the traditional monastic communities.

We need Anglican Jesuits!

Nothing fires me up like a new, unlikely opening. There had to be a new way of doing community, a way that was not stuck in the past, that touched the world more than I had experienced at my former community. So, when Elizabeth called, I said no. I don't want to be a stable, quiet Benedictine. The wound from the convent was still fresh; I wanted nothing that smelled of constraint or enclosure. I was still trying to find ministry in "the world."

"Well," she said, "let's keep talking anyway. I've been in conversation with two other women who live near San Francisco, and they're interested too. Why don't you join us and see if there's anything there?"

A month later, I was on my first Skype call. I met Stacey, a priest, and Liz, a schoolteacher in Oakland. The four of us talked about what we might like to do together and settled on some reading and discussion for a monthly meeting.

By November, we had agreed to get together in person at the monastery for the week after Christmas. Elizabeth and I both knew Don Bisson, a Marist Brother whose community was just down the road, and Elizabeth asked him to facilitate a meeting for us. Don was excited at the thought of a new women's community, and he agreed.

That same fall, I got a call from one of the leaders of the 'Making A Difference' course. She was calling to invite me to apply for the Mastery Foundation School for Leadership.

The Foundation brought its tools to people serving in faith communities like myself, but also to people working in contexts where religion was a source of division. They worked in the United States, Ireland and Northern Ireland, and Israel and Palestine. The three-year course of the School involved an annual five-day gathering in Northern Ireland, another three-day gathering in each region, and regular group calls. Each participant also got coaching from a senior member, mostly people who were successful in business or coaching or organizational development. Everyone offered their time for free because they believed in the work. Still, the School had expenses, so there was a hefty fee.

I was interested, but ouch! I had just begun earning a living again after giving away my money at life profession. How could I do this? Then I calculated: if I were in therapy, I'd likely pay $100 a week. That's $5,000 a year. And therapy was great, but I wanted to build some other muscles. I wanted to manifest what I felt inside me, to free it up to create. The School seemed to offer more of that than therapy.

A month later, I was on my way to Northern Ireland.

I arrived in a foreign country. I don't mean Ireland, although it was that too: I landed in Dublin and found the money exchange, changing dollars into Euros. But the bus was taking me to Northern Ireland, so I needed pounds too. Plane: dollars. Bus and airport: Euros. Taxi: pounds.

But that wasn't the foreign part. I had landed among people unlike any group I'd known before.

My cohort included a Bedouin social worker, a Christian Palestinian school principal, Israeli peace activists, a minister of the Northern Ireland government whose job was to keep the opposing factions talking rather than killing, a singer, and several people who ran businesses, sat on boards, and used their positions to try to heal the rift between Catholics and Protestants. The Americans included a hospice chaplain, a Presbyterian minister, and a Cambodian-American woman who had lived through the Khmer Rouge and was organizing the Cambodian community in Los Angeles. In short, I was in the midst of extraordinary people. I wondered how I got in. They must have been desperate. Apparently, they saw something in me.

I was bedraggled when I arrived. I had caught a cold, and it blossomed that first night. I woke the next morning barely able to breathe, or think. But I had come all this way, and I had spent a pile of money, and I was going to be there. Each day, I went to the daily yoga, the meals, and the classes. I joined in the twice-a-day centering prayer times. Then I went back to my room and collapsed.

I don't know that I managed to take a lot in. The language of the course can be subtle and hard to get even at the best of times, and I was not at my best. But even in my woolly-headedness, I could sense that something big was happening here. In that room, I smelled the possibility that I could do anything I chose, one step at a time, if I dared.

All my life I had lived a contradiction. On the one hand, I had risked my life doing stupid things while drinking or drugging; I had taken the risk of leaving academia; I had left the convent with virtually nothing in my 50s. On the other hand, I had often turned from the sort of challenge that leads to achievement or growth, fearing failure.

Growing up, I had been told to tone it down; to keep safe; to stop scaring people, as if I were too smart and too determined and too direct. As an adult, people said I was intimidating. Here, for the first time, I was surrounded by men and women who were at least as bold and direct and intelligent as I was, and by men who were comfortable with women like that. Everyone was bursting with possibility, and eager to manifest it, and ready to embrace one another's dreams.

For the first time, I felt really welcomed. My intellect was welcome. My enthusiasm was not too much; in fact, others had at least as much as I did. The rooms of recovery had given me a place to share my weaknesses and wounds and to grow into a more complete person. Now, I had a place that demanded my strengths, without denying my vulnerability. I could feel new leaves unfurling.

On the last day, we met our coaches for the year. Ed, my coach, and I would meet every other week on the phone to deepen my use of what I was learning. Through focusing on an area where I would practice, the tools of Mastery would become a reality for me. I would be able to contribute to others more effectively, and to be more alive myself.

I dutifully plotted my course. My practice field was the church. I envisioned a new future for it, in which the two congregations had fully joined together and drawn new people and energy and purpose. I followed the steps outlined for me to declare the vision, to enroll others in it, to develop concrete steps. I was "being a good student," but I didn't feel energized or like much was happening. And, of course, I was talking with Elizabeth, Liz, and Stacey about something else altogether.

After four months of working together on my practicum about the parish, Ed opened my eyes. He asked, "I get where your plans serve the concerns of your parishioners. But where are you in this? Does this fulfill your concerns, the future you want to live into?"

And I knew instantly, and answered: "No."

I'd been doing this for the congregations, to realize my hopes for them. I'd been doing it to look successful, to ward off any feelings of failure. But no, the future I wanted to live into was life in religious community. When I first arrived at the School, I had known that; I had declared, "I am the possibility of new forms of Anglican religious life." But I had forgotten it and used my practicum to "succeed" at something that was not my most basic concern. The church was concrete; a new community was so nebulous I couldn't commit—even as I took steps, with Elizabeth and Stacey and Liz, toward that future.

Once Ed asked me that question, I knew what I had to do. I threw out that practicum and focused on moving toward a new community.

So many hands and chairs helping me reach a new window! Thank you, all of you, for blowing new life into my world. Thank you, God, for all these messengers of your loving creativity. Please make me a messenger in turn. Give me the grace to share the possibility of new life in you.

Bless my readers—you all, you right now—to see the windows awaiting you. Too high up, you say? Ask God for a chair.

The night after Christmas of 2011, I drove to the airport and met Stacey and Liz for the first time.

Stacey was big in frame and in energy; she rowed, and her build showed it. Her silver hair was distinctively styled, with one side cut close to her head and the other hanging straight past her ear. She bounded over with a big grin on her face.

Liz was softer, more rounded, with long dark hair. She brought a quiet focus quite different from Stacey's extraverted enthusiasm. In person, in the small space of a car, I got much more awareness of them than I had via the internet. These were two powerful women, women who loved their work and ministry, but also wanted spiritual community. I couldn't wait to see what we might create together.

We had arranged to meet Elizabeth at a diner right off the New York Thruway. We pulled in, got out of the car, and immediately took our first group photo, standing in the parking lot under the diner's lighted yellow sign.

Our excitement carried us through the awful food—bad hamburger patties, wilted iceberg lettuce. The waiter tried to flirt with us until he saw us holding hands and saying grace.

After dinner, we headed to the monastery and straggled off to our assigned rooms. I tossed all night; what were we doing? What was I doing?

On the next morning, we gathered in the small private room assigned for our work together. The Brothers were gradually converting the room and the one next to it into a library, so hammers and drills punctuated our conversation. Don was there, with an easel and flip-chart for making notes.

He began at the beginning: What did we desire? What did we dream of that had led us to come together? As we each talked, we began to see common threads. By the fourth day, we had a list of things that mattered to us. We wanted to foster the spiritual journeys of all people, not only Christians. We wanted to use contemporary technology to connect people who wouldn't ordinarily meet. We wanted to foster inclusive, expansive images of the Divine. And we wanted to uphold women who served, lay and ordained, in the current context of declining church resources.

We were fired up, ready to keep meeting and talking. Our goal was residential community, but we hadn't fleshed out any of that. We agreed that in April, Elizabeth and I would fly out to California, and we all would meet again. Don was planning to be out there, and he agreed to meet with us for one of those days. We were on our way!

Over these days, other guests started to notice these four women and a man going into this room. We began getting questions and requests: "Are you starting a new Episcopal community?" "I've thought about joining community but never found one that fit." "Can I come listen?" We said, "We don't even know what we're doing yet. Stay tuned." We became celebrities of a sort for the week, women doing something exciting. And we, in turn, heard the possibility of others coming—when we were ready.

Somehow, I knew my time in the parish was short.

In February, Liz decided to leave the group. She realized that teaching high school in Oakland was her true vocation, and she wanted to give her energy to her students. So now it was Elizabeth, Stacey, and me. As Jesus says, wherever two or more are gathered in his name—it's enough.

Things got more complicated when we met in San Francisco. Stacey still wanted to belong to a community with us, but she didn't want to leave California or her work as a parish priest. Elizabeth and I didn't want to lose her, so we began talking about how we could make this work. We decided that our commitment to use technology could make this viable somehow.

When we met with Don, we told him where things stood. He didn't seem optimistic that our plan would work, but he didn't try to deter us. He referred to a classic definition of residential community: "One kitchen, one roof," and asked whether any of us wanted to go forward with that. Elizabeth and I nodded. He didn't rule out our attempt at long-distance community, but urged us to focus on getting started with the residential part.

In June, we returned to the monastery. We wanted to be with the Brothers while they were in their annual chapter, to get their advice.

Again, we went to the diner. We had the same bad hamburgers, the same waiter, and vowed that we wouldn't eat here on future trips.

Our top agenda item was choosing a name for the new community.

Liz had dubbed us "ORCS": The Order of Really Cool Sisters. But that wasn't really going to work . . . so, what would we call ourselves?

We wanted a name that made clear our feminist commitment. We also wanted words that didn't imply the tight boundary between "insiders" and "outsiders": words like "order," even "community," seemed to signal such boundaries. So, we generated some candidates and began to pray.

The next morning, we met with the Brothers. Thirty-five men listened as we told them of our dream. "What's the name of your community?" they asked. We looked at one another and raised our eyebrows. "We don't know yet," Stacey said. "We're praying about that." "What Rule will you follow?" "We don't know yet." I could see some of them looking a bit baffled. Everyone belongs somewhere, in some tradition, don't they? But they themselves had begun in 1887 without a Rule; eventually their founder wrote one, which they followed until they adopted the Benedictine Rule in 1985.

Finally, the Superior asked, "What do you want from us?" We looked at one another. Elizabeth answered, "We want your blessing." Brother Roy stood up, and everyone followed. They all stood and gathered around us. Those closest laid hands on us, and the others laid hands on them, to form a human chain. The Superior prayed, and we all said, "Amen."

Everyone stepped back and grinned. I looked at the faces around me, faces I'd known for years, and saw the love and the hope on them. Andrew grabbed me and hugged me. I was once again with people who understood—who shared—my desire to center my life in the quest for God. I was beginning to become legible again.

We returned to our little meeting room and took up the question of a name. We looked at the possibilities we had generated the day before, and we instantly knew which one was ours: The Companions of Mary the Apostle.

Mary Magdalene turned out to be our matron saint. In the years since I had entered the convent, her position in the church had grown.

The old stories about her being a prostitute had been challenged (though many still had heard them). Her history of "possession" and healing was a powerful sign of what God could do. She followed Jesus at great personal cost, right up to the cross. She was the first witness to the resurrection.

Writings, long lost and recently discovered, made her even more central to Jesus' ministry. According to these new sources, she was Jesus' closest disciple, sent to teach the others.

She seemed the perfect foremother to our desire to proclaim resurrection and healing, as well as women's place in the Church.

I realized later that I began my recovery journey on Mary Magdalene's feast day, July 22, in 1985. It turned out she had been there, all the way back.

And "Companions"? Well, it was less bounded than words like "society" or "community." We wanted a more porous line between "in" and "out" than traditional communities had. Companions may or may not live together, they may not all live in the same way, but they are bonded. They travel together. They share bread (com + pan, bread).

So: Companions of Mary the Apostle, sent to proclaim resurrection to a world and a church that fear death and decline. I felt the curious melding of past and future, the threads of my life beginning to blend into a new tapestry. My past struggles were becoming a platform for potential ministry. My "Jesuit" desire to serve was blending with the more "Benedictine" thread of settled monastic life. Perhaps these did not have to be opposed.

The Brothers agreed to rent us the tiny house at the top of their winding driveway. Elizabeth's lease ran out in September, so she would move then. I decided to stay with my churches until the end of the year to help them transition.

Ah, my churches.

In between our spring meetings, people were dying. I had to leave our June meeting early to perform a funeral. The deaths echoed the larger decline in the churches. All around me, I was seeing the end of an era for these churches and for the "mainline" denominations as a whole. I saw, too, the emotional and physical and financial toll on members trying to keep a shrinking church going.

My contract was due to expire in March 2013. The two churches and I were supposed to be engaging in mutual discernment about whether I would continue. I was pretty sure I wouldn't, but until our plans were firm, I didn't feel I could be sure. The two church bodies seemed to be assuming I would continue; it's a hassle to find someone else, and things are fine, aren't they?

The "normal" way clergy leave churches is to give a couple of months between announcing and leaving. This gives time for some preparation, but doesn't draw out the suspense. Once someone has announced their departure, their agenda basically stops: they're a lame duck. Plus, people's emotions go wild, whether it's grief or anger or fear of the future.

Ah, but I knew better. I couldn't keep quiet. These people were discerning in good faith. If I knew I was not going to stay, I reasoned, I needed to let them know so they could look into the future realistically. Perhaps this would push them to really consider the big questions: did they want to continue together? Did they want to officially close the Lutheran Church and become a sort of hybrid? Did they want to have one clergy person or two half-time people? Who were they, and who did they want to be?

I thought they should know now, six months before I planned to leave.

It didn't go well.

There was a lot I didn't know about being a parish leader, and I didn't know I didn't know. I made the announcement to the whole congregation, not telling the wardens or council leader first. I had struggled to build relationships with the wardens, and I just didn't think to take them into my confidence. I was still living in an old world where I was alone and independent.

I told everyone my hope, that they would now really move toward discerning their larger futures. I soon learned I had no power to move things forward anymore. Worse than a lame duck, I was in the way. I had thought I could lead them to do the work they needed to do, but I learned that my days of leading them were over. Sure enough, I should have left sooner or announced later.

Aiee! I'm finally beginning to learn that there is wisdom in experience, and I should pay attention.

Finally, on the last Sunday in 2012, I said goodbye to the two churches. What I found left me stunned.

People who had never come to me for help or invited me into their homes told me how important I had been to them. One couple came over with their two-year-old daughter. I had baptized her. She reached greedily for the consecrated wafer at every Eucharist. Now, her parents told me that whenever they drove near the church, she wanted to come in. She wanted the wafer, and she wanted to see me. Jeff said, "Thank you for being such a loving presence here. We're so sorry to see you go. Shannan especially—we don't know how to explain it to her."

Really? I'd tried to reach out, but never got in the door of their family. I'd had their son in Youth Group, but I had no idea I had connected.

On it went: Danielle, the 10-year-old acolyte I had danced with to Lady Gaga; David, the 13-year-old energy bundle, another dance partner. These I understood and loved. But I hadn't felt connected to the adults. Anything I had felt for them, or they for me, had gone unexpressed, even unfelt, until the time of leaving. Perhaps, when the fear of future intimacy was over, I could feel affection. Perhaps the same was true for them.

I walked back into the church, where Rich and Sue remained in their pew. Rich had been there from long before my arrival, for decades: he was our self-appointed handyman, willing to work on things whether he had experience or not: garage doors, boilers, whatever needed a little help. Rich and I had spent a lot of time together, sometimes talking buildings, sometimes talking about personal and spiritual matters.

Sue and I had had some hard moments, but we'd also had some

mysterious trust between us. She had recently told me that I was the first woman priest from whom she had received Communion: there had been a woman there before, an assistant, but Sue managed never to receive Communion from her. She was not fully on board with the direction of the church, but she was trying.

As I approached, Rich turned to me and grinned. He said, "You were our most spiritual priest." He meant it as a compliment, but I suddenly understood the gap I had felt between me and the congregation.

I had preached about God, about prayer, about living a life centered on our relationship with God. A lot of priests focus more on contemporary issues, on social justice and service. There's nothing wrong with that. But I talked about God and prayer. I invited them to prayer, to worship, to retreat and reflection; I took them to the monastery and to the Cloisters in New York City. I went to places that are foreign territory for a lot of faithful church-goers. I lived like a nun, in my sparsely furnished house, and I talked like a nun to people who weren't looking for a monastery.

As I left, I felt I had missed something big—some place where my love of God, and my love of them, might actually have been connecting without my knowing it. I had missed the connection. I never landed there, really, never made a home—if there was a home for me to make there. I was a fish out of water, but something real and powerful had happened in that place.

Now, as I went out the door and drove up the Palisades Parkway, I began to realize what I had missed. I tried to trust that God was somehow at work in that. Had I thrived there, had I been able to help them thrive, I might have buried that part of me. I prayed to pay attention to love and to let myself be led.

Thank you all. I believe I brought some gifts to you, but I'm more certain that you enabled me to settle and find a new direction. I learned so much from my time with you, knowledge that serves me as I work with people in parishes. I am a more effective spiritual director and companion because of you. Bless you as you continue to worship together.

Chapter Seventeen

Building the Container

FROM THE UPSTAIRS WINDOWS of the Companionary, I can see the Hudson. A ten-minute walk down the hillside, and my feet are wet. I'm surrounded by trees. The bells of the monastery ring across the fields. Before they begin their day, the wrens and cardinals, the indigo buntings and finches, have begun their chant. I can't wait to get up each morning.

I arrived at the little house on the Hudson. Three days later, we joined the monks in their annual winter retreat of five days. After three days of settling in, Elizabeth and I entered into silence. I developed a terrible cold and spent most of the retreat in bed, sneezing and blowing. Some new beginning! Beneath my cold, though, I was relieved and excited. Another chance to live the life I felt called to! A chance to build a contemporary women's community, a place where I, and others, could express all of our selves.

I had a lovely bedroom, large and full of morning sun, looking out on a grove of maples and oaks. I had room for my bed, my beloved Papasan chair, and a tiny desk that Pat and Colleen had given me. The walls were that neutral beige that people paint when they won't be living there, but that was fine; I was used to bare walls. Eventually, I would get out some pictures and make a home here.

After the retreat ended, we began to dream. All we knew was that we both wanted to live in community, to pray, and to see how to serve. We knew we needed a plan of formation for ourselves. Don had offered to help us with this, but the final choices were our own. I had books, and I had experience in religious life. Elizabeth had 40 years connected to the monastery, five of them in residence alongside them. Stacey had been close to the Brothers in California for decades, so she knew the outlines of religious life.

Elizabeth and I started following a monastic schedule of prayer based on the Brothers' pattern: Matins at 7 a.m., Eucharist with the Brothers at 9, Diurnum (noonday prayer) at 12, followed by lunch at the monastery, back for Vespers at 5, and Compline at home at 8. We observed the Great Silence from after Compline until breakfast, so we had quiet time to sleep, pray, and reflect.

I began to notice my previous formation when it ran counter to Elizabeth's experience at the monastery. I had whole psalms, whole cycles of psalms, burned into my brain. Now, we had different psalms, a different cycle. While both communities shared ancient hymns, St. Helena had modernized and adapted some verses. To this day, if I close my eyes while singing these hymns, I'm likely to use the "old" words. I still associate certain psalms with certain plainchant tones for singing; I not only know the words, I know the tune for each verse.

I had been using the St. Helena Breviary with this new cycle since coming to my parish, but it was different praying with Elizabeth. Saying things out loud with another makes them vivid in a way that solo silent prayer can sometimes evade. Now the differences, though tiny, took on meaning for me. "This was how 'we' did it"; I had left the convent, but I found I was still identifying with that community. It would take quite a while for my "we" to shift to "they."

Outside of offices, there were all the other adjustments that go with living with others. Sharing a kitchen and a bathroom demands patience and tolerance. After three years of living alone, I was in a new situation. I knew about living alone and making decisions on my own. I knew about entering other people's space and learning to fit in. But this, this truly mutual decision-making about furniture, meals, visitors—everything—this I had not done since Karen and I had separated.

This time was even different from that. Elizabeth and I weren't lovers. We didn't have a strong personal connection or even much knowledge of the other. We had spent a total of less than a month together, in four-day chunks, before we jumped into this new arrangement. We were joined by purpose, not by affinity.

This was actually a good place for me to start. My intimacy issues were less likely to be provoked. I could gradually grow into a relationship that was not about Elizabeth and me, but about God, her, me, and any others who might share our life. It offered the emotional distance I needed to develop trust.

Into this new landscape, I brought my experience in living religious life. I had practice in organizing life in a way that others might join, in living in silence with others, in following patterns. Most especially, I had experience living with vows that reflected values: values of simplicity, of listening, of devotion to God first and foremost. I brought my understanding of these, but I was not in a position to dictate what they meant in our context. I had years of experience, but I had to jettison some of it to meet Elizabeth as a partner. I had to allow myself to be new again. I watched her work to claim her own vision and understanding in the face of my certainty. It was an uneasy balancing act, but we kept going. Elizabeth was forthright, initiating conversations that I might have avoided, so she pushed us along the path of relationship.

We were on fire. We'd start talking at breakfast, and the next thing we knew, we'd be deep in some project, the dishes forgotten on the table. Elizabeth started to tease me because I'd begin each day with "I've been thinking . . ." Elizabeth, for her part, "wondered" a lot. The next thing we knew, we'd be rearranging our tiny chapel, or the guest room. We might start writing up plans for ministries or projects we wanted to start. It might be about what books to read next. Whatever it was, it wasn't the dishes.

We read books and articles on the state of religious life, and on the Rules of various communities, to see how we wanted to orient ourselves. We didn't feel called to follow any existing Rule, so we listened for pointers to help us write our own.

Of course, we couldn't make decisions about community structure or formation on our own. Stacey was still in the mix, meeting with us for an hour a week on Google Hangouts. Quickly we began to absorb our first lesson: founding a community takes more than an hour a week. We could broach a topic for discussion, but Stacey's schedule didn't allow us to really sit and ponder together. Plus, we were living very different lives. Trying to write a Rule or make plans based on two different contexts was more than we could handle. Frustration simmered within me.

In January, Stacey flew out to be with us, and we made the first public declaration of our intention to live this new life. We thought of it as a postulancy service, asking for six months to explore and learn whether we wanted to continue. It was not, exactly, postulancy, though. We weren't learning about an existing community; we were building a new one as we lived it. As one of our School for Leadership mentors said, we were building the plane as we flew. We wrote the service in Mastery form, as a declaration rather than a request. We declared ourselves learners in the Companions of Mary the Apostle.

In the chapel at the monastery with one of the Brothers and a Sister from another Episcopal community, we followed the familiar form: "What do you desire?" This time I answered, "I desire to know God and serve God with my whole being. I desire to walk with others on the road of discipleship and to learn about life as a Companion of Mary the Apostle." Then I declared my commitment to "live for six months in simplicity, celibacy, and accountability to my companions"—updating the traditional vows of poverty, chastity, and obedience to name the spirit of each vow. Elizabeth and Stacey made the same commitment, and the gathered community prayed for us to be guided and to persevere.

We were Companions! For now.

Three weeks later, Stacey told us that she was stepping away. She had realized that she couldn't immerse herself in creating this community from a distance while serving a parish full-time.

In one way, I was relieved. I had seen the unworkability of our current way of being, and I couldn't see a way to overcome it.

But another part of me was terrified: just two of us? I would never have done this with just one other person, especially one I hardly knew! Three was small, but at least it was three. Two sounded less like a community than a partnership. Coyote giggled.

Another fear was more concrete. After working for three years, I had enough savings to last a year and a half. If we didn't start earning money or receiving donations, I'd have to find "outside" work, work with a salary. I didn't like that thought, but for now, it was out in the future.

I prayed, and my fear subsided. God knew that we wouldn't have started if there were only two of us, so She cleverly lured us by giving us companions until we had committed. Somehow, I believed—hoped—the money would appear. For now, we were set in this house, invited to create.

But what was our long-term future? For that matter, what was our short-term future? What was God leading us to?

A month later, a woman knocked on the door of our little house. She was tall and slim. Chin-length gray hair framed her face, a face that seemed to have seen a lot. I'd seen her around the monastery a bit, but we hadn't met yet.

"Hi, I'm Amy. Can I talk to you?"

"Of course!" We sat down, the three of us almost filling our tiny living room.

Amy and her husband had recently moved to Newburgh, about a half hour away, to join a small community dedicated to serving people living with homelessness. Together, they ran a day shelter, served food, and arranged for beds overnight. Amy had been involved with this work in Connecticut before they moved, but she was excited to be part of a residential community that met her passion for ministry.

"I love what you're doing," she said. "It's really inspiring to see women starting a new community."

Then Amy came to the point. "Let me tell you why I came to you. I just completed four years of EfM (Education for Ministry, an Episcopal program to equip laypeople with knowledge of Scripture, church history, and theology, and practice at thinking theologically). I loved my group, both the learning and the community. Now that I'm done, I don't have a structure for any of that. I want you to start a group."

We looked at each other for a second. I could feel my eyebrows raise a bit.

"What kind of group?"

"I want a group for women to share deeply and grow in the love of God, a place to renew ourselves for ministry. I think you two might be the people to host such a thing."

Wow. I thought about what we had said we wanted to be about: supporting people's spiritual journeys, fostering women's authority, connecting people, offering inclusive visions of the Divine. This seemed to have room for all of that. It seemed to me that the Holy Spirit had just knocked on our door.

I wanted to jump up and say, "Yes! Yes, let's do this!" But I knew we needed to talk. *Festina lente*, as Elizabeth always said—make haste slowly. So instead, I waited for her cue.

"This sounds exciting," she said. "Can we think about it and get back to you?"

"Of course," Amy said. She gave us her phone and email, and we said goodbye.

I turned to Elizabeth, gobsmacked. "What was that?" I asked.

"That was the Holy Spirit," she replied.

"Yup. That's what I thought. HHS!"

Oh, I need to explain that. Somewhere in our first gatherings, one of us exclaimed: "Hallelujah! Holy shit!" We agreed it expressed exactly how we felt: jubilation and trepidation in one package. It had become a shorthand phrase for those times when we saw some big new opening, when we needed to acknowledge our terror and excitement. This was definitely an HHS moment.

Two weeks later, we hosted our first gathering for women. That's what we decided to call it; a gathering. Not a class, or a society, or a program. A gathering. Every other Friday at 3, we would meet for shared conversation and worship.

Elizabeth had been connected to two local churches for years, and I had begun to do priestly supply work, so I was meeting some people. We put out the word via our brand-new Constant Contact account. We had no idea who would come.

Our living room could comfortably hold four people. The tiny kitchen afforded two more chairs, and we could fit a few people on cushions. By the end of a month, 15 women crowded into our little space. And it worked, in a way: we got very familiar with one another! The feeling of welcome grew quickly.

We had heard from many women that they would like to participate, but work prevented them from joining us on Friday afternoons. In response, we scheduled a gathering for a Saturday afternoon. Knowing the limits of our living room, we reserved a space at the monastery. That was a good move: 25 women showed up! We followed our familiar format for part of the meeting, but another part was given to sharing about the new community for those who had questions.

We had drafted a covenant, rather than a Rule; we had learned that many people are allergic to the word "rule." The covenant named three faces of love that we saw as the ground of the traditional vows. Chastity, as we saw it, is about love of God. We give ourselves to God above all others, letting that love fuel us to love and serve one another and others. We had a section listing commitments that followed from that, such as daily prayer and worship. Poverty we connected to love of creation, not using more than is needed. We listed recycling and composting, buying with a view to sustainability, and maintenance of what we possess. "Obedience" translates the Latin for "listen," focused not so much on submission as on honoring the divine in others. The covenant included practices of reconciliation, forgiveness and apology, respectful listening, and honoring authority within the community.

It was a long, challenging list. The covenant concluded with the acknowledgment that we would fall short, and a pledge to keep trying and to ask forgiveness.

As we shared the covenant with the group, several people said, "I want to live like this!" They started to ask, "How can we be with you without becoming residential members?"

This possibility hadn't occurred to me, to us, but it was exciting. We wanted to make something new; and here these women were inviting us, asking us, to do that. By the end of the gathering, a "dream team" had formed to follow up on this idea. In July they met, and dreaming began.

By now we had several balls in the air. In the spring, we had formed a non-profit corporation in order to receive donations and also to divest ourselves from private ownership; from now on, all we received went to the Companions. In place of the traditional chapter, we had a Board of Directors, made up of friends with spiritual wisdom and organizational savvy. So, they were one circle. Then, there was the community of women gathering, some of whom wanted a more formal connection. Another circle.

Then there were the people reading our newsletter and following our Facebook page. I had begun the newsletter almost as soon as we started, and people were signing up. Now we were connecting in one way or another with more and more people. It felt good.

It also felt a bit confusing. The same conflicting impulses that confused me in New Jersey were back. I wanted to pray; at the same time, I was on fire to organize, to build something. Now in my second year in the School of Leadership, I wanted to show "results." My head hurt, trying to make sense of all the different shoots of growth.

As we responded to the desires of the "dreamers," we began to see a bigger picture of what the Companions could be. We saw the possibility of an intentional, dispersed community for ongoing formation as Christians. We studied some models and visited a few communities, and we plotted how to move forward, thinking about communications, funding, facilities, discernment, liturgy, and, centrally, the values leading us to conversion of life. By November, we had a plan: we would begin a monthly covenant group to study the covenant together, to live by the covenant, and, eventually, to lead other groups.

More questions arose in that first year. We had begun by seeing ourselves as an Episcopal women's community. By May 2013, though, we had our first challenge. Jenny, a UCC pastor, was a regular at the gatherings. She asked, "Could I be a member?"

Huh. Clearly, she could belong to the gathering and to the covenant group. But would we admit non-Episcopalians to vowed life, to full membership? We still weren't clear whether we wanted to be recognized by the Episcopal Church. In order to be "official," communities had to have as members only Episcopalians or other members of the Anglican Communion. But what were the advantages of being official? We weren't sure yet. So we said, "We don't know."

The next month, a trans man I knew asked if he was included. I wanted to say, "Of course!" But my voice was no longer my own; I needed to consult with Elizabeth. I said something like, "We want to connect with you in some way, but we don't know the exact shape yet."

In fact, "We don't know" became one of our catchphrases for the next few years. I grew to revel in it; it freed me from needing to provide answers, or sounding like I have answers, when I'm unclear. For our new community, it signaled that anyone who wanted to join with us should be prepared to live with uncertainty.

We had none of the things that people often associate with monastic communities. The two questions we heard most frequently were: "What is your habit?" and "What Rule are you following?" Everyone who knew something about Anglican religious life "knew" that communities have habits, and that they live by a certain Rule handed down—Benedict's Rule or Augustine's Rule or somebody's. We didn't have habits yet (though we made some attempts), and we didn't want to just adopt someone else's Rule, so we had to say either "We don't know" or "We don't know yet."

And then: "Where is your monastery/convent?" Well, we live in a little house. There's room for one more person. Oh, and we don't have an endowment, so you'd need to bring an income, at least a modest one, with you.

In short, we didn't have what most people were looking for when they got ideas about monastic community life. What we did have was what I had asked for: time to pray and someone to pray with.

That first fall, the fall of 2013, one of the Brothers told me a story. He had been to an event in New York City and ran into some of my former Sisters. He referred to me as "Sister Shane," and one of them balked. "She's not a nun!" she exclaimed. He replied that we declared ourselves to be nuns, and everyone referred to us as Sisters. "Well, anyone can *call* themselves a nun," she replied.

His story stung. I wondered why he needed to tell me this story. Did he not see that it could be hurtful to me? Or did he secretly agree with her and want to share the message from a distance? I didn't know.

Then I thought, she's right! Anyone *can* call themselves a nun! No one has the authority to withhold this name from me! Others may not acknowledge it, I may not be on any official church roster, but I know what I am. I knew that throughout the history of the Church there had been women who had gathered together without Church sanction, living under vows unacknowledged by "the authorities." I was proud to find myself in that lineage.

This awareness actually made my vocation more precious and real to me. I was following as faithfully as I knew how. I was striving to live the vows I had made, in this new way and place. Without an official stamp of approval, my stand for this vocation became its own solid ground. We were creating the container, as hundreds of people had done before us.

"Monk" derives from a word that means "one." A monk, or a nun, is someone whose single-hearted devotion belongs to God. While churches may officially acknowledge some people as monks or nuns, many people live their lives in this way, alone or with others, with no official sanction.

I was—I am—a nun, a monk, as surely as the Desert Mothers and

Fathers, as surely as the Beguines and other women who refused to be cloistered. Many of them risked persecution for their independence. We merely "suffered" from our lack of access to the Church Insurance Company.

If some sniffed at our project, others did acknowledge my vocation. Don, who helped us to get started and guided our formation, believed that our call was authentic. A Jungian, he was enthralled with the prospect of what he called "a fully conscious women's community," committed to inter- and intra-personal growth (no pressure there!). He stood for us, reminding us that God had called us. Our spiritual directors and those we ministered to saw us as "nuns." We didn't need an official stamp from a Church body.

Psst. Yes, you. Does this stir something in you? Have you been waiting for someone to authorize you to follow God or to give you a stamp of approval? Or maybe it's lack of resources, of financial certainty, that holds you back. Whatever. Just roll this around. Your desire is enough. God loves the search, the hunger. Let it lead you.

When Elizabeth and I moved in together, there was a lot we didn't know about each other. I found out quickly that she didn't eat wheat or sugar; she was fine with artificial sweeteners and gluten-free treats, but she didn't touch many of the things I loved. No matter; I got regular sugar fixes down at the monastery, where they had desserts on Sundays and feast days and cookies by the coffeepot. But still, Elizabeth's choices impacted me. It turned out that she, too, attended a 12-Step program, one that I had been advised to try back in the 1990s. I had gone to one meeting, but I didn't identify with the people I saw there: "I'm not that bad." I never went back.

I had put on a lot of weight since then. I'd lost it through Weight Watchers, but I didn't keep it off. I spent most of my sober years in the neighborhood of 200 pounds. I thought, "So what? I'm sober, I'm not smoking. I get some exercise. So, I carry some extra weight; no one's perfect."

As I talked with Elizabeth, as we shared the occasional story, I began to see the parallels between alcoholism and compulsive eating. She would share about a behavior, some incident, and I'd say, "I drank like that." My drinking was like her eating—or, her eating was like my drinking. We shared a path of recovery, but with distinctive foci.

There was a problem, though. I wanted chocolate. I was used to chocolate candy, or ice cream, every day. Living alone, I had graduated to buying large gift boxes of Russell Stover candy, lying to the clerk about how I was buying them for parishioners (as though she cared), hiding them in my pantry in case someone stopped by—I didn't want to share them! I had my lonely life with a solitary chocolate habit.

Now I was living with someone, and that someone didn't eat chocolate. I began buying candy bars when I was out and eating them in the car. I'd find ways to dispose of the wrappers or hide what was left. Gradually, I was able to confront the fact that this wasn't normal.

One day, I was driving home from New Paltz, eating my candy bar, when a radio show began talking about diabetes. I had never worried about diabetes before; I hadn't really thought about whether I ate more sugar than other people. As I listened, I began to get nervous. So, I wasn't diabetic yet, but I knew that I sometimes suffered low blood sugar. I began to wonder if I was in danger. I began to get that I ate a lot of sugar, more than other people.

Still, I wasn't ready to take action. All around, people encouraged me to share their delight in food. Brother Andrew would always say, "Would you like me to get you another?" Brother Rafael and I would take a bite and roll our eyes at each other, signaling the rush on our tongues. Eating was—is—a communal bonding event as much as nourishment.

And, underneath all that, I was just terrified. I had given up alcohol and drugs and cigarettes—I couldn't give up anything else!

God had to step in. I guess She'd been stepping in already, in her sneaky way, or I wouldn't have even been thinking about this. But I needed a pull as well as a push.

It came over New Year's. In Albuquerque, I always attended an Alkathon over New Year's Eve. These are all-day, all-night events to help people stay sober over holidays like Thanksgiving, Christmas, and New Year's. I loved going at 2 or 3 in the morning, when the streets were deserted, and sitting in a folding chair and drinking bad coffee (and, of course, munching on something from the heavily laden food table). I loved the gratitude that I heard from those who showed up. I wanted that experience again.

Rather than find a local Alkathon, I decided to offer a retreat for people in all the 12-Step programs. It turned out that one of the Brothers used to lead such a retreat, but he died in 2006, and no one else had picked it up, so there was an opening. I called it "Welcoming the New Year." We began on the evening of December 30 and ran through midday on January 1.

When the retreat began, I asked people to introduce themselves and include whatever 12-Step groups they belonged to. Two women identified as alcoholics and as compulsive overeaters. I didn't think much of it at the time, but as the retreat went on, my ears opened. Jean talked about the similarities between her craving for alcohol and that for food, the mental obsession that led her to focus on the table rather than the people she was with. She recalled isolating to eat. She described her attempts to control it, and her failures.

Suddenly I got it. I remembered my friend in Massachusetts saying, "If you have to control it, it's out of control." That was the phrase that broke through my denial about my drinking. I had struggled for control for years, though mostly, I had just accepted that I would drink, blackout, and do awful things.

Now I saw that I had been doing the same thing with food. I tried desperately to contain myself within my latest pair of jeans. I tried to eat sane portions of healthy food. But more often than not, I could not overcome the craving and the obsession. When I thought about the craving, I felt a tightness in my chest. I remembered that I had that same tightness when I used to "need" a drink, when I was headed for one. It's a physical craving, carrying with it a feeling of desperation. I had to have that piece of cake, just like I used to need a drink.

"Oh shit," I thought. I'm a compulsive overeater. Now what? What does that mean? What do I need to do about it?

The day after the retreat ended, we went into our annual winter retreat. I had a week of silence in which to ponder this terrifying new realization. I began to notice my feelings and thoughts a bit more. Sure enough, they were familiar from my drinking. When the retreat ended, I went to a meeting.

It was so strange! I had been in recovery for 28 years, but I was a newcomer too. I knew the Steps, the spirituality around the program, I had a Higher Power, but I was just now beginning to see the shape of this other issue in my life. Walking into that room felt as vulnerable as when I first got sober. But people were friendly, and I knew one person, so I didn't feel completely alone. I took some pamphlets home to read.

There was a pamphlet with lots of sample food plans. This was a new phrase to me—"food plan." Is this a diet? The pamphlet said no. It's a pattern of eating for life, a pattern that allows me to rest free from the compulsion. But there's no one plan: some people need five little meals a day, some people eat three larger ones. Some people have a snack, some people don't. It would be up to me to find out what worked for me.

I didn't have a sponsor, someone to guide me, so I decided to just try a plan. I decided I would eat three meals a day, anything I wanted, but nothing in between. I had been a snacker, a grazer, for years, so this seemed pretty ambitious, but doable.

I couldn't do it.

I'd have my big lunch—the monastery's main meal, dinner really—at 12:30. By 4:00, I'd be thinking about whatever dessert was lying on the counter in the pantry. We went down for Vespers each day at 5:00, and it would be easy to go a little early and pick up something. Some days, there wouldn't be any dessert but there might be a nice loaf of bread.

My craving was up. Some days, I'd hang on and make it to dinner, but my knuckles were in danger of going permanently white.

I knew I needed a sponsor to help me. I looked and listened at the meetings I went to. Finally, I heard someone I liked, someone who seemed gentle. I thought she'd be easier to work with than some of the people I heard who were really strict, measuring and weighing their food, no this, no that. I wanted someone who would help me without asking too much.

Sneaky, trickster, Coyote God. I asked Ramona to be my sponsor. She agreed to talk with me about it.

Early in the morning of February 27, 2014, I called her. I told her how I was trying and not succeeding. She asked me one question:

"How much recovery do you want?"

Well, put that way, it seemed clear. "I want it all."

"Okay then, here's what I'd like you to do." And in her gentle, patient voice, she shook me to my core. Follow the food plan she would send me: No sugar, no refined flour. No artificial sweeteners except stevia. No fruit juice or dried fruit, nothing to mess with my blood sugar. Tons of vegetables. Weigh and measure my food, to head off the disease of "more."

That was just the beginning. I had to read program literature every day and write on it. I had to send her my writing. Two phone calls to other people in recovery every day (I talked her down from three). Talk to her three times a week. Report every day on how my food went, what I planned to eat, phone calls I'd made.

Ramona turned out to be one of the people I feared! Oh, my precious Jesus. No way could I do this. But I'd said I wanted it all.

"Okay," I said.

Ramona promised that if I did these things, my life would open up. "You are going to enjoy your food in a whole new way," she said. "There is a lot of wonderful, healthy food waiting for you to discover. This is not the end." But more than food, she promised that I would find friends and experience joy and serenity in a way I had not yet done.

Right. Sure.

I couldn't see another way, so I decided to try.

I sat in terror until the bell rang for Eucharist. I went down to the monastery and approached the chapel. Brother Bernard was by the entrance. I went up to him, grabbed his arm, and said, "Pray for me." He smiled and hugged me and sent me into the chapel.

How can I ever thank you, Ramona? You have been my precious guide for ten years now. Everything you said is true—about food, about my habits and thoughts and struggles. Now, I share your wisdom, and people treat me as wise. I share your patience and gentleness (well, not fully), your careful, loving attention. Thank you for being a (Jewish) face of Christ for me.

I soon found that the food itself was not so hard as the social challenges that arose. Before, dinner with the Brothers had been a nice time together. Now, one of the Brothers would try to get me to eat dessert, and he looked sad when I said no. Well, not sad exactly; he'd shrug his round shoulders and look at me with that sort of embarrassed look that people get when they're doing something they suspect isn't so good in front of people who aren't sharing in their guilty pleasure. It was a sort of helpless look, an "I can't help it" look, warding off potential judgment. I knew that look; I had worn it for years.

Andrew had a different reaction. True to form, he was blunt and clear. He made known that what I was doing was stupid and excessive.

"What's wrong with a little pleasure? I think you're being rigid." I stared back at him, this man I loved and I knew loved me, and said, "Would you say that if it was alcohol?" That shut him up, but it didn't mollify him. He sat up and stiffened his spine. Then he ate his cake and glared at me.

After a year on my food plan, I had lost 70 pounds—one third of my earlier body weight. I was back to what I weighed in my 20s, before I got sober and started eating sugar and driving instead of walking and biking.

I haunted the Salvation Army, as my size changed every two months. After years of hating to shop, to confront my growing girth, I looked forward to these trips. I liked seeing muscles gain definition as the fat around them shrank. I liked feeling that I didn't need to hide my stomach. I liked feeling strong and energetic again.

As I lost weight, a weird thing happened. I began to turn into a girl.

I had always struggled with gender. Whether I identified as straight or lesbian or queer, I had never really reconciled with femininity. I'd been a "tomboy"; I'd worn "masculine" clothes long before I came out. I had definitely been on the butch end of the spectrum in more ways than my clothes. I had a period of real confusion in the late 1990s as trans people began to come out.

Now, I was being drawn to clothes I'd never worn before. I could fit in women's sizes, unless the legs or sleeves were too short. I bought a pair of crops—the first in my life. Then I bought another. I bought women's T-shirts. I bought a cardigan sweater.

I liked how these clothes made me feel. Not like a "woman," but like a girl. I felt young and open and beautiful.

I felt young inside too. I could feel this happy girl in me now. I could feel the way my face opened; I could feel the delight and love in my eyes. Thanks to the meetings and phone calls, I had friends beyond the immediate circle of the monastery. I had Christian community, and I had another, wider spiritual community. I became aware of all the love that surrounded me, all the people who believed in me and in what we were doing.

I was happy, and safe. Barbie began to crawl out of her tomb.

Of course, that did not mean everything was easy. Elizabeth and I moved in together on the basis of a shared commitment. We barely knew each other. We followed a monastic schedule, we tried to live in a way that others might join, but on a daily basis, it was just the two of us learning to live together. We each brought our histories with us, of course. My ways of doing things sometimes upset her, and vice versa. In the past, I would likely have shrugged off these feelings, denying them until the pressure built and I thought of leaving. But now, I was living with someone who not only felt things, but named them and tried to actively address conflicts.

I was stuck. Or, I was confronted with a choice. Was I prepared to work at this relationship, to undergo the feelings, to cooperate in my own growth? Or would I walk away, or worse, avoid in place?

At bottom I was clear. This was where I belonged, what I was meant to do. Now I had tools, both from recovery and from Mastery, to help me meet the challenges of relationships. I had a partner who would push me to do that. I believed that this was God's invitation to me, to grow into abundance of life.

We fought. Hard. I occasionally dissociated, sometimes for days, but each time we fought, Elizabeth would open a door of communication, and I would return. Gradually, I learned that my companion was trustworthy, even when I was activated. I wailed to my sponsor and my spiritual director, but I didn't really reach the point of thinking I should leave. Rather, my respect and love for Elizabeth deepened. I learned to name my feelings and to share them. I began to see how God was leading me into wholeness.

Life was full. Each day, we continued to organize as a community, writing a Rule for vowed members, running the covenant group, blogging, offering retreats and quiet days, filling in at local churches when they needed a priest, getting a website. All this, plus our routine of prayer and common meals, filled my days.

And slowly, slowly, I began seeing people in spiritual direction.

That first impulse, back in New Mexico, had never materialized in the convent or in parish ministry. I had felt called to offer spiritual direction, but then got diverted. I took courses, but no one course offered a credential. But as soon as I arrived on the banks of the Hudson, people began to come. Some I met through the monastery or local churches; others came to our events or read our newsletter.

As I began to direct more regularly, my confidence increased. I joined a monthly supervision group, a place to bring questions and concerns, and to learn more. Inch by inch, I moved toward realizing my initial desire.

Still, I was uneasy. Shouldn't I be more "in the world"? What about people's needs for food and shelter and safety? I wrestled with the desire to be "relevant," to not be seen as living a life of indolence under the cover of prayer.

My new spiritual director had to listen to this for months. She pointed out that "spiritual works of mercy" were as important as "corporal" ones, that people came out of a felt need. It helped, a little. I knew I was more alive in those capacities. I knew that working out of guilt never brings joy. But still. Was this what God wanted from me?

I followed my time-tested pattern: I asked God to show me the way. If I was supposed to be doing something different, I needed clarity and energy. If the impulse arose from guilt or the need to look good or just the desire to help in ways that didn't belong to me, I needed clarity about that.

I waited for an answer.

Over time, I got clear. My role was to support the people doing that crucial frontline work. By offering direction and retreats and hospitality, by preaching and presiding at Eucharist, I could help those people to do the work they were called to. We are, in fact, one body, all of us, and my part is not the same as anyone else's.

I was flourishing.

After two-and-a-half years, I felt ready—we both felt ready—to commit to life in this fledgling community. We didn't know what the future would bring, but I knew this was the life for me. God had answered my prayers—again, and again, and again. Don and Susan, our primary mentors, agreed we were ready.

We sent out formal invitations, with the restrained language of the Church: "By the grace of God, on the feast of Mary Magdalene, July 22, 2015, Shane Phelan and Elizabeth Broyles will make their life professions in the Companions of Mary the Apostle." For ourselves, we had another: "By the grace of God, on the feast of Mary Magdalene, Shane and Elizabeth will jump off a cliff into the loving arms of Jesus."

And so, we did.

Chapter Eighteen

Dancing in the Light

July 22, 2015 opened with a bright sun, promising heat later on. The Hudson River gleamed in the sunlight.

After breakfast, we all went to the monastery chapel.

The covenant group had been meeting for a year and a half. When we had announced that we would be making life vows, they had chorused: "We want to make vows!" We didn't feel ready to have people make vows after this brief time of meeting online, but we loved that they wanted to go deeper together. We designed a program called Covenant Companions, more intense than "Associates" but not like living a monastic life. It included weekly meetings on Zoom, an annual retreat together, living the Covenant accompanied by a vowed Companion, reading, and theological reflection. We envisioned that these people would be co-creators with us of this developing community. No one had asked to join in residence, and this offered us a way to journey more deeply with others. We may not have more monastic members, but something was happening.

Elizabeth and I left the group in the chapel and took refuge in the parlor, a little room with air conditioning and comfortable chairs. It was our last chance to talk and pray before we entered the swirl of bodies and purposes that would carry us through this day.

Two years before, we had come to this place and made our novice commitments. We had designed a "habit" that reflected our body images and our sense of "appropriate" monastic wear: basically, big bags of tan linen, below the knee, with white shirts underneath. As we had both lost weight and the cheap fabric began to fall apart, we had reassessed what a habit should be. It should be simple and easy to produce—none of the elaborate folds and gathers of traditional habits. We decided on "black off the rack," clothes that would be easy for new members to purchase but still marking a distinct way of being.

Today, we dressed in black T-shirts and pants that fit. The spiritual and emotional growth of the last two years was matched by our bodies. I felt clear, unconflicted, joyful. We had worked hard so far, and we were committed to "continual conversion of life," as our vows said. The monastic journey of prayer, self-examination, letting ourselves be changed by the encounter with one another and those around us, was already bearing fruit. I knew that the journey was lifelong, one day at a time, and I felt ready to face into that.

After some brief and fervent prayer, we moved down the hall toward the chapel. We poked our heads in to see who was there. The place was packed. Friends had crammed into the chapel, and extra chairs had been brought in. We had designed the service. Today was our day, to declare and share the joy we had found.

I remembered coming to this chapel back in 2000. I had felt that this was where I belonged. I remembered Brother Andrew, who had died two months before; he not only helped us find one another, he made our first donation—$25—out of his Christmas money in 2012.

Now, I was getting ready to make my vows here. I had come full circle.

And yet, I still didn't belong here. I was a guest in this chapel, not a member of the community. I came to this chapel every day, but it was not my home. Even today, on our big day, we had had to accede to the wishes of another group that wanted to come for the service. I was coming home, but not to this place. I was coming home to God, to myself, to my vocation.

As the music began, everyone stood. We entered the chapel in the usual order for such services: Brother Jose, swinging the incense, led the way.

Then Elizabeth and I entered. We moved slowly to give the Brothers time to get to their places, and then we went past them to face the altar. To the left of the altar were our five soon-to-be Companions. To the right were those who would ask the questions and receive our vows: Don and Susan, our "abba" and "amma"; Kathy, an Ursuline Sister and my spiritual director; and Robert, the Superior of the Order. With them stood Chilton Knudsen, now our "Bishop Companion."

As we came to the altar, we prostrated ourselves on the floor. I had longed to do this for years, to give bodily expression to my desire to give myself to God, but it was not part of the tradition in my former community. Finally, my body and my heart were in synch.

After the readings, Don delivered the sermon. In his religious habit, with its long black robe, distinctive white chest panel and preaching tabs, with a big silver cross, he looked very different from our everyday mentor.

"This is a unique day," he began. "In the course of history, there have been very few times in which a congregation of Christians have witnessed the founding of a religious community, and the birth of a movement of covenanted men and women." While we were recognizably in the monastic tradition, he said, "Benedict [the founder of Western monasticism] could not have imagined that two women priests, under the title of Companions of Mary the Apostle, in a digital world, could create a community of covenanted companions on Skype! The spirit of God continues to create and recreate."

Don testified to our journey of transformation. Our bodies had visibly transformed from our beginnings, but Don told us that our spirits had also been transformed. I welled up as the enormity of what had happened in my life really landed.

Then, the questions and answers began. We had written these vows ourselves, based on tradition.

"I desire to know God and serve God with my whole being, and to walk with others on the road of discipleship.

I desire to give myself to God wholeheartedly, following the Rule and the covenant of the Companions of Mary the Apostle.

I commit myself to opening to continual conversion of life under vows of poverty, chastity, and obedience for the rest of my days."

After prayers, Bishop Chilton blessed our crosses and the shawls we would wear in chapel, red for Mary Magdalene, and put them on us. I bent deeply to receive the cross, partly from reverence and partly because Chilton is about 8 inches shorter than me.

Then, we turned to the other side of the altar, where our five new Covenant Companions were standing. We who had been "received" now received them as they announced their desire to know and serve God, to let Christ transform them through sharing in community. We gave them crosses and small icons of Mary Magdalene.

Then, all seven of us knelt and held hands as we said the prayer we had written for the community, a prayer we say at Vespers every day:

"Pour into our hearts, O God, the Holy Spirit's gift of love, that we, clasping each the other's hand, may share the joy of companionship, human and divine, and draw many to your community of transforming love; through Jesus Christ our Savior. Amen."

After the Eucharist, we danced out to drumming, "marching in the light of God" as the African hymn had it. We danced down the aisle, and back up the side, gathering others as we went. My new red shawl swirled as I spun around and clapped to the drumbeat.

Fifteen years before, I had left New Mexico almost by stealth, heading out without companions other than my dog. Now, I was surrounded by companions. I had begun my journey without spiritual guidance or direction other than my own heart; now, I stood with people who gave me counsel and prayed for me. I had left behind obligations; now, I was choosing commitment.

Nine years earlier, I had made life vows in a community that I struggled to belong to, for reasons I wasn't exactly proud of. Now, I felt clear and unconflicted. This was right. I could finally trust God, and my companions, and myself. I could give myself in that trust.

This was the service I needed, a service that followed an ancient tradition while bringing it into this new time. This was the kind of community I needed, one where I was free to express my devotion and commitment with full-bodied joy. I could be all of me: grateful, devout, irreverent, queer. Now, finally, I could be the big queer nun that God intended, and rejoiced in.

We danced, God and me and Elizabeth, in the company of other dancers. Jim stood up with his cane and danced while Bob clapped to the music. We danced in the sight of those who didn't understand or appreciate the dance. We danced before those who longed to dance but didn't yet dare.

We danced.

Epilogue

"THE LITTLE GIRL IS NOT DEAD; she is asleep" (Mark 5:39).

Last fall, I visited my brother and sister-in-law. Ann is a whole health provider, focusing on mind/body/spirit connections. One day, as we stood in the kitchen, she showed me a pendulum she uses to help people discern their truth. You make a statement, or ask a question, and the pendulum moves one way for yes and another for no. I know, it sounds creepy, but there it is. Ann demonstrated by saying, "My name is Ann." The pendulum swung one way, affirming her answer. When she said, "My name is Dave," it swung the other way.

Of course, I had to try it. "My name is Shane," I said. The pendulum swung yes. Then I blurted out, "My name is Barbara." Again yes. Ann and I gaped at one another, our mouths making matching circles.

I had seen little Barbie in the mirror; I had felt her innocent joy in me, but I had ignored Barb, and Barbara, all those other selves that had come before. The shut-down eight-year-old, the furious adolescent, the rebel looking for a cause—all of them lived still. I knew from therapy about internal dynamics, but I didn't really pay attention.

At that moment, I realized they're all still with me. No, not with me; they *are* me. And, I can welcome them. "I contain multitudes," as Walt Whitman wrote, but more than that; the multitudes are all me. All of me is present in each of those stages, either as a past or as a potential.

Before I knew her, Shane was present in Barbie. The Shane of my stories was a golden child, the light that shone in the darkness. Later, as Barb acted out the dangerous part of Shane's stories, that light kept me from total implosion. Somehow, windows always opened just enough, and Barb, Barbara, and Shane together managed to crawl through.

It's not just the Barbaras and Shane who live in me, however. Professor Phelan is there, teaching and writing about identity and community. Sister Shane Margaret is there, seeking God, finding meaning in the tradition. Pastor Shane lives in my work with churches, in preaching and leading worship. They're all there. I'm sure there are others I've never claimed. My ancestors and teachers, opponents and guides, all have their part in this swirl that shows up in one body. I welcome them. I answer to "Shane," but I revel in the knowledge that all of "me" is present whether I'm aware of it or not.

Joseph Campbell writes, "The two—the hero and [her] god, the seeker and the found—are thus understood as the outside and inside of a single, self-mirrored mystery, which is identical with the mystery of the manifest world." The point of the hero's journey, he says, "is to come to the knowledge of this unity in multiplicity and then to make it known."

I'm as great a mystery to me as God is. I can experience and encounter "me," but I can't grasp myself any more than I can grasp God. And you know what? I don't need to. My job is to open, to be a channel, to let God move through me however God chooses. I don't have to be able to parse or define God; to do so would be idolatry, or simple hubris. Stories and poetry come closer, but they can never completely encompass the mystery of God, or of any person—really, any being. Some look simpler than others from our point of view, but that's just our limitation. The mystery is where the juice of life is.

Each year, I spend a week in silence on a beach in Connecticut. I let the mystery rise up, first in the multiplicity of herons and egrets and whelks and rocks, and then, eventually, in the unity of the whole. I let my own multiplicity rise up as thoughts and feelings, letting God direct me. Then, one day, in a flash, the unity is manifest. I am one with all of creation. In that moment, I know that to be true of you as well. You and I, you and I and all the others, are one. I cry with joy and gratitude.

Then I examine the tide pools again.

There's no question in my mind. I belong here, in this tiny community, with this Companion and those others sent to us. The Covenant Companions are gone; that program, that experiment, has given way to the more traditional Oblate model. We meet online with our Oblates for prayer and conversation, and try to meet in person each year. Our local community, the "Coffee Table Communion" community, gathers regularly for study and prayer. We are surrounded by opportunities to love and be loved.

If no one else comes for vowed membership, God has still answered my prayer. I get to pray. I get to live a life of prayer with another person whose spiritual hunger matches my own. I get to walk with others in their spiritual journeys. I am swimming in abundance. I sit in the sun, I take walks, I get excited over birds, and I weep with joy.

In the wake of COVID and the horrors of the past years, and the social and political horror that seems to deepen each day, I have become clear about my place. Through hospitality, through prayer, through writing, I can be a channel of peace. This requires that I cultivate peace in myself, that I remain faithful to the disciplines that Jesus named and all religions highlight: meditation, study, prayer and worship, giving of my time and treasure. I do this not only for my sake, for my own sanity and health, but for the sake of the world.

The Big Book of Alcoholics Anonymous promises that if we pursue recovery, "We will not regret the past nor wish to shut the door upon it . . . No matter how far down the scale we have gone, we will see how our experience can benefit others." I know this to be true. It is precisely my past that has equipped me to work with others going through their own struggles. Accepting my own hurts, the ones I've received and the ones I've given, accepting my mistakes and my resilience, enables me to serve others. My whole ministry, including this book, is a product of the road I've traveled. I'm grateful for all of it.

It's been a long time since the little voice gave me direction. I think as I've continued to heal, it doesn't need to break in in the same way. As I pray and "improve my conscious contact with God" that voice doesn't need to break in.

I do hear something, though. Sometimes, as I walk up and down our lane before Matins and I say good morning to God, I hear with my inner ear: "I love you."

I'm not always sure whether I'm saying that to God or God is saying that to me. It doesn't really matter. Love rises and speaks. I know if I stick close to that love, my decisions will likely be solid. If I'm not sure, I ask others for guidance. I listen for love.

It's possible that one day the money won't be there. It's possible—it's inevitable—that I will one day no longer be able to preach and write. One day I might be struck deaf or blind. I might lose a limb. Elizabeth, my beloved Companion, might die before me; I might find myself alone in this life. It's possible that our friends and supporters might vanish. All of that is possible.

What is not possible is for me to be separated from the love of God. God spoke to me when I could not, would not, acknowledge Her. As "my little voice," as Coyote dancing through my dreams, as Mary Magdalene leading me into recovery, as Jesus in the chalice, as kind and generous and challenging companions, God has invited, cautioned, and encouraged me all my life. And, when I can no longer hear or see or taste or move, God will continue to uphold me and shine in me.

This is true not only for me. God is at work in each of us. So often, Her work does not conform to our hopes or plans. And there are disasters and traumas, not delivered by God. Nonetheless, She is at work recycling all our trash, the refuse of our lives and this beautiful, fragile world. God is in the strangers who leave their lives to help in disaster areas, in plants that take root in the hard ground of volcanoes or fires, in all whose love holds or heals others. She is present in the small voices in us that do not want to give up, and She holds those in whom the voices can no longer be heard. She does not eliminate danger and injustice, but She insists that they are not the end or the truth of our lives. She continually proclaims the promise of new life.

When I got sober, I didn't believe in God. I was willing to concede something—an energy, a guiding force—but I was not going to buy the whole "God" story. For me, that was the story about an old White man pulling strings, a fairy tale turned grim for too many. Then I prayed, and I felt my fear relieved immediately, viscerally, as though a breath had swept through me. This was too personal an encounter for me to refer to it in the third person or simple description. This mystery seemed to know me and respond to me. I needed to know and respond in turn. I needed to give thanks and to address gratitude to someone. I used the word "God" because it was in my heritage and in the rooms in which I recovered. I followed the advice of others who said to explore this God for myself rather than just accept or reject what I had been taught. As I prayed, as I addressed God, I found the story of God in the Scriptures speaking to me. "God" became not just a word, not just an abstract benevolent force or energy, but a living presence.

When I let Jesus into my world (or when I entered Jesus' world), I found more love, more strength, more direction. I found words that matched my feelings, and words that created new feelings. I was, I am, empowered by living in Jesus' world.

I don't live in the world of the hellfire preachers or the imperial Church; I live in a world where the poor receive good news, where prisoners are freed, where we are healed of our demons and illnesses and filled with abundant life. I live in a world where resurrection is possible, beyond my understanding but not beyond my hope. I live in a world aching for justice and reconciliation, continually falling short and yet starting over again and again.

As a Companion of Mary the Apostle, I am called to proclaim the renewing and transforming power of God in our lives and in the world. This is not optimism, or denial. It's hope, hope grounded in certainty. God is big enough to hold it all, to hold us all, to hold all of us.

I'm not so stereotypically visible as a lesbian anymore. I'm not so legible as a nun as I was when I was in habit. I'm not even as big as I have been at times.

Nonetheless, I'm still queer. In a world where gender is mandatory and sexual activity becomes a required and defining part of one's life; in a world where Christianity is becoming either a nightmare or invisible, the path of religious life itself is becoming queer. For many, like the doctor I met in the emergency room, it looks like escape from the demands of the world. For others, its only justification is active ministry. Beyond that, though, it is simply incomprehensible. Like LGBTQ people, monastics can be invisible, or scorned—or strangely attractive. Monastic life is deliberately counter-cultural: in a world of inexhaustible consumption and appetite, aiming to live simply; in a world where sex is an ultimate (consumer?) good, loving Christ first; in a culture that makes an idol of autonomy and individualism, choosing to be accountable to others for our choices—it's a pretty queer thing.

And that's good. The first monastics were not looking to be respectable, or even useful. They fled the imperial Church in order to follow Christ. They refused to be contained or defined by others. They were queer as queer can be.

Queer is where holy lives. Living into the holy messes up everything settled and respectable and comprehensible. Living into the holy is where we find the awesome mystery, not only of God, but of ourselves. The word breaks off, and we become still.

Queer is a place big enough for each of us, for all of us, for all of each of us. The reign of God that Jesus announced is totally queer, upside down and sideways, from the ways of "the world." It's a space (not a place) where old identities are irrelevant, where healing happens, where new possibilities arise.

Welcome.

If anyone has told you that you aren't welcome in God's world, remember this:

That's a lie.

You belong here, with the rest of us. You are loved. Your love is needed; your love is a blessing to the world.

Go ahead, make mistakes. Make some big ones. I surely have—but I'm not exactly sure which ones they are. Sometimes my worst moments have brought the most growth; I wouldn't have missed them. God remains, waiting to recycle and reuse whatever we've got.

I want to keep telling you: *You are loved. You belong.* You are magnificent, in all the ways you don't fit; especially in the ways you don't fit. Jesus didn't fit. He did much better than that.

Go ahead—live your life. I dare you.

I do pray that you who read will find your heart on fire, your spirit inspired, your soul longing for the living God (or at least, a little curious!).

Yet, in the end, I find I have written this memoir to sing God's song back to God, to use my voice to speak to the little voice that speaks to me.

God, thank you for my life.

Thank you for rescuing me from the horror of incest, from the pain of addiction, from all the trauma that accompanied these, and from my own horrible and petty sins.

Thank you for calling me beyond my comfortable life, for not letting me settle, again and again.

Thank you for upholding me, for sending people to guide me and encourage me and support me. Thank you for friends. Thank you for my family, for bringing me back to them.

Thank you for Elizabeth (now simply E).

Thank you for opening me to see and receive all these companions.

Thank you for the bluebirds and sparrows and cardinals who sing by my window, for the fox creeping and trotting across the lawn, for the hawks nesting in the little marsh next door, for the eagles poised above the church on the highway.

Thank you for the hard times and the lush times.

Thank you for the seed of love you planted in me and for all the ways you water it and make it grow.

Thank you.
I love you.
I love you.
I love you.
Amen.

Acknowledgments

So many people have contributed to this project and to the life I've described here. Where to start?

Thanks to the many saviors who have shown me a path when I saw closed doors: my teachers, therapists, sponsors, mentors. Thanks to all my spiritual directors and companions over the years. Dearest Sister Susan John, thank you. May you rest in peace. You were truly my amma, as Sister Helen was my grandmother.

Thank you to everyone who was a part of writing this memoir. Beverly Donofrio, who led my first memoir retreat; Nadine Kenney Johnstone, writing coach extraordinaire, and the Monday Writer Workout Group; my local memoir buddies, Charlotte, Jodi, and Darcy. Any fluency or grace in this writing is due to all of you.

Thanks to my first intrepid squad of readers: Sarah Gardner, Kappa Waugh, Anne Kadet, and Emilie Trautmann. This book is nothing like what you read; I hope you like it!

To Lyn Brakeman, who hounded me to stay on point, to Suzanne Guthrie, who believed in me and pushed me to become a writer. Thanks to Ann Overton, for your leadership over the years in Mastery and your gracious interest in this project.

Thank you to my local communities, especially the Coffee Table community, and to our followers and friends on Facebook and the Companions newsletter. Your support has kept me going when I wanted to give up.

Thank you to my brother and sister, Dave and Jan, and my sister-in-law (and in fact), Ann. Being family with you is a precious gift. Thanks to Ann and Dave for the blessing of writing retreat time.

Thank you to all the retreatants and partners in recovery who told me to write this story. You're the ones who convinced me to do it; here it is. Thank you to our donors and supporters for your belief in this project.

Saying "special thanks" doesn't begin to cover my gratitude to my Companion, my sister, E(lizabeth) Broyles. Our shared life has grown me beyond my wildest dreams. Your stubborn insistence on the importance of this work has kept me going. Your careful, thoughtful reading of drafts has added immeasurably to any merits that may be here.

Finally, thanks be to God. I know it can be a cliché, but really. My life is nothing without you. You have rescued my feet from stumbling; you have pulled me out of the nethermost pit and made my footing sure. You have shown me the path of life. Every breath I breathe is a gift from you.

Glory to God whose power working in us can do infinitely more than we can ask or imagine! (Eph. 3:19).

www.ingramcontent.com/pod-product-compliance
Lightning Source LLC
Chambersburg PA
CBHW071145130626
46553CB00004B/1524